MW00809498

Image
and
Reality

in Plato's
Metaphysics

Image
and
Reality

in Plato's
Metaphysics

Richard Patterson

Hackett Publishing Company

Copyright © 1985 by Richard Patterson
All rights reserved
Designed by Mark E. Van Halsema
Cover and jacket designs by Jackie Lacy
Printed in the United States of America
For further information address the publisher
Hackett Publishing Company, Inc.
P. O. Box 44937, Indianapolis, Indiana 46204

The paper in this book meets the guidelines
for permanence and durability established by
the Committee on Production Guidelines for Book Longevity
of the Council on Library Resources

Library of Congress Cataloging in Publication Data

Patterson, Richard, 1946-
   Image and reality in Plato's metaphysics.

   Bibliography: p.
   Includes indexes.
   1. Plato — Metaphysics.   2. Metaphysics — History.
1. Title.
B398.M4P37   1984   111   83-26654
ISBN 0-915145-72-3 (alk. paper)
ISBN 0-915145-73-1 (pbk. : alk. paper)

For Cindy

Acknowledgments

It is a pleasure to acknowledge the advice, support, and helpful criticism of a great many people – if not to reflect on how many years these debts have been accumulating. The principal creditors are Charles Kahn, William Rumsey, Michael Rohr, Paul Woodruff, and Howard Stein. During the course of several expansions and contractions of the manuscript substantial contributions were received also from Edwin Hartman, E.N. Lee, Kevin McTighe, David Palmer, Steve Cardin, Richard Kuhns, Isaac Levi, John Cooper, Michael Frede, Martha Nussbaum, James Higginbotham, J.M.E. Moravcsik and Fabrizio Mondadori.

For generous financial support I am grateful to the Machette Foundation, to Columbia University for three summer grants, and to the Center for Hellenic Studies. For their work in transforming my scribbles into more legible notation I thank, and hold rather in awe, Dan Brown, Mike Lasser, and Mildred Garcia.

Three scholars whose names do not appear above, but whose writings are in large part responsible for anything of value in this book are Harold Cherniss, Gregory Vlastos, and G.E.L. Owen. Although they (and especially the last two) are usually quoted here in order that I may explain why I disagree, the fact remains, for reasons obvious to all who now work in this field, that as a student of Plato's philosophy I am very much a follower in their footsteps.

Contents

1

Introduction

Sometime early in the fourth century B.C. a certain Plato, son of Ariston of the Athenian deme of Kollytos, advanced the singular proposition that the world and its contents, the reliable objects we see and handle every day, are only images of "truly real" things—so-called "Forms" or "Ideas" (*eidē*)—possessing no perceptible properties, existing nowhere at all, and accessible in their purity to pure reason alone.[1] Some readers have insisted, with charitable intent, that Plato's talk of perceptible images (*eikones, eidola, mimēmata, phantasmata*) of intelligible models (*paradeigmata*) is "only metaphor,"[2] or merely one of several "nontechnical . . . synonyms and metaphors which Plato used to express the inexpressible."[3]

One can sympathize with this reaction in the name of a more down-to-earth Plato. And yet from a Platonic point of view, good common sense so often appears in the end common nonsense, the wisdom of *hoi polloi*,

that one comes to suspect serious intent especially where Plato has pro-
vocatively, even "paradoxically," stood accepted views on their head. In
any case, metaphor cannot be lightly dismissed as "mere" metaphor: If a
figure is carefully constructed, as some of the most celebrated images in
Plato certainly are, it may prove a valuable guide in the interpretation of
its author's philosophical intentions. Even if it should be designed to "express the inexpressible" (illustrate the primitive or undefined terms of a
theory?), one ought not neglect it but, on the contrary, treat it in that
special way a dog treats a marrow bone (to borrow a metaphor freely
adapted by Rabelais from Plato's *Republic*), inspecting it devotedly, gnaw-
ing it diligently, seeking out whatever precious matter it may contain.

Some of those who do take the analogy more seriously believe it reflects
a fundamental flaw in Plato's theory of Forms, at least as the theory appears in such works as the *Phaedo, Symposium, Republic,* and *Timaeus.*
The alleged error is that of treating Forms both as abstract, non-spatial,
common natures shared in or exemplified by worldly individuals *and,*
where the image analogy is invoked, as paradigm cases or unqualified
exemplars of those same natures—worldly individuals being only non-
paradigm specimens of those same kinds of thing. Unfortunately for any
such theory, it is not in general possible for abstract natures or essences
to exemplify themselves: the invisible, non-spatial nature of Humanity
itself is not *a* human, the nature of Hotness not itself hot, Bedsteadity not
a bedstead. (Other abstract natures constitute exceptions, but do not affect
the point as stated.)

Such an interpretation of Plato's intelligible *paradeigmata* appears already in Plato's own dialogue *Parmenides*, where a venerable and dialec-
tically superior Parmenides exploits it to show that if young Socrates'
Forms resemble their worldly participants (and Socrates agrees that they
do, if sensibles are images of Forms taken as models) they will not be
unique, but each only one of an infinite series of Forms. The issue has
given rise to intense debate ever since, among prominent members of the
early Academy (Speusippus, Xenocrates, Aristotle, and others), in medi-
eval controversy over "reification of universals," and in our day as the
question of "self-predication" (that is, as most commentators use the
phrase, the question whether each Form is a paradigm example of itself,
or whether the *onoma* of each Form is truly *predicable of* or truly *describes* the Form itself). I think it is fair to say the interpretation of Forms
as paradigm cases of themselves—recalling that covers a variety of differ-

ent specific readings – is today dominant in English-language Plato studies, and has substantial support elsewhere.[4]

Taking the comparison of participation to imaging as a serious philosophical analogy does not, however, commit one to any version of a paradigm case interpretation of Forms. A third response would concede that imaging *does* involve the kind of similarity pivotal to that regress argument of the *Parmenides*, but would maintain that such similarity is irrelevant to the intended point of the analogy and so should not be read into Plato's metaphysics. After all, philosophical or scientific analogies ordinarily aim at illustrating certain specific ideas; it is not normally intended that every property of a proposed analogue should find a counterpart in the subject illustrated. Bohr's (or Rutherford's, according to Bohr) solar system analogy for atomic structure illustrated what he took to be the orbiting of electrons about an atomic nucleus; he was perfectly free to deny that the forces holding electrons in orbit were the same as those acting on the planets, or to leave that an open question, even though gravitational force plays a central role in the theory of the solar system. Similarly, Plato might not have believed Forms were similar to their homonymous participants (except in trivial ways not involving the problems sketched above) but used the image analogy anyway in order to stress the role of abstract natures in the generation of sense objects[5] or, more broadly, to underline some sort of ontological priority of Form (model) to participant (image).[6]

A final alternative takes the bull by the horns, asserting that the relevant concept of imaging does *not* in itself consist in or imply the sort of similarity between image and model assumed by Plato's Parmenides, by paradigm case interpretations of Forms in general, and even by the friends of the Forms mentioned just above. This reading begins with the observation that the specific respect in which a Form and its sensible participants are somehow alike or akin is the respect signified by the *onoma* ("term" or "name" in a non-technical sense) common to both: Sensible beauties and Beauty itself are somehow alike with respect to their all being beauties, sensible equals and the Equal itself with respect to their all being equals, etc. But if one considers the term "landscape" or "horse" or "god," one may notice that a painted landscape – what Plato calls a *phantasma, eidōlon, eikōn,* or *mimēma* of a real landscape – is not a real landscape at all; a reflection of a horse is not a real horse at all; a dream image of Zeus is not in the least a god, not even an imperfect or non-paradigm one. Thus one intended point of the analogy would be that intelligible model and sensible image or imitation, although related in a manner justifying the sensible's being called by the *onoma* of the intelligible nature, are *not* similar in the respect indicated by their shared *onoma*; they are not akin or like to one another in the manner of perfect and imperfect horse, or of paradigm and non-paradigm shuttle.[7] This much is consistent with various interpretations of Forms as abstract natures or essences, and of participants as embodiments or exemplifications of those natures.

Given the importance of Plato's image analogy not only for his metaphysics but also for his attendant theories of knowledge and perception, of craftsmanship in general (including cosmology, statecraft, and all less exalted "useful arts") of the fine arts or "imitative arts," of moral education, and of rational action in general, serious concern with any major aspect of Plato's thought will lead in time to questions about his notion of imaging as such and thence to its non-figurative philosophical implications. My excuse for entering into this hoary debate is that, first, despite the antiquity of some of the issues involved, there remains a good deal of relevant textual material yet to be appraised properly — material sufficient to settle fairly securely some basic controversies about Plato's views on imaging and on corresponding aspects of the theory of Forms. Second, detailed elaboration of the image/model analogy reveals a much more fully articulated and precise figure than even its defenders have argued, one that integrates and vivifies virtually every aspect of classical Platonism. Third, and most important, the analogy serves in some instances not just as an illustration of theoretical points already made clear in other ways, but as an independent aid to proper understanding of Plato's views. Cases in point include the nature and perfection of Forms, the imperfection of sensibles, the contrast between time and eternity, the activity and authority of craftsmen whether divine or human, and the nature of participation itself.

Chapter 2 prepares for discussion of all these matters by distinguishing various sorts of *paradeigmata* found in the dialogues or in ancient usage generally. Illustrative or pedagogical examples, standard instances, structures or patterns, and models or originals constitute a broad array of alternatives capturing many historically important readings of the nature of Forms; the chapter attempts to clarify some main consequences of identifying Forms with one sort of *paradeigma* rather than another.

Putting these results to work, chapter 3 examines in detail the suitability of the image analogy for illustration of a genuinely Platonistic metaphysics. The initial aim will be to establish three points fundamental to the interpretation of Plato's own version of Platonism. First, the *paradeigmata* of his "paradigmatism" (his view that Forms are in some sense *paradeigmata*) are models or originals whose correlates are images (*eidola, eikones*) or imitations (*mimēmata*). Second, the distinction between image and original (or image and "real thing") does illustrate a strong difference in type between sensible participant and intelligible Form. Third, the specific analogue to a sensible's *participating in* a Form, the relationship that both grounds the kinship of image to model and justifies calling the image after its model, is the image's *being an image of* its model. Investigation of Plato's own examples of images, his use of such terms as *eidōlon* and *eikōn* in the dialogues, and his infrequent but revealing comments on the nature of images as such will all help show that the image analogy is designed to illustrate a theory of abstract essences or natures and their particular worldly namesakes. This is hardly a novel conclusion. But because it is fundamental, and is nonetheless so often asserted or denied on what appear to be inadequate grounds, it seems worthwhile to attempt as secure a demonstration of its truth as the evidence will allow. The chapter then considers some consequences of that basic conclusion for the *Parmenides'* "regress of similarities," and for Plato's talk of likeness between image and model.

We shall then be in a position to examine more directly in chapter 4 the nature of Forms and their perfection, beginning with the vexed issue of how each Form can be said to "have its own nature" (the phrase is from Plato's *Sophist*) or how the Form for any given property F can be said to "be F." I will suggest that such statements follow simply from the fact that each Form F is real, that it is distinct from all other Forms as well as all worldly things, and is the nature F itself rather than some other nature. The chapter will also maintain, in contrast to the apparently universal view of friends and foes of the Forms alike, that "F" can be truly predicated of, and does not merely name, the Form F construed as an abstract nature or essence. But if one is to import talk of predicates here (Plato did not formulate any theory of predicates as opposed to proper names) then one must respect the particular manner in which Plato distinguishes among kinds of F, or among things rightly labeled "F."[8] To that end one may follow Plato's lead where he has in effect provided three different predicates, appropriate to his three different kinds of F: "intelligible F" (or "F-in-nature", "what-is-F," "F itself," "nature of F", or "*eidos* F"); "sensible F" (or "image of Form of F"); and "image of sensible F" (or "image of image of Form of F").

It is not that "*F*" is baldly ambiguous, applying to different sorts of *F* by bare equivocation; it is rather that if one must cast Plato's theory in terms of predicating "*F*" of various subjects, one must appreciate that "*F*" might stand for any of three larger predicates of which it is a part. One sort of predicate will truly apply to Forms considered as abstract natures, another only to sensible participants in Forms, a third only to phantasms or *eidola* of sensible participants.

Means will be provided, however, for expressing the same point in genuinely Platonic terms. To wit, there are different kinds of things one may justly, rightly, or correctly label, call, or dub (*onomadzein, prosagoreuein*) "*F*," and three of these (Form of *F*, image of Form of *F*, image of image of Form of *F*) have related, even if very different, sorts of claim to the *onoma* "*F*." Plato seems happy enough to allow in *Republic* X that a variety of things labeled "*F*" rather than "*G*" will be *F*s of one kind or another. But only the abstract nature of *F* itself enjoys a claim to the *onoma* that is not qualified as to time, respect, relation, or context: sensible embodiments of the Form have other, variously qualified, claims to the *onoma* insofar as they exemplify a given Form in some respect, relation, or context, or at some time, while paintings or reflections of sensible *F*s can make only a still more derivative claim to the *onoma* "*F*," based on the fact that they are images of some embodiment of the Form.

Either way the important question is not simply whether Plato calls both Form and sensible by the same *onoma*, or whether he says they are two different kinds of *F*, for on *any* interpretation of Forms one may maintain that in *some* specifiable sense Forms are different in kind from their sensible participants. The issue concerns rather the precise nature of the alleged difference in kind, and the corresponding basis for homonymy between *F*s of different kinds. Chapter 4 proceeds, then, to a description of that type distinction, with particular attention to the perfection of Forms, to Plato's related distinction between being and becoming, and to some potentially troublesome cases in which Forms earn their *onomata* not only by being the particular abstract natures they are, but also by exemplifying themselves. Finally the image analogy returns, this time bringing into focus one strong Platonic intuition behind talk of the Form as the "really real *F*." Plato's emphatic application of *onomata* usually reserved by right-thinking people for the "real" *F*s and *G*s of our workaday world to his own intelligible Forms shows no concession or subservience to an impoverished philosophical vocabulary. Quite the opposite: it makes a calculated, positive point of its own, being in fact the linguistic complement to Plato's radical view of the superiority and ontological priority of Forms.

We descend then into the world of becoming for a closer look at the inferiority of sensibles, now with an eye to the perfection of Forms. Chapter 5 traces several different marks of that inferiority, emphasizing their variety, in part as an antidote to a common and natural tendency to fix on some feature(s), such as sensibles' being not only F but also in one way or another the opposite of F, at the expense of others. This is a matter of utmost importance, since too narrow a view of sensibles' inferiority can, in very specific ways, foster a mistaken view about the nature of Forms themselves and about Plato's philosophical motivation for postulating such entities in the first place.

Having perceived this variety, it is necessary also to explore several important interconnections among the various *stigmata* of sensibles. Here Plato's theory of the receptacle, the place in which all worldly things eke out their inferior existence, comes to the fore. We shall see how the theory applies to a range of very different sorts of worldly participants and that the "scatteredness" (lacking Plato's rhetorical motivation we would probably say "extendedness") of things that come to be in the receptacle is closely related to other marks of their inferiority: to their ontological dependence on Forms, their mutability, their being sensible rather than intelligible. The receptacle occupies a key position in Plato's image/model view of reality, making explicit the need of some place (*chōra*) or medium in which sensibles may come to be, and consolidating some important convictions already familiar from the *Phaedo* about the divisibility and mutability of corporeal things.

Although all sensible Fs are, in their manner of being F, inferior to F itself, some sensibles are also perfect in their way. The paths of the fixed stars describe perfect circles, the sensible world as a whole is, according to the *Timaeus*, perfectly spherical, and (as maintained in appendix A) some objects are exactly equal to others in one respect or another. If so, even "perfect" sensible Fs are still inferior in their manner of being F—in their scatteredness, dependence, mutability, perishability, and opacity to pure reason—to the Form of F. These neglected cases of perfection in the sensible realm strikingly reinforce the conclusion that sensibles (even considered at that time, and in that precise respect, relation, or context in which they are F in the manner open to sensibles) are still inferior to their corresponding Forms in all the usual ways. But more positively, these cases can help one see how Form and sensible differ in type, how they differ in their manner of being *F*. A closing section brings together results from chapters 4 and 5 for a discussion of Forms as the standards by which sensibles are to be judged better or worse specimens of their kind, parallel to everyday use of models or originals in assessing the correctness of images.

With a rather detailed picture of the nature of Forms and of the fundamentals of the image analogy in hand, chapter 6 addresses the very old but still pressing question of whether separate abstract natures can be the (formal) *aitiai* of, or factors responsible for, the very being of their sensible participants—what is sometimes considered *the* problem of participation. This role of the Forms differs from that of craftsman's model, and poses different philosophical and exegetical problems. It will have been observed in chapter 3 that an image's *being of* some model is the analogue to *participation in* some Form as a formal *aitia*, or what Socrates calls in the *Phaedo* his "simple" and "safe" *aitia*. Chapter 6 considers some further issues in the handling of this point of the analogy, but is primarily concerned with philosophical problems in the theory illustrated.[9] In particular it will undertake to explain how participation in separate (roughly, non-locatable and independently existing) Forms can "make" sensibles be what they are. Separate Forms are in no way efficient causes of sensibles; nor do they make sensible *F*s be *F* in the manner of immanent universals, or particular property instances, or Anaxagorean bits. Granted they *are*, as others have put it, the abstract natures sensibles *have*, how are we to understand this "having" of separate Forms? Surely it is significantly different from any having of immanent forms, however that is explicated; but it is not at all obvious how it *is* supposed to work. Here again critics since antiquity have claimed that Plato's theory cannot possibly work,[10] or that although it is internally consistent its workings must ultimately be left a mystery.[11]

Although the image analogy will prove useful in addressing this problem, too, positive explication of participation will draw more heavily upon introduction of a somewhat different "intuitive model" (one suggested by Socrates' construction of the just city of the *Republic*), along with certain carefully proscribed aspects of Plato's views about nature, about the Good itself, and about the relation of the Good to other Forms. Herein lies what I take to be Plato's single most important reason for postulating separate Forms, a bedrock conviction about the objectivity of goodness and its articulation. Precisely how such a conviction leads to the theory of separate Forms may not be immediately obvious. But once this has been explained I believe we shall be able to see also how sensibles may participate in *separate* abstract natures as a kind of formal *aitia*, and why it makes good sense to say, as young Socrates does in the *Parmenides*, that sensible participants are in fact only images of "intelligible models fixed in the nature of things."

A concluding chapter draws together various explicit and implicit conclusions of the study in order to underline some important general facts about Plato's classical theory of Forms: that Forms as *paradeigmata* fill a wide range of philosophical roles; that one should not worry lest two sorts of object (at least) be required to perform all these labors, since separate, abstract, intelligible Forms are quite equal to the task; that the image analogy does illustrate all the main aspects of the metaphysical theory as well as its chief applications to epistemology and value theory — the important points of analogy numbering about eighteen without, I hope, undue splitting of any whiskers in Plato's dense but well-kept beard. Because the philosophical work performed by Forms often overlaps with that assigned to similar objects in other versions of Platonism, I shall try to explain, finally, why Forms should be spoken of as Forms, rather than as structures or patterns, sets, universals, Fregean concepts, or eternal possibilities. Here some may sense the spirit of Prodicus; but something like his penchant for drawing distinctions is needed to keep Forms apart from their metaphysical next of kin.

2

Varieties of *Paradeigmata*

There is little agreement on even the most fundamental implications of
Plato's paradeigmatism. In part this is due simply to the difficulty of the
issues involved, which include all the thorniest problems surrounding the
theory of Forms. But it is due also to neglect of Plato's method of division.
To use a metaphor from the *Phaedrus*, one is tempted to assume at the
outset that one knows the relevant sense of *paradeigma* and to proceed
directly with its analysis and application, without having first divided the
subject "along its natural joints," and consequently without having taken
into account the large philosophical differences implicit in different uses
of the term — even, perhaps, without having confronted some of the most
serious alternative readings. The following sections attempt to sort out
various kinds of *paradeigmata* mentioned by Plato and his contempo-
raries, along with the principal modern readings of the term, not in order

to narrow the field (though some partisanship may be detected), but to clarify alternatives and draw out the consequences of regarding Forms as one kind of *paradeigma* rather than another.

A. Illustrative Examples

By simple head-count illustrative or pedagogical examples are the most common of Plato's *paradeigmata*. They are an interesting and important breed, but no one would mistake them for Forms. *Gorgias* 525c contains a graphic occurrence in which extreme wrongdoers are "made examples of." Those guilty of the most heinous crimes, and quite beyond cure, may yet serve some good purpose if their subsequent torment can provide a cautionary *paradeigma* for other bad men. Such *paradeigmata*, selected in all likelihood from tyrants, kings and politicians (525d), are vivid examples as they "hang there in the prison house of Hades" of a type whose utter wickedness is rewarded finally with the greatest of suffering.[1] So also in the *Sophist* 226b-c Plato's Eleatic Stranger introduces the general notion of an art of separation by citing several specific arts: sifting, winnowing, straining, threshing, and others. Theaetetus is at first puzzled: "What do you wish to show about them, setting out all these *paradeigmata* about which you asked?" The Stranger replies that each is a type of separation and that this single art common to all deserves its own name, *diakritikon*. Theaetetus, a "promising lad," catches on, and the hunt for the sophist resumes.

In both passages one moves from a number of examples (*paradeigmata*) to the more general types of which they are illustrations.[2] The Stranger varies this proceedure in the *Politicus* (278c), comparing a single familiar example of a certain activity with an unfamiliar one so that the factor or property already apparent in the former (the *paradeigma*) may appear more clearly in the latter. There he adopts weaving as his familiar *paradeigma* of the activity of "plaiting together"; this he sets alongside kingship (279a) in hopes that young Socrates, starting from a grasp of the art of plaiting together as illustrated by the example of weaving, will see the relevant similarity of kingship to weaving, and so learn something about kingship.[3]

Familiar *paradeigmata* are helpful not only in recognizing but also in constructing new instances. For example, the process of defining the angler constitutes an illustration (*paradeigma*, 218d) of the method to be used in capturing that more elusive quarry, the sophist. Theaetetus gets some preliminary practice on an easier case, the angler being a relatively guileless sort, before attempting to track down the wily sophist by the method of division.[4] So, too, Meno is urged to answer the question "What is virtue?" in the same way Socrates had answered a corresponding question about shape: by embracing all its parts in one formula. "Do not give me a plurality," says Socrates, "but a whole, as with the *paradeigmata* I have given you" (*Meno* 77a, 79a). Socrates had already (75a) encouraged Meno to try the question about shape, so as to get in some practice at giving the right sort of answer before taking on virtue itself.

In general, these *paradeigmata* point beyond themselves either to a general type or principle of which they are more specific illustrations[5] or to another, less easily apprehended, coordinate instance of the same general type as the initial *paradeigma*. Their philosophical interest rests on this fact, which accounts for their role in Socratic *epagogē* or "induction" (where they serve as the base cases agreed on by interlocutors), in arguments from analogy in general, and in the use of examples for teaching or suggesting new lines of investigation.[6] Plato makes free use of illustrative *paradeigmata* throughout the dialogues, from early to late, and comes eventually (*Politicus* 278c) to analyze explicitly one of their most important pedagogical uses. There is, however, nothing peculiarly philosophical about the use of *paradeigma* for "illustrative example"; it is familiar from a broad range of ancient authors. Sophocles gives us, in Oedipus, perhaps the most striking case of all:

> What man, what man on earth wins more
> of happiness than a seeming and after
> that turning away? Oedipus, you are
> my *paradeigma* of this, Oedipus, you and
> your fate! (*OT*, 1189 ff., trans. David Greene)[7]

B. Paradigm Cases and Standard Instances

Greek architectural practice will illustrate a second sort of *paradeigma*. Apparently on at least some occasions the architect of a temple requiring, say, twenty-four Corinthian capitals would have one made to his own specifications, then instruct his masons to produce twenty-three more just like it. Their success would be determined on the basis of similarity or dissimilarity to the original taken as standard.[8] In common parlance the masons could be said to imitate the action of the mason who produced the standard or, alternatively, to produce copies, duplicates, imitations, or more or less exact approximations of the standard capital. All twenty-four artifacts would be Corinthian capitals of such-and-such design (the particular design embodied in the architect's standard), all similar and comparable to one another in that respect.

As I shall use the term, it is a sufficient condition for a thing's being a *standard* for the type or property F that instances of the type are classified on the basis of similarity to that particular F in respect F. Thus items a yard long (e.g., shop yardsticks) are classified as such on the basis of similarity to the Standard Yard with respect to its length; blue objects might be classified as such on grounds of similarity, with respect to color, to a standard sample of blue; all non-paradigm capitals would be classed as "Corinthian" just in case they resembled the standard in having a certain design. There are other types of standard for which such similarity is not a necessary condition, as will be seen in sections C and D.

Perhaps the best example of this second sort of *paradeigma* still extant was discovered only recently in the ancient water tunnel of Eupalinos on the island of Samos. Most of the tunnel consisted of a series of sections of identical design; on the section with which construction began excavators discovered the archaic inscription, ΠΑΡΑΔΙΓΜΑ. In their opinion, that "can only mean that this section of the wall provided the model for the rest of the structure."[9] Here the model or *paradeigma* is a section to be *duplicated*, in relevant respects, by the workmen: In the finished work all sections of the tunnel, including the standard or paradigm, will help to convey water. The difference is that although the initial section and all other well-made sections illustrate a certain design, in the manner of *paradeigmata* of type A, the initial section also serves as a paradigm case, in that its design is specified as the one that all other sections are supposed to duplicate or copy.[10]

One can see how identification of Forms with paradigm cases leads directly to the issue of self-exemplification. Paradigm cases, standard instances, or perfect particulars are still cases, instances, or examplars of a given kind of thing, right along with their non-paradigmatic brethren: The Standard Pound will itself weigh one pound, as the Standard Yard will itself be one yard long. The standard F may be F "by definition"; it may be known to be F without our having to compare it to anything (as when we define some length as the length of a certain bar at a given time or under certain conditions). It may on these grounds be considered ontologically and epistemologically a different kind of F from non-standard Fs. Still it is similar to other Fs, and comparable to them in respect F. Indeed the standard instance *must* resemble and be comparable to other instances in respect F since that is the very basis of its utility as a standard.

It is in view of the special role of a standard in picking out members of a given class that P.T. Geach and R.S. Bluck (and ultimately Wittgenstein) have suggested that "F" can be predicated only "analogously" of the standard F and all the other Fs.[11] While this helps bring out an interesting fact about the different bases for attributing "being F" to a standard of F-ness and to other Fs, it does not affect the present point. The standard F will still be comparable to non-standard Fs with respect to being F. Or again, standard F and non-standard F will share the property of being F, even if non-standard Fs are F only because of their similarity to the standard while it is F "in and of itself."

The familiar notion of Forms as "perfect particulars" is closely related to the concept of a standard instance, in that any stipulated standard instance of being F will be exactly or perfectly F (putting aside the fact that a concrete standard could change with respect to being F, as bronze standards of length do in fact contract slightly during the first few decades after fabrication).[12] But these are nonetheless two distinct conceptions, since not every perfect particular (e.g., a stick perfectly equal in length to some other stick) need be a standard of F-ness. A perfect-particular interpretation usually preserves uniqueness of the Form by supposing that nothing else could possibly be exactly or perfectly F; other Fs are presumed capable only of *approximating* perfect F-ness. But one might well admit there could be many perfect Fs, as there could in principle be many yardsticks exactly duplicating the length of the Standard Yard, while ensuring uniqueness of the Form by making it the *sole standard* of F-ness. Like a unique standard of length, it would play a unique role in the objective classification of all other Fs, including any perfect Fs. (In actual practice one might designate several standards of, say, weight or length, rather than one, but Plato's Form of F is a unique standard.)

So one has immediately two sub-species of the familiar notion of Forms as paradigm cases, one allowing for, one disallowing, exact embodiment of the character in question (justice, equality, circularity) by Fs other than the Form of F itself. But both notions require some degree of similarity with respect to being F between standard and non-standard instances.

There is yet a third reading on which Forms are F, and similar to non-Forms with respect to being F. Here Forms are cases or examples of being F without being un-F in any way (such as being equal without being *unequal* in any respect, relation, or time.) Accordingly Forms are now referred to as "unqualified exemplars." By contrast, sensibles are F only in some context, relation, or respect, or at some time, and are also un-F in some other context, relation, or respect. Insofar as they are F they need *not* be only approximately F; but their being F is necessarily qualified in one or more of the ways just indicated. Although this gives a different sort of paradigm-case interpretation than the two mentioned above, it results in property-sharing between Forms of F and sensible F with respect to being F, and so is still vulnerable to the Third Man Argument.

Despite the role of similarity in all three readings, the Form is always different *in kind* from sensibles. Either it is the sole specimen capable of perfect F-ness (the approximation view), the sole standard for classification of all Fs, perfect or imperfect (a view usually combined in the literature with the approximation view), or the sole specimen of being F that is not also, in some way, un-F. We shall have to inquire in due time whether these views preserve as strong a difference in kind between Form and sensible as Plato intends, and whether Plato's difference in kind does not preclude the sort of resemblance common to these readings.[13]

C. Patterns or Structures

In a last attempt to meet the objections of "Parmenides," young Socrates of the *Parmenides* turns to Forms as *paradeigmata hestanai en tē physei*, often translated as "patterns fixed in the nature of things." (*Paradeigmata* could of course be translated here as "models"; for the moment let us see what conception of Forms goes best with a "pattern" reading.) At least four different interpretations might be given to this phrase. With emphasis on the 'in,' Forms may become forces embedded in nature, somehow guiding, shaping, or directing natural processes from within. The motive would not be simply to avoid a charge of superfluousness laid to separate Forms by critics from Aristotle onwards, but also to unite being (the internal guiding factor) and becoming so as to make being *immediately* responsible for the directedness of processes in the visible realm — and (if sensibles *are* simply directed processes of various sorts) for the very being of worldly *F*s.[14] However, aside from the difficulty of making Forms actually inhabit the visible cosmos (an assumption already in conflict with the *Phaedo*, *Symposium*, and *Timaeus* — see chapter 6), a Platonic teleology would not require that Forms intervene in the hurley-burley of becoming in quite so direct a way. At least, a Platonism based on separate, independently existing platonic entities need not give up teleological explanations of natural processes. Plato's picture of the cosmos and much of its contents as the product of divine or human craftmanship conducted according to Forms gives separate Forms a crucial (even if indirect) role in all purposeful directing of the flux. Moreover, the only factors Plato recognizes as dynamically guiding things from within would seem to be the souls of living things; these are at any rate the only sources of self-motion, hence of goal-directed self-motion, in Plato's created cosmos.

A second variation on the "pattern" interpretation is again concerned to relate Forms to the generation of sensibles and to such orderliness as one finds in the development and behavior of sensibles, but does so by treating Forms as laws of nature rather than immanent directors of worldly flux. The position is held, for example, by Paul Natorp, whose central thesis is that "die Ideen Gesetze, nicht Dinge bedeuten."[15] A more recent representative offers the following example: the "pure form of the Greylag exists in another sense [from that in which particular Greylag geese exist], namely, as that very law which describes the optimal functions of the Greylag goose."[16]

A persistent problem for this interpretation is that of making clear the nature and ontological status of such laws, then reconciling the natural law reading with what Plato says about the nature and status of Forms. It may well be true that Plato wanted to express in terms of Forms certain thoughts about nature or the cosmos that later writers would normally express in terms of laws of nature. But it is a long way to the conclusion that what Plato called Forms are what we would call laws of nature — rather than, say, what we would call abstract essences or paradigm cases. The natural law interpretation will not be developed further here, although we will see later that it contains an important insight captured by the theory of paradigmatic Forms.

Patterns in the nature of things can be immanent without being dynamic or impelling causes. A third "pattern" interpretation would construe Forms simply as the formal aspect of objects having both a formal and material aspect. Once again, the charge of superfluousness (of separate Forms) is avoided, since Forms as formal structures can be the formal *aitiai* of sensibles in a markedly Aristotelian sense.[17] Here again the question arises whether the Forms in *any* of the dialogues, even late ones such as the *Philebus*, are reasonably seen as formal aspects of participants, or as immanent in, rather than separate from, sensibles. And there is a serious question whether immanent Forms could do all the things Plato wants Forms to do (such as serve as eternal, objective standards of justice, beauty, and the like). For the moment let us simply note it is possible to interpret paradigmatic Forms as immanent, but not causally active, patterns.

Finally, a pattern or structure might be a separate, independent, abstract object embodied in or conformed to by things and motions in this world, but neither literally present to them nor guiding them in any sense from the inside. We are now back among the august and holy, the solemn and aloof occupants of "noetic space" (*noētos topos*, *Republic* 509d). Unlike standards and unqualified exemplars, these abstract structures are not similar to worldly Fs or Gs with respect to being F or G. They are rather what concrete things are supposed to satisfy or embody perfectly — as a house may "wish" or "strive" (in Socrates' metaphor of *Phaedo* 74-75) to embody precisely the structure specified by a blueprint. On this reading visible participants strive not to possess properties already possessed perfectly or unqualifiedly by a paradigm case but rather to embody, satisfy, or conform to a fixed abstract pattern or structure which does not exemplify itself.

This fourth pattern or structure reading subdivides in an interesting way. On one branch the abstract pattern is highly specific, as if spelled out by a blueprint indicating not only shape but also a definite size, so that any building satisfying it perfectly would have *these* precise dimensions (and not be just a house of the "Colonial type"). A Form of Shuttle itself would determine the precise shape, size, and texture that every shuttle ought to possess, rather than specify only a particular shape or function for shuttles. Thus all perfectly crafted shuttles would be congruent.

A second branch is more flexible, allowing a less precise stipulation of the relevant structure. Circle itself would determine a shape, but no precise radius; the pattern or structure that is Shuttle itself might determine a shape but no precise size (though perhaps specifying an allowable range of sizes). Consequently a circle or shuttle of one radius or size would be as good a specimen of its kind as one of another size, and there might be many varieties of perfect circle or shuttle. [18] In the case of Shuttle there would not be, on the more flexible pattern or structure interpretation, a single perfect shape and size that each of the craftsman's products ought to possess.

Either of these two abstract structure readings will preserve a great deal of what Plato says about Forms. *Separate* abstract structures can easily be conceived as independent of the concrete objects embodying them. They would be a different type of F from concrete Fs (being the pattern F itself rather than G itself, but not in general an F embodying itself). They may be eternal, immutable, intelligible. They would be that to which a craftsman looks in producing artifacts, and they would serve as standards for classifying and evaluating particulars. Notice that their use as standards would not be based on similarity to their embodiments with respect to being F. Classification and evaluation of participants would turn not on similarity in respect F to a standard instance, but on the extent to which some structure is realized in a worldly participant. In addition the more flexible pattern or structure reading allows for different sorts of Fs (different sorts of triangles, bees, or shuttles) all of which embody a common general structure. Since for many Forms there will be participants of various sorts, this flexibility has a clear advantage over a more rigid pattern or structure interpretation and over paradigm-case interpretations on which, for example, every shuttle would try to embody the same detailed structure, or to duplicate the same paradigm shuttle. (On the varieties of shuttle that share one and the same *eidos*, see *Cratylus* 389b-c.)

It is a serious question, however, whether all Forms can be regarded as structures of some kind, or whether a more general notion of abstract natures — one covering functionally as well as structurally defined natures — is necessary. But let us turn now to a reading that enjoys all the advantages of the more flexible abstract structure reading, and can be made as general as one likes: the notion of Forms as intelligible models of worldly images.

D. Models

It is frequently stated or implied that a model is related to its images, imitations, or likenesses in much the same way that a paradigm case is related to its non-paradigm kin. Hence the assumption described in the Introduction that Plato's image analogy was intended to illustrate a theory of

Forms as paradigm cases. Plato's own usage, like common English usage, encourages that conflation to some extent, for not only can the same word *paradeigma* ("model") serve for both a standard instance to be duplicated and a model to be imaged, but the term "imitation" (*mimēma*) can apply both to duplicates or copies of a standard and to images or likenesses (e.g., paintings or reflections) of a model. But there is at least one sense of "image" and "model" prominent in the dialogues and found in common English according to which images of a model must be sharply distinguished from duplicates or copies of a standard instance. Indeed Plato's stock examples of images—paintings, statues, drawings, reflections in mirrors or water, dream images, songs, images in poetry or prose—are in no case related to their models as copies to standards or as qualified to unqualified exemplars. In these cases the image *F* is not "another real *F* such as its model" (the phrase is from *Sophist* 240a9), nor does it resemble its model with respect to being *F*: the reflection of Cratylus in the mirror or on water is not another Cratylus; the black-figure warrior on a vase is not another, only qualified or imperfect, warrior; the marble Hermes is not itself a god. Put another way, the mirror reflection of a bed is no more a "real" bed, a worldly participant in the Form of Bed itself, than is the mirror reflection of a horse, since neither fulfills the function or does the characteristic work of a carpenter's bed. The contrast between model and imitation (*mimēma*) or image (*eikōn, eidōlon*) is not that between perfect and more or less imperfect instance, or between unqualified and qualified exemplar, but between real or true or genuine *F* and something that is called "*F*" rather than "*G*" even though it is not a real or true *F*. To avoid a possible misunderstanding: This is not to say "image" and "imitation" (or *eikōn, eidōlon*, and *mimēma*) have the same meaning, or that they are co-extensive. All these terms have a variety of uses, some of which are nebulous in themselves. The specific claim is that on at least one point these terms overlap, namely, when each is used to contrast images (likenesses, imitations) with "real things themselves." Notice also that while *we* might not apply the terms "image," "imitation" and "likeness" freely to paintings, statues, reflections, dreams, and dramatic performances alike, Plato does not hesitate to refer to *all* of these by *mimēma, eidōlon*, or *eikōn*. (I have encountered native informants who found "image" much more natural for mirror and water reflections than for paintings and statues.) These points are documented in chapter 3.

The use of "real *F*" as applied to a model or *paradeigma* of this sort (for example, an artist's model or original, as at *Republic* 500c, *Timaeus* 48e-52, *Sophist* 253d) is what J.L. Austin called the "ellipsis excluding" use of "real," while "image" or "imitation," as contrasted with "model" or "original," is akin to our usage in "imitation diamond" or "imitation leather."[19] To call the former "ellipsis excluding" is to observe only that the statement "this is a diamond" will in certain contexts be elliptical for "this is an imitation, but not a real, diamond." A portrait labeled "Napoleon" is not a real Napoleon, but only – if we fill in the ellipsis – a portrait of Napoleon. On the other hand when we say this is a real (true, genuine) diamond we mean to exclude any such addition: This is no mere imitation, no piece of cut glass that only sparkles like a diamond, but the genuine article – truly, in one antique phrase, a girl's best friend. "If something is a real dog then it is not a gasometer, a rose-bush, a stuffed dog, a model dog, a toy dog, a dream dog, a picture of a dog, an ice cream dog; its being a real dog excludes its being any kind of non-dog. . . . "[20] On this use of "image" or "imitation" as opposed to "real," it is essential to something's being an image *F* or an imitation *F* that it *not* be a real *F*, that it not share the property of being *F* with the model or real thing itself.

Accordingly, the *Oxford English Dictionary* lists this use of "image" as something "simulating the appearance of someone, *or considered as unreal*," and provides memorable illustrations:

Those most miserable men (yea, rather
Images, and pictures of men, than very men in dede).
(Cunningham, *Cosmographical Glasse*, 1559)

Hearyng that this feyned duke was come,
and had heard that he [Perkin Warbeck] was
but a peinted ymage.
(Hall, *Chronical*, 37b, 1548)

The spelling has changed but the usage is still comprehensible: Images and pictures of men are not men at all, so that the hyperbolic metaphor of the first passage depicts men so miserable they are no longer even human. As for the feyned duke, he is no more a real duke than is a peinted ymage of a duke. It is probably not a coincidence the *OED* lists no more recent examples. The use of "image" to convey that a thing is "considered as unreal" seems not to be common anymore; it is not listed in most modern dictionaries. Perhaps this is part of the reason many readers of Plato think immediately of resemblance between image and model rather than of the *contrast* between real thing and mere image (i.e., the *lack* of similarity with respect to being *F*). If this is so it is all the more important to observe carefully how Plato illustrates and discusses his contrast between image *F* and model *F*, putting aside as far as possible any immediate associations the term "image" may have for us.

Three additional remarks may help sharpen the use in question. First, it entails more than that the image *F* does not *exactly* resemble the model *F* respect to being *F*, or that it has only some *lesser degree* of *F*-ness. It implies rather that the image *F* (the painting of a horse, dream of a treasure, drawing of a castle, reflection of a dagger) is not itself another real *F* (horse, treasure, castle, dagger) at all. Second, the image *F* can perfectly well resemble its model *F* in respects *other* than *F*. Plato frequently points out that a painting can have the same colors as its model, and a statue the same colors and proportions in three dimensions. Although a portrait of Cratylus is not another real Cratylus, it may be another real white thing, having color in the same sense as Cratylus. But however much the image *F* may resemble its model in other respects, it must always, so long as it is to be only an *eikōn* or *eidōlon* of *F*, fall short of its model in not being another real *F*.

Third, it does sometimes happen, in apparent exception to the principles just stated, that images of *F*s are also real *F*s: A painting of a painting (not a fake or a copy, but something like a painting of "the artist's studio" depicting other paintings) is itself a real painting.[21] A shadow or reflection of a triangle could well itself be triangular, and "functional art" itself performs the function of the sorts of objects it represents (as with a three-dimensional chair-shaped statue of a chair, the representation being itself serviceable as a chair). These examples do not nullify the general contrast drawn above. Indeed functional art actually highlights the intended conception, since it relies for its effect precisely on one's expectation that a painting or a statue will be an image *F as opposed to* a "real" or functional *F*.

Now Plato may not have thought of such cases, and he may have mistakenly thought that no shadow or painting of a real *F* would also turn out to be a real *F*. But that seems unimportant for his task of illustrating an ontology, and to ours as his interpreters. So long as his examples and discussions of images make clear that he intends the sort of image/reality contrast described above (a thesis to be argued at length in the next chapter) these exceptional cases should have no effect on our understanding of the image analogy.

E. Overlap of Types

These classifications are not mutually exclusive. One important overlap is that of examples and paradigm cases (A, B) with models (D). Many examples of a certain kind of thing (animals, plants, landscapes, including any perfect specimens or standard instances that may be put to use as examples) can also in other contexts be the models depicted in paintings, reflected in water, and so on. And if participants in Forms (e.g., "real live lions"), are construed as images of Forms as models, then illustrative examples and standard instances (these live lions, or this perfect specimen of the breed) will in turn be images as well.[22] They could all be *paradeigmata* (examples, or in some cases, paradigm instances) and at the same time images of Forms taken as *paradeigmata* (intelligible models). Such predictable overlap of terminology should cause no confusion if the distinctions surveyed above are borne in mind.

3

Image and Reality

There is a notion abroad that metaphor really ought to be dispensed with when we stick soberly to the task of making our ideas clear. As Max Black remarks, "to draw attention to a philosopher's metaphors is to belittle him — like praising a logician for his beautiful handwriting."[1] But in fact even the most arid prose can hardly get along without metaphor. More to the present point, although use of metaphor can sometimes mask obscurity of thought or engender an illusion of understanding, it also serves less shady purposes, including some for which it is peculiarly well suited. I have in mind, for example, the illumination of primitive terms of a theory — terms for which the theory provides no further explicit definition. Within the theory of Forms, "participation" (itself a somewhat less complex metaphor than "imaging") is such a term. Or again, a metaphor of sufficient complexity may draw together numerous points of theory so as to facilitate appreciation of their underlying unity. This, too, seems a deliberate and important feature of Plato's image/model imagery. And, contrary to the attitude noted (but not endorsed) by Black, a properly controlled metaphor can help avoid important misunderstandings, even where a given claim can in some manner be stated without recourse to metaphor.

In the following discussion of these and other claims, I will often speak of Plato's image "analogy" as well as his image "metaphor." Here "metaphor" covers transfer of expressions from one subject matter to another, the new usage being conditioned more or less strictly by the old. By an analogy I will mean any statement in which the same relationship is said to hold between one pair of items as holds between some other specified pair. Thus where a metaphor is also an analogy the transfer of terms is governed by the fact that two original items are related, in certain respects, in the same way as their proposed analogues. I hope by the end of this chapter to have shown that Plato's use of the concept of imaging amounts to a carefully wrought and versatile philosophical analogy illustrating a detailed, highly ramified version of extreme Platonism.

Against the background of alternatives described in chapter 2, two elementary points will provide a secure foundation for the interpretation of Plato's image analogy. (1) The *paradeigmata* of paradigmatism are analogous to models or originals or "real things themselves" whose correlates are images, imitations, phantasms, or likenesses. (2) On Plato's view of imaging, model F and image F are two different types of F such that they do not share the property of being F. With these two points established (sections A and B, below) it will be possible to see what Plato does and does not mean by the "likeness" of model F and image F (section C) and how a friend of the Forms would deal with the regress arguments of the *Parmenides* (section D). A third basic aspect of the image analogy will emerge in the course of the chapter, and come to prominence in chapter 6: The relation between image F and real F which underlies their kinship as Fs and corresponds to a sensible F's participation in the Form of F is the image's *being of* some genuine F. It is its being of a certain sort of object that "makes" an image be the sort of thing it is. Its being a drawing of a horse "makes" a given drawing what it is: a (drawn) horse, rather than a cow or a man, or simply a collection of lines on paper. Treatment of these three most basic points will bring to light several subsidiary uses of the analogy.

A. The *Paradeigmata* of Paradigmatism

The first point is scarcely controversial and can be established by a quick review of passages dealing with paradeigmatism in general terms. Let us proceed directly to the *locus classicus* of the doctrine, *Timaeus* 48e:

> Then [in the beginning] we distinguished two types (*duo eidē*), but now a third kind (*triton genos*) must be revealed. Those two were adequate for the earlier discussion, one *eidos* posited of the *paradeigma* . . . a second the imitation (*mimēma*) of the *paradeigma*.

Timaeus also likens participants to images (*eikones*, 52c2) and to phantasms (*phantasmata*, 52c3).[2] Therefore they will, like images, require a "medium" in which they come to be (52c). Finally, the creator in Timaeus' creation story is the divine artisan or craftsman (*dēmiourgos*) who fashions visible and spatial images (*eikones*) looking to noetic, non-spatial models (*paradeigmata*, 29a-b).[3]

The image analogy also dominates the central books of the *Republic*, where it is fundamental to the similes of both the divided line and the cave. Within the lower section of the divided line the shadows and reflections correlated with *eikasia* are images (*mimēmata*) of the objects (animals, plants, artefacts) of belief (*pistis*), while the latter objects are in turn used by the soul as images (*eikones*) when it is forced to "start from hypotheses" (510b2-9). Thus geometers "use visible forms and talk about them . . . The things which they construct and draw, of which there are shadows and images (*eikones*) in water, these they use as images (*eikones*) though they wish to behold those things themselves which no one may behold except in thought" (510d5-511a1).

Whatever one may wonder at in this text, it is the relation of images (such as shadows and reflections) to their originals (plants, animals, and artifacts) that is supposed to illumine the use of man-made images of intelligible originals, as well as the relative ontological and epistemological status of sense objects as opposed to intelligible Forms.

The same relationship underlies the simile of the cave, which rests on a more elaborate hierarchy: Within the cave one finds shadow-images, then wooden images which cast the shadow-images, and finally fire as a source of light. These strata parallel those found above ground: the shadows and reflections in water, the "things themselves" which cast shadows and are reflected, then the light of the stars and moon and

ultimately the sun itself (515c-516c). Without entering into the difficult
issue of how the details of the three great similes of sun, line and cave fit
together, it is safe to say that the basis of the simile of the cave, as of the
divided line, is the relation of image F or imitation F (shadow, statue,
reflection) to genuine F or "real thing."

The epistemological side of paradigmatism is reemphasized later in the
Republic:

> And when you are accustomed to the darkness you will see immeasur-
> ably better than they; you will recognize each image (*eidōlon*), what
> it is and of what it is the image, once you have discovered the truth
> of Beauty and Justice and the Good (520c4-6).

Again the opposition is between that which is real or true and that which
is only an *eidolon* (here a shadow) of reality.

Moreover, in the *Republic*, as in the *Timaeus*, productive activity is a
matter of craftsmanship conducted with an eye to appropriate Forms. The
statesman-philosopher looks to the Good and the Just and, like a painter,
"mixes his pigments" to create the good and just citizens of his city.[4] In
similar fashion the carpenter of *Republic* 596-7 makes a bed looking to the
Bed-in-nature; his activity, too, is analogous to that of the painter, whose
painting of a bed is only an image of the carpenter's bed, which is in turn
only an image of the "really real" Bed-in-nature or Form of Bed (cf. 600e5
on the poets as imitators of images, *mimētas eidōlōn*).

Phaedrus 250a-d adds that among things of which there are likenesses
(*homoiōma*, a6) in this realm, some, like Beauty, provide us with many
distinct visual images. By contrast Justice, Temperance, Wisdom and
everything of value in the soul, in whose likenesses (*homoiōmata*, b3;
eikones, b4) there is no luster, have given us no clear visual image
(*enarges eidōlon*, d5) of themselves.[5]

Elsewhere the image theory makes a cameo appearance (*Symposium*
212a on the *eidola* of true virtue for example), or appears thinly veiled—
as at *Phaedo* 74-75, where the recollection of Form from sensible is illustrated by Simmias and "drawn Simmias." Recall also the pointed declara-
tion in Socrates' "intellectual autobiography" (*Phaedo* 100a) that by studying things in *logoi* he is no more studying them through images (*en eikosi*)
than those who study *erga*. Studying things in *logoi* is implicitly agreed
by all to be a study of things in images, the idea of *logoi* as *mimēmata* of
things being entirely commonplace. Socrates' reply is that those who sup-

pose they study sensible things directly are just as much involved in the study of images as he.[6] But the dialogues in which the theory is most explicit leave no doubt that Plato held an image-model theory of participation.

B. Image *F* and Real *F*

The second and more controversial claim was that on Plato's view of imaging, image *F* and model *F* are two types of *F*, not similar with respect to being *F*. This is in direct conflict with what many commentators, and *hoi polloi* as well (if I may link the two without offence to either party) appear to assume. Certainly resemblance is often a conspicuous part of the relationship between an *eikōn* or *mimēma* and its model. It is also a complicated question whether Plato assumed that *some* sort of resemblance was essential to imaging, and if so what exactly this would mean for the interpretation of his metaphysics. But if one agrees that resemblance must always be resemblance *in some specific respect*, and then considers what Plato has to say about the respects in which an imitation *F* may or may not resemble its model *F*, I believe one will conclude that Plato's *eidola* or *eikones* are *not* supposed to resemble their models in the respect presumed by paradigm-case interpretations of Forms and by the regress arguments of the *Parmenides*. In fact Plato will be found to insist that model and image are not so related, as one essential part of his Herculean attempt to convey for the first time a conception of an abstract intelligible realm. Evidence for this basic claim is of three sorts: (1) Plato's own examples of images; (2) specific applications, often of interest in their own right, of the image-model contrast in non-metaphysical contexts; and (3) two passages from the *Cratylus* and the *Sophist* which discuss explicitly the nature of images.

Plato's Examples of Images

Plato's own examples – paintings, drawings, statues, reflections, shadows, dreams – are already quite revealing. For in none of these specific examples does the image *F* share the property of being *F* with its homonymous model.[7] The shadows and reflections of the lowest section of the divided line are not real "plants, animals, and implements" such as one finds in the next section above (*Republic* 510a-b). Naturalistic scene paintings and mirror images of a landscape are not real landscapes (*Republic*

596d-e). The painter's bed is not a "real" bed, because it is not naturally suited to perform the work of a bed; nor is the actor who imitates a rooster or a clap of thunder, strut or rumble as he may, a real rooster or clap of thunder. The implication of such examples is that image *F* and model *F*, however else they might resemble one another, must be different types of *F*, since image *F*s are not real *F*s at all.

It is worth noting at this early stage the variety of Plato's image terminology (*eikōn, eidōlon, phantasma, homoiōma, mimēma*), since some of his terms (or their translations) may carry for us vagrant and misleading connotations. *Phantasmata* will perhaps suggest most clearly the *contrast* between a mere image (or phantasm) and a real thing of the sort imaged. By contrast the word *homoiōma* might put one in mind rather of some supposed similarity (*homoiōtēs*) between image and original. But even the latter term always applies in Plato's dialogues to items which, though they may look like their originals and in some respects be like them, are not similar to them in respect of being *F*. These items are in fact always images such as paintings, statues, or dramas (*Cratylus* 434a; *Sophist* 266c-d; *Laws* 812c. At *Parmenides* 132d, 133d – the second regress argument – Parmenides, perhaps for tactical reasons, does not mention any examples).

The use of *eidōlon* is broader, applying also to various wraiths and ghostly appearances (*Phaedo* 81d), and to sensible embodiments of things unseen. So actual speech makes manifest a thought or opinion in the soul, as at *Theaetetus* 208c spoken sounds are a kind of sensible image of the affection in the soul (cf. *Republic* 382b). When speaking of (deliberately) deceptive images or counterfeits Plato prefers *eidōlon* to *eikōn* (*Gorgias* 463d, *Lysis* 219d, *Phaedo* 66c, *Republic* 586b-c, 587c, d), although he may also use *phantasma* or *mimēma* for this purpose. (None of these words necessarily implies any attempt at deception.) *Eikōn* applies to all the sorts of images mentioned so far and also to comparisons, similies, or parables. The latter could be thought of as verbal images to bring out their kinship to such *eikones* as paintings, statues, and reflections.

Mimēsis, as indicated in chapter 2, could cover both copying (as when the *paradeigma* is a specimen whose manner of being *F* is to be duplicated) and imaging. To imitate the colors of a model is, in some cases, to copy or duplicate them, though on the other hand the resulting *mimēma* taken as a whole will be only, say, a painted Simmias and not another (real) Simmias at all. Similarly, one could imitate (try to copy) a model of good behavior in order to become well-behaved oneself. Common language, like

Plato's, is flexible: One will sometimes say that the good imitation of the model, in the "copy" sense of "imitation," *is* another actual specimen of the same sort of thing as the model (perhaps a second well-behaved little boy). But one may sometimes wish to contrast the imitator of a good man with an actual good man (as in "the imitator of the true legislator is *not* another legislator," *Statesman* 300d-e). Likewise one could contrast merely imitating some wicked person with actually being another wicked person: "Don't imitate so-and-so lest you become wicked yourself, and not just an imitator of an evil man" (see *Gorgias* 513b, *Republic* 395c7; cf. *Protagoras* 326a). The latter uses are the sort relevant to the analogy between imaging and participation, and Plato will often use the term *mimēma* alongside *eikōn, eidōlon*, or *phantasma* in such contexts. Thus all four terms occur together at *Sophist* 241e, where paintings, reflections, and sculptures are in view (from 239d) and where an image is said not to be another genuine thing of the same sort as its model. (For discussion of the passage see below; for other pairs and trios of these terms including *mimēma*, see *Republic* 382b, 509e-510a, 599c-d, 601b; *Timaeus* 52c; *Laws* 836e; *Cratylus* 430c.)[8]

It is surprising how often the evidence of Plato's own examples is overlooked. Even some of the most detailed and able discussions of Forms as standards take no notice of that commonplace fact about reflections, paintings, dreams, and the like. Meanwhile the relation of *copy* to standard is repeatedly analyzed, sometimes with great sophistication, on the assumption it would tell us what Plato intended or was committed to by calling sensible objects images of Forms. Of course the copy/standard relation and the image/model relation do have some important things in common. But concerning the critical feature of resemblance in respect *F*, they are directly opposed: the former necessarily includes it, the latter excludes it.[9]

Some Practical Applications: Semblances of Virtue

In Plato's hands the opposition of image *F* or imitation *F* to real *F* becomes an effective weapon against pretense and fakery as well as an instrument of philosophical exegesis. He wields it with special relish against pretenders to virtue or wisdom. So rhetoric and sophistic are attacked in the *Gorgias* as deceitful *eidola* of true justice and legislation, practiced only by the man with knowledge (464b-465b). Lacking knowledge, the sophistic pretender lacks one property essential to being a genuine or true legislator; this human *eidolōn* is no more a true legislator than cookery is medicine – or than a certain *eidōlon* fought over at Troy was (in Stesichorus' version) the real Helen (*Republic* 586b-c). *Politicus* 300d-e makes the same point about imitation statecraft: Without knowledge, one can only imitate the genuine statesman (*to alēthes*); with knowledge, one no longer has an imitation, but the real thing (*ouk esti eti mimēma all' auto to alēthestaton*). In the same vein Socrates quotes, at the very end of the *Meno*'s inquiry into virtue, Homer's description of Teiresias in Hades, likening the seer to a man in this world who could instill virtue in his fellow citizens: "With respect to virtue such a man would be like a real thing among shadows" (*hōsper para skias alēthes . . . pragma . . . ,* 100a7). In this context Socrates' point is that there are no men on earth who really teach virtue, though some may appear to do so (the sophists, for example, or Themistocles).

Perhaps the most interesting application of all is Socrates' attack on the so-called courage and temperance of the many (*Phaedo* 68d-69b). Their apparent virtues are not really courage and temperance at all, but cowardice and intemperance; the "virtue" of the many is only a deceptive scene-painting (*skiagraphia*) which in reality has nothing sound or true in it. Genuine (*to . . . alēthes tōi onti*) virtue is something altogether different; it is based on wisdom (*phronēsis*) and is not at all a matter of trading off pains, pleasures, and fears against one another. Socrates does not mean to allow that *hoi polloi* are virtuous, but virtuous only to a limited extent, or in a certain respect, or that they are halfway to virtue, or anything of the sort. He says they are not virtuous at all. Even worse, without *phronēsis* their apparent courage and restraint is in fact the opposite of virtue: Their "courage" is only fear of some greater evil, their "self-control" only desire for some even greater pleasure. Similarly, a scene-painting, even a very good one, is not an imperfect landscape, or halfway (or more) toward being a landscape; it is not a genuine landscape at all. Socrates' reference to *skiagraphia* actually evokes the manner in which illusions of courage or self-restraint arise. As *skiagraphia* apparently consists in the use of contrasting light and shade (or contrast of colors) to present an appearance of solidity (when viewed at a distance), so the virtue of the *kosmioi* really is not virtue at all, but only the playing off of pleasures against pains, pains against pains, fears against fears, and so on. It may appear to be virtue, however, to those who do not or cannot look closely into the matter.[10]

Mention of *skiagraphia* may remind one of an even more extreme case, the cunningly wicked man of *Republic* II who secures happiness by cultivating a reputation for justice—that is, by drawing about himself a deceptive *skiagraphia* of virtue (*Republic* 365c). From a distance the facade may look like the real thing, but it is only an image in paint, and is no more a real landscape than Adeimantus' utterly unjust man is just. So, finally, the sophist may succeed in making people think he is wise even though he is only an imitation wise man, and not really wise at all (*Sophist* 233a-c). In his seeming ability to discourse and dispute on any subject whatever he is like that deceiver of innocent children who appears able, with his drawn imitations and homonyms of real things (*mimēmata kai homōnuma tōn ontōn apergadzomenos tēi graphikēi technēi*, 234b7-8), to produce all things. But each is in fact only an imitator of real things (*mimētēs on tōn ontōn*, 235a1).

We are not yet directly concerned with image metaphysics, but rather with the force of labeling something an *eidōlon, eikōn* or the like. I suggest that any reading of image *F*s as imperfect *F*s or as qualified *F*s would spoil every one of the vividly metaphorical passages just reviewed. The point Plato wishes to emphasize is not that the image or imitation of human virtue is more or less virtuous, or virtuous in one respect but not in some other. It is that the imitation is not virtuous at all—does not resemble the truly virtuous person with respect to his virtue—and may even be the opposite of virtuous.

These examples do call, however, for one forward-looking terminological caveat: The imitation just man is not, in the language of the image theory of participation, an image of Wisdom, Statesmanship, or Justice. The human being who is actually just, and not an imitation just man, is an image of Justice itself. (It is real leather, not imitation leather, that would be an image of a Form of Leather.) By contrast the imitation just man is often the opposite of just, in which case he constitutes an image of the Unjust, if there is such a Form.

The Image Maker

Our friend from the *Sophist*, the artist who seemed to produce every sort of thing, introduced a contrast between producing mere *mimēmata* and producing real things themselves. The *Republic* also speaks of a wizard able to produce everything—at least everything under the sun. With the sun overhead he simply brandishes his mirror and "quickly produces the sun and everything in the sky, and you, and the earth, and every plant, animal, and implement" and "everything produced by any handcraftsman" (596c-e). He is thus a marvelous *sophistēs: panu thaumaston . . . legeis sophistēn.* (The translations of Shorey and Grube as "marvelous Sophist" and "marvelously clever man," respectively, reflect Plato's double *entendre* — and the frustrations of translation.) The trick is that he really produces only *phainomena,* not the real things *(phainomena, ou . . . onta . . . tēi alētheiāi, Republic* 596e). Plato's real target in the passage, the poet, imitates most beguilingly the several arts — those of the cobbler, carpenter, smith, horseman, general, legislator — and, like our friend with the mirror, in a sense produces anything you like *(Republic* 598b-c). But in reality poets do not produce doctors, armies, bridles, or shoes. By imitation they produce only phantasms and not realities; they merely "imitate doctors' talk." Those who actually possess the art of making shoes or houses or legislation produce real shoes and real cities, not phantasms, and insofar as they make real shoes or cities they are not imitation craftsmen but real cobblers and legislators.[11] Socrates even goes so far as to claim that no one would *want* to produce these imitations if able to produce the real things (599a-b).

Plato's insistence on this point would have been all the more vivid against a contemporary background of art as imitative, in the sense of striving after realism. "Certainly the *practice* of art (whatever may have been the theory about it) becomes more and more 'realistic' from the late fifth century onward — the schools of illusionistic painting, the proverbial hare of Polygnotas — and we can trace the change from the time of Euripides as it persists through the Hellenistic period and beyond, whether in comedy or sculpture. . . ."[12] Plato forceably brings us back to our senses (he might prefer to say back *from* our senses), reminding us that the artist's illusory work *is* an illusion — that it falls short, at least, in not being another genuine thing of the sort it imitates, no matter how lifelike it may be. He also reminds us of the artist's lowly aspiration: not the creation of real things, of genuine articles, but only the production of *phainomena* of real things.

Craft and Authority

Plato's contrast between true and imitation craft, whether in statecraft, handcraft, or world-making, has interesting consequences for how one conceives the craftsman's procedure and authority, and forms a natural bridge to image metaphysics. It is a Platonic commonplace that the *technitēs'* craft is based not just on experience and practice (though these are important for the exercise of any art) but on knowledge of relevant Forms. Still, how is that requirement to be understood? Does the craftsman try to embody in all products exactly the same specific pattern, design, or structure? Is he an expert copyist of a single paradigm artifact, earning our respect through production of copies virtually indistinguishable from his model and from one another? Or does his knowledge somehow leave room for discretion over how to proceed in an individual case?

Cratylus 389 is a crucial passage, dealing explicitly with several key elements of Platonic craftsmanship:

SOCRATES: Where does the maker look when he makes a shuttle? Is it not to that sort of thing naturally suited to do the work of a shuttle (*pros toiouton ti ho epephykei kerkidzein*)?
HERMOGENES: Certainly.
And what about this: if he breaks the shuttle in the process of manufacture, will he make another looking to the broken shuttle, or to the *eidos* to which he looked before?
Toward the latter, I think.
Then we would justly call that one what-is-Shuttle (*auto ho estin kerkis*)?
Yes.
So when there is need to make a shuttle for thin or thick coats, or flaxen or woolen or whatever type, all these shuttles ought to have (*echein*) the *eidos* of shuttle, and whichever nature is appropriate for each case, that is the nature (*physis*) the maker must give the shuttle.
Yes.
And for each kind of web there is by nature a corresponding type of shuttle. . . . (389a6-d2)

If the Form is a highly specific pattern, structure, or design, then the maker of shuttles will try to make all shuttles exactly alike. The maker will try to produce each and every one in exact conformity with the single pattern, design, or structure of a perfect shuttle. The better the craftsman the closer the shuttles will come to perfect conformity with the pattern (perhaps even conforming perfectly in some cases) and the more nearly the products will be exactly alike. Besides knowing what every good shuttle should be like, this craftsman maintains the highest standards of quality control. There is room here for fuller or more precise knowledge of the model than the layman has, and room for superior skill in embodying the model, but none for "custom work." Departure from strict conformity to the single pattern will produce inferior shuttles. If the Form is a paradigm case of itself then the same results follow, the only difference being that the craftsman will now be, literally, a copyist.

I believe the passage shows Plato has something quite different in mind. For it says not only that the craftsman looks to an *eidos*, but also that the maker must produce a variety of shuttles for a variety of webs (389b8-c1). Therefore there cannot be either a single specific pattern, design, or structure, or a single paradigm shuttle which all his products must embody or duplicate. On the contrary, the carpenter must make different sorts of shuttles for different sorts of webs, all of which must nonetheless have the same *eidos* of shuttle. Common to all shuttles, of whatever make and model, is possession of the *eidos* Plato calls "What-is-Shuttle," defined by reference to a certain use, function, or natural capacity—namely, that of carrying the woof thread back and forth between the threads of the warp (388b). This is what the carpenter looks to in making a wooden artifact which will have that *eidos* or serve that function. For a craftsman, to look to the Form is to be cognizant of the function the product will be called on to serve, and to fashion it accordingly.

Once the implication of *Cratylus* 389 on the making of shuttles is appreciated, other passages of similar import come quickly to mind. There are, for example, different varieties of clay for different purposes. So while the *Theaetetus* provides a single *logos* satisfied by all sorts of clay, (water mixed with earth, 147c) it also mentions three varieties of clay: dollmaker's, brickmaker's, and potter's clay. There can be no such thing as *the* unqualified exemplar, standard instance, specific pattern, or design (here, a single precise ratio of earth to water) for the making of clay, since there is no such thing as *the* perfect clay. If some clay were perfect for the dollmaker, it would be unsuitable for the brickmaker and potter; if it were perfect for the potter it would be unsuitable for the dollmaker, and so on. But all clay, of whatever sort, still satisfies the same definition or follows the same generic recipe.

The image theory of participation is well equipped to accommodate these observations. As there may be a variety of ways of imaging a Form, so a single original may have many varieties of image in various media and a variety of equally faithful images within one medium. Analogously, the Platonic artisan has knowledge of a single abstract intelligible nature, from it producing a potentially large variety of images: sensible objects embodying that intelligible nature.

Knowledge of the same sort of object underlies the *technē* of the handcraftsman, the philosophical legislator, and the divine composer of the cosmos. It underlies the *authority* also of the expert in any field, be it navigation, medicine, or generalship. That is, in part, why the expert can determine what is right in each individual case, and can cope with new situations—determine the right sort of shuttle, legislation, or medical treatment for a given case. The expert may, of course, discern certain standard types of shuttle, or stock treatments, or strategic manoeuvres for use in common situations; there will certainly be some of these in the repertoire of most *technitai*. The handcraftsman might even create paradigm cases for his own use or for the use of apprentices: Recall from chapter 2 that Greek architects may sometimes have made one section of a structure as a *paradeigma* (in the sense of "paradigm case") to be duplicated by the masons and builders. Similarly a maker of shuttles or shoes or clothing may envisage certain specific standard patterns, or even produce corresponding paradigm cases of different shoe styles or shuttles (see *Phaedo* 110b8 on the painter's "color samples," *deigmata*). But in the first place it will be only on the basis of his knowledge of the single intelligible Form that the craftsman can settle on this or that as the pattern or paradigm. Moreover the true *technitēs* is not limited in the manner of an apprentice who knows only how to copy paradigm cases or embody specific given patterns. He could in principle make a shuttle or cloak of a new sort (there is a place in Plato's *Republic* for custom tailors), devise a new kind of treatment, or modify the law if the nature of a given case demanded it.

These discussions of imitation virtue and of Platonic craftsmanship may try the patience of readers anxious to get on to the metaphysical message. But they prepare the way for that topic, since they help show what Plato did and did not mean by "imaging." They show, too, that a basically negative point (about lack of resemblance in respect F between image F and real F) does not arise simply as a point of contention among interpreters of the Forms, but was much on Plato's own mind, and was put to good use in a variety of other contexts worthy of attention in their own right.

Image and Reality in the Cratylus *and the* Sophist

There are two passages—*Cratylus* 432 and *Sophist* 240ab—in which Plato seems concerned about possible misunderstanding of the sharp contrast between image F and real F.

Cratylus 432 is especially interesting since it takes up the correctness of images in part precisely to show that the criterion for them cannot be the same as for copies or duplicates of a model. Socrates argues

> with regard to any image . . . it must not render in every respect that of which it is an image, if it is to be an image (*eikōn*) of Cratylus. . . . Now what if some god should make an image having not only your colors and shape, like a painter, but should also make all the things inside just like yours, softness and warmth and movement and soul and intelligence, and in short all of your characteristics, and should set this next to you: would we have then Cratylus and an *eikōn* of Cratylus, or two Cratyluses?
> Two Cratyluses, it seems to me, Socrates.
> . . . Do you not see, then, to what extent images fall short of having the same characteristics as that of which they are images?

Here is a concise rebuttal of the common sense opinion that the criterion of truth or correctness for an image is simply similarity to its model. It is an easy mistake for Cratylus to commit, especially since Socrates had started him out with paintings, which are explicitly said to reproduce the colors and shape of a model with varying degrees of accuracy (431c). Given also that there can be better or worse images of a given model, it is tempting to suppose the better image is simply that which more closely resembles its original, so the perfect god-made image would be an exact double of its model. But this eminently reasonable line of thought is deftly squelched by Socrates' observation that the perfect image—perfect by Cratylus' criterion—has become "another Cratylus" (a real Cratylus), not an *image* of Cratylus at all: We now have two Cratyluses rather than one Cratylus and an *eikōn* of Cratylus. The image F, as we have had frequent occasion to observe, is not a real F; the real F is not an image F.[13]

The fact that the opposition of image F to real F lies behind Socrates' contrast between "another Cratylus" and an image of Cratylus is, however, consistently overlooked. Even some readers who realize the importance of the passage seem drawn instead to what is in fact a second argument, that the god's image would be an exact duplicate or a double (*ditton*, 432d7) of its model and therefore indistinguishable from it (aside from differences as to spatial location or past history). As applied to Cratylus' theory of names as images of their bearers, such duplication would entail the ludicrous conclusion (d5) that one could not tell a thing from its correct name (432d5-9).

We have not one, but *two* arguments. The first (432a8-d1), based on Plato's notion of an image (specifically, on the notion that another F cannot be an image of F), taken together with Cratylus' similarity criterion of correctness for images, leads to the contradiction that a perfect image is not an image at all.[14] After drawing the moral (c7-d3) that we must seek a different criterion for the correctness of images, Socrates proceeds (d5-9) to a second *reductio* argument, this one based on Cratylus' similarity criterion taken together with his position on the "natural correctness" of *onomata* as images of their bearers. The second absurdity Socrates draws out — that we could not distinguish anything from its correct name — is perhaps the more striking of the two. But given the results of our discussion of *paradeigmata* in chapter 2, the first, which in effect uses the contrast between image and reality to show that an *image* is not a *duplicate* or copy, should now stand out clearly.

Others have noted the implication of this passage that an image must be *different* from its original.[15] It is worth emphasizing again that the passage says more than that the image F must be different from, or distinguishable from, the real F. For if, as the passage implies, an exact duplicate of an F cannot be an image F *because* it would be instead another real F, then it is one condition on being an image F that it not be a real F. And just being different from the model does not guarantee a thing will "fall short" in the sense of failing to be another real F. A mason's copy of a paradigm Corinthian capital might show some slight defect and yet be another real capital; the two might even sit atop adjacent columns in some temple of Apollo. But an image or imitation capital — a painting, dream image, or shadow of a capital — will fall short of its model to the extent it fails to be a real capital at all.

Theatetus learns a similar lesson in the *Sophist*. At 239d the Stranger gives as examples of images (*eidola*) those "in the water or mirrors, and those which have been painted or sculpted and all others of that sort." But at 240a7, having described the sophist as a maker of images, our sophist hunters encounter a difficulty:

But what, Stranger, would we say that an image (*eidōlon*) is except
that which, being made like (*aphōmoiōmenon*) the geniune (or true
thing, *t'alēthinon*) is another thing such as it (*heteron toiouton*)?
Do you mean another such genuine thing (*heteron . . . toiouton
alēthinon*) or what do you mean by this *such* (*toiouton*)?
By no means genuine, but like (*eoikos*).
And by genuine you mean really real (*ontōs on*)?
Yes.
Well, then isn't the non-genuine the opposite of the genuine?
Certainly.
So you say the like is not really real, since you say it is not genuine?
But it is in some way.
But not truly (*alēthōs*), so you say.
No—except that it really is an image (*eikōn*).
So not being really real, it really is that which we call an image
(*eikona*; 240a7-b11).

Now a copy or duplicate of some "real" object would be in the Stranger's
phrase "another genuine thing such as" the original—another real man,
tree, shuttle, or Corinthian capital. But as the Stranger says, *images* of
some *F* will not be other genuine *F*s. If they are to called "*F*" at all—and
paintings, statues, or even reflections may be called after their models—
they are *F*s of a type different from their *paradeigmata*. The image is not
another true or genuine or real *F*; it really is only an image *F*.[16]

So just as in the passages examined earlier from the *Phaedo* to the *Sophist* and *Statesman*, and just as with Plato's stock examples of images, the
distinction between image *F* and genuine *F* indicates not only that images
fall short of exact duplication of their models or that they are distinguishable from their models, but that they are not real *F*s at all, not even imperfect ones or qualified ones. They cannot, so long as they are images
or phantasms, be similar to real *F*s with respect to being *F*.

C. The Likeness of Likenesses

The metaphysical moral of the preceding sections would be, once again,
that sensible *F*s are a type of *F* different from intelligible *F*s, not sharing
with them (even qualifiedly, or imperfectly) the property of being *F*. The
image analogy, understood in the way defended here, does provide suit-

able illustration of a truly Platonistic theory of intelligible Forms and sensible participants, reinforcing rather than conflicting with the sort of difference in type indicated by Plato's categorical distinctions between Forms and worldly things in terms of non-spatiality, immutability, intelligibility, eternality, and so on. But it is equally important that sensibles do have some claim to be called "F" rather than "G," and that it is possible, as Plato often says in the *Republic*, *Timaeus*, and elsewhere, to hold true opinions about them. Thus it would be quite misleading to say simply that sensible Fs "are not Fs at all." They are not "really real" Fs at all, not abstract intelligible natures at all; but they are image Fs, sensible embodiments of Forms. Analogously, portraits, statues, dreams, or reflections of Cratylus or of a horse are not real Cratyluses or horses at all, but only drawn Cratyluses or horses. This does qualify them, however, for labeling as "Cratylus" or "horse" rather then "Simmias" or "ox," and determines the truth or falsity of various opinions as to what sort of image they are (that is, *of* what real things they are portraits, shadows, or the like).

This positive counterpart to the negative point about resemblance in respect F may also be expressed in terms of a likeness or kinship between different types of F. As Plato put it, sensibles are somehow "like" the Forms in which they partake, where this likeness or kinship has to do with their being Fs. In the *Phaedo* visible equals are said to be like (*proseoikenai*, 74e3) the Equal itself, only unable to be equal as it is (74e1), and recollection of Forms from visible participants is represented as a case of recollecting like from like (*homoios*), where drawn Simmias and Simmias (73e) provide the worldly example of recollection of like from like. At *Phaedrus* 250a-b the images (*eikones*) of Forms are called *homoiōmata*; at *Timaeus* 52 visible *mimēmata* (called also *eikones* and *phantasmata*) are said to be not only homonymous with but like (*homoion*; 52a5) their *paradeigmata*. Certainly image Fs (sensible Fs) are somehow like their model Fs (the Form of F). And while Plato sometimes speaks of resemblance in respects other than F (as when a painter reproduces the colors of a human model, as opposed to the model's humanity) it is clear that in the passages just quoted from the *Phaedo*, *Phaedrus*, and *Timaeus* Plato is talking about some likeness in precisely that respect indicated by the common *onoma* of homonymous Form and sensible, namely, with respect to being F.[17] Accordingly, the first *Parmenides* regress, and probably also the second, produces an unending series of Fs starting from visible Fs.

Plato's talk of likeness between image and model in respect F is presumably one reason (so I have argued) why commentators have often conflated the notions of copy and image, and taken the *Parmenides* regress of similarities to be a fatal objection to classical paradigmatism. It is ironic that Aristotle does not press the objection in quite this way (his interpretation of Forms as eternal particulars stems rather from assumptions about the necessary results of separating Forms from sensibles), and in fact tends to emphasize, in his own comments on images, the *lack* of similarity to a model in respect F. In this he *agrees* with Plato on the key point documented above. But in omitting notice of any positive kinship between image and model F in respect F, Aristotle takes a position actually more extreme than Plato's. For Aristotle, image F and model F are bare homonyms. By contrast Plato wants to emphasize not only a lack of resemblance in respect F (a lack of resemblance such as would obtain between two worldly participants in the Form of F) but also a positive relation between image and model F such that they can be called "different sorts of F," and the painter's bed called a bed "in a way" (as in *Republic* X), or such that "F" does rightly apply to both, but not by bare equivocation. They would be, to borrow Aristotle's important conception, *pros hen legomena*.[18]

It seems to me Plato was right about this. One can see why he might have spoken of "likeness" in respect F even as he recognized a strong type distinction between image F and real F. The positive link that removes image and model F from the realm of bare homonyms is the image's *being an image of* its model. This relationship is not defined by Plato (or anyone else, as far as I know), and it may involve different factors in different sorts of image. For example, causal factors are paramount with shadows and reflections; artists' intentions will presumably figure in the cases of painting and sculpture. Whatever its genesis in a particular case, the relation does justify calling or naming the image after its model: We label the drawing "horse" rather than "cabbage" because it is a drawing of a horse.

Likewise, the relation justifies grouping together real and imitation Fs in a way that does not justify grouping together image Fs and image Gs, or image Fs and real Gs. By way of illustration, suppose one is confronted with a gallery of images of presidents along with those notables themselves and told to sort out all the Washingtons, Coolidges, Roosevelts, and so on, in the room. There is a positive basis for grouping Washington himself with the Washington portraits, Coolidge with pictures of Coolidge, and so on, even though we can tell, in most cases at least, that one member of the group is animate and not just an image president. One might even speak of an umbrella property *being an F of one sort or another*, where the sorts share an *onoma* not by historical accident (as with river banks and savings banks) but because they are linked by the relation of imaging. In Plato's hierarchical ontology the Form is an intelligible model, the sensible participant an image of the Form, the painting of the sensible participant an image of an image of the Form. There is thus an extended family of *F*s held together, despite differences of type, by the relation of imaging.

I suggest this is an adequate explanation of Plato's speaking of "likeness" with respect to being *F* between two things that are in another sense definitely not alike in that respect. Here it is instructive to contrast the use of *toiouton hoion* ("such as") at *Republic* 597a with that at *Phaedo* 74e1: The former says the sensible couch is *toiouton hoion* the couch-in-nature, the latter that sensible equals cannot be *toiouton hoion* the Equal itself. In *Republic* X Socrates had stressed the type distinction between image *F* and real *F*, and at 597a emphasized that the carpenter's couch is not the "real" Couch. Still the carpenter's product, being a couch rather than a pruning knife, is naturally akin to the "really real" Couch. It is like or such as (*toiouton hoion*) the real Couch in that both are couches of one sort or another; both are rightly called "couch," even if they are different types of couch.

In the *Phaedo* Socrates had emphasized that recollection of Forms is a case of recollecting "like from like." It had to be made clear that the sensible equal, though its being equal makes it in some way akin to the intelligible Equal, cannot be equal in the same manner as the Equal itself (*houtōs ison einai*, 74d7), cannot be "such as" the Equal itself (*ou dynatai toiouton einai [ison] hoion ekeino*, 74e1). Thus each passage expresses both the kinship of sensible (image) *F* and intelligible (model) *F* (since both are *F*s of one sort or another) *and* the type distinction between image and real *F*. The *Sophist* passage discussed earlier (240a-b) displays both sides of the coin: Although it is true that the image *F* is in *some* way "like" (*eoikos*) the model *F*, it is not "another real thing such as" its model (*heteron . . . toiouton alēthinon*, 240a9).

Chapter 4 will treat in greater detail Plato's naming of images after their models, and develop positive reasons for his application of neuter adjectival terms to Forms as well as sensibles. For the moment I wish to stress the centrality of the of-ness of images as a positive complement to the strong type distinction between image and real *F*. Being of a particular model is what entitles a certain quantity of pigment to the *onoma* "grapes," a certain inanimate piece of marble to the label "Cratylus," or a given region of light playing upon the water's surface to the *onoma* "shuttle." Likewise, it is the image's being of some model that "makes" it what it is — a (drawn) Simmias (*gegrammenos Simmias, Phaedo* 73e), a dreamt treasure, a painted landscape, a marble goddess. Since these items really are only images of real things (*Sophist* 240b), it is no surprise that what *makes* them what they are is their being images of real things. This should remind the reader of Socrates' "safe" and "simple-minded" explanation of why sensible *F*s are *F*: They are *F* for no other reason than that they participate in the Form of *F*. (See *Phaedo* 100c. The passage and its philosophical difficulties occupy most of chapter 6, below.) Just so, the reflection, statue, or painting is a horse only in that it images or imitates, or is a phantasm, *eidōlon*, or *eikōn* of a horse.

I am not sure the positive point of a parallel has been isolated in precisely this way before, even by supporters of the analogy. The point is different from, because stronger than, the familiar generic claim well-put long ago by Cook Wilson that images as such are relational entities, that they are what they are only because of a relation to some original.[19] That is true so far as it goes and is entailed by the *Timaeus* passage Cook Wilson had in mind:

> For an image, since even that which it is supposed to be does not belong to it (*epeiper oud' auto touto eph' hōi gegonen heautēs estin*), and it exists as the ever shifting phantasm of another (*heterou de tinos aei pheretai phantasma*) . . . (52c).

Cook Wilson writes,

> "Now an image or semblance (*eikōn*) is what it is (i.e., a semblance) of something else, and therefore of it, as of every relative term, it is true that ἔστιν οὐδ' αὐτὸ τοῦτο ὅπερ ἐστὶν ἑαυτῆς. Thus we have the very formula of the text *[Timaeus* 52c2-3] — except that instead of saying ὅπερ εστιν we find ἐφ' ᾧ γέγονε."

But an image or imitation is not *only* an image. It is an imitation *horse*, or a *shuttle* image. The present claim, then, goes beyond that generic position. The portrait's being an image depends upon its being an image *of* some original of the appropriate sort. So also does the portrait's being a Napolean, or the dream image's being a centaur, depend upon this. *Timaeus'* phrase ἐφ ᾧ γέγονε ("that with an eye to which it came to be, that which it is supposed to be") refers to the image's status *as* the kind of semblance it is supposed to be, not simply to the fact it is supposed to be a semblance. Thus also in *Laws* III the Stranger remarks that in passing judgment on any work of imitative art one must know what the work is, that is, "what it wishes to be and of what it is in fact an image" (*tēn ousian, ti pote bouletai kai hotou pot' estin eikōn ontōs* 668c6-8). His example is a painting which one must first recognize as being of a human being before one can judge either its correctness (accuracy) or its beauty. The striking *bouletai* at 668c6 is reminiscent of Socrates' *bouletai* at *Phaedo* 74d9; sensible equals "wish" to be such as the Equal itself, but cannot be equal in the same way it is. This metaphorical "striving" of the image F—its being an image of some model F whose manner of being F it cannot duplicate no matter how much it otherwise resembles it—determines what it really is: an image F rather than an image G, and rather than nothing at all.

Harold Cherniss' view is compatible with what I have proposed, and may look very similar, but is in fact significantly different:

> The point . . . here . . . is that any particular image stands for something, refers to something, means something and that this meaning the image has *not* independently as its own but only in reference to something else apart from it and not dependent upon it but of which . . . the image is always a transitory adumbration. So, for example, a human image is not itself *human*; but it is a human *image* precisely because it does not have as its own the 'humanity' that it signifies. Or, to take an example from this section of the *Timaeus* itself, an igneous or aqueous image . . . is such because, not having as its own what fire or water is, it signifies or means fire or water.[20]

There is much here with which I enthusiastically agree. My one reservation is that in speaking of the "meaning" of an image one may fail to explain *how* the being of a sensible participant depends on a separate Form, and perhaps overlook the fact that the metaphysical parallel to this point about imaging demands an enormous amount of explanation. It may be that the being of an image F, considered as an image F, *is* its meaning or signifying some real F. (In fact its being an image of a real F would be a narrower relation, since there are ways in which an image might come to signify, mean, or represent its model independently of its being an image of that model.) But on the side of sensible participants it seems that *being a sensible F* and *signifying or meaning the Form of F* are distinguishable. The latter would be associated, for example, with the use of sensibles as *paradeigmata* (in the sense of illustrative examples); sensible participants can suggest, and help reveal, the nature of *F* itself. But a sensible's being a participant is different from, and independent of, that sort of meaning relation: A sensory fire would be an image of Fire itself even if there were no one alive for whom that fire meant or signified Fire. And it is the dependence of a sensible *F*'s *being* a sensible *F* upon the Form of *F*, rather than its meaning or signifying *F* itself, that has presented the greatest problems for interpreters and critics.

Having said this I must add that there *is* a way of viewing the being *F* of sensible *F*s as a kind of meaning relation to a separate Form, but that is a *makros logos*, a long story, as Plato would say. *Explaining* how that might be so, and defending such a view as an interpretation of Plato, are the principal tasks of chapter 6.

The interpretation defended here differs also from the more recent views of R.E. Allen and E. N. Lee, who rightly stress the images' being of a model, but who require assimilation of other images to mirror images (Allen) or exclusion of "substantial" images, those that can survive destruction of their originals (Lee), on grounds that many sorts of images simply fail to illustrate Plato's point. The issue is that participation is supposed to be a continuous relationship, lasting for the lifetime of a participant and involving essential dependence on a Form. But, goes the argument, the point is lost in cases where the image can actually survive its original, as may happen with paintings, statues, and dreams, but not with reflections or shadows.

One large textual problem with both views is that neither the assimilation nor the restriction they require is to be found in Plato, who appeals indifferently in most relevant texts to paintings, statues, and the like, as well as to reflections. (Detailed replies to Allen's specific argument for assimilation based on Plato's theory of art, and to Lee's appeal to *Timaeus* 48e-52, are contained in appendix 2.)

The philosophical problem with these views is twofold. First, they do not, in my view, do justice to the of-ness of images. Supposing it agreed that a certain portrait in the Frick is a Thomas More only so long as it is a portrait of Thomas More, the portrait does not cease to be *of* that original or cease to be a Thomas More when the original dies. Rather the portrait is still of Thomas More, even though More has long since gone to a presumably glorious reward. Thus illustration of Plato's metaphysical point does not require preferential treatment for images that cannot outlive their models; the requirement of continuous dependence can be captured by the of-ness or intentionality common to *all* the sorts of image to which Plato habitually appeals.

Still, Plato's implicit assumption that there will be (or will have been) some model for the image to be an image of does call for further comment. We speak of pictures "of " chimeras, gorgons, and centaurs (such images are mentioned at *Phaedrus* 229d-e, *Republic* 488a) even though we know that there never actually were and never will be any such things. So we may wish to distinguish between being an image *F*, where we do not assume the existence of any actual *F* even *sub specie aeternitatis*, and being an image of *F*, where we do assume the existence of the model.

Plato himself shows no concern with such a distinction in any discussion of metaphysical parallels to imaging. But we may note its possible implications for the image analogy. One possibility is that Plato intended only images of some particular actual model as his analogues to participants, even though in some other contexts he mentions images of non-existent models. Or he might have been slightly less strict, allowing for images of things of sorts that are represented in our world, even if they are not images of any particular thing of that sort (such as a bed painting that is not a painting of any particular bed). Or he may have taken a very liberal attitude toward the existence of models, allowing them to exist in the artist's imagination or in myth, even if not in the "real world," simply acquiescing in and using the flexibility of common parlance. (A slightly stricter version of this last alternative would require that fabulous subjects be compounded of elements of actual things, as with centaurs, minotaurs, and the polymorphous beast of *Republic* 588c-e.)

Although I do not think resolution of this question has much bearing on how we eventually understand Plato's metaphysics, comparison of these alternatives can at least clarify one shared implication that Plato does intend. On all of these alternatives the image will be of some "second level" object – on the scheme of *Republic* X – some "real" as opposed to "imitation" *F* (so that an image of Pegasus would depict Pegasus rather than another image of Pegasus). On any of these readings the image will be what it is – an image F – only because it images, or is of, a "second level" F, whether that second level F actually exists, or once actually existed, or never has existed anywhere but in the artist's imagination. Consequently any of the alternatives listed above will harmonize with the Platonic hierarchy of *Republic* X consisting of Forms, images of Forms, and images of images of Forms.[21]

A second philosophical problem with restricting the analogy to reflections, or assimilating other images to the nature of reflections, is that it introduces a serious disanalogy in the way sensibles depend on Forms for their being. Plato reminds us in many places (including *Timaeus* 49 ff., the passage on which Lee relies) that there is a great deal of motion and change among participants, whereas there is none among the Forms (the Form of Motion cannot move, since it is a Form). And since Forms are not themselves the efficient causes of any motion of their participants, those participants will have an independence of motion not enjoyed by reflections. Unlike shadows or reflections, it is not true that their every move is determined by the motion of the model (or medium): Sensibles undergo many changes in their interaction with other sensibles even while Forms remain utterly immutable. (The point is perhaps sharper in the case of self-initiated motions of living things.) So the particular way in which reflections and shadows depend on their models, far from being the preferred analogue to participation, is on this very point seriously disanalogous to it. The specific manner in which reflections depend upon their models is too abject to preserve a parallel with participants.

The problem facing every interpretation is that there are two important aspects of participation: one a continuous dependence of participants upon Forms, the other a certain ability of participants to move and change in a way not determined by a Form (or any interaction of Form and receptacle). These may seem to be illustrated separately by different sorts of image, but not together by any one type of image: continuous dependence by reflections and shadows, independence by statues or paintings, stage actors, or dream images. The trouble is that reflections and shadows are too utterly dependent on their models while statues, paintings, songs, and dream images seem too independent, since they may actually survive their originals. The solution lies in recognizing the image's *being of* its model as the counterpart to a sensible's *participating in* a Form. As explained above, this captures the aspect of continuous dependence even where a substantial image survives its model, while allowing for various independent motions among worldly images of Forms. Moreover in operating at a more general level, by utilizing a property common to all sorts of image, it remains faithful to and vindicates Plato's appeal to statues and paintings as well as to shadows and reflections.

D. Primary and Derivative Likeness

These observations about the essential of-ness of images imply in turn an important point about similarity. No doubt Plato was right in thinking that "the many" would never be able to view the visible, tangible objects they see, handle every day, and consider to be as real as things get, as mere images of some intangible, invisible, non-locatable "Forms." And along with the strong, natural, and usually ineradicable tendency to view corporeal objects as at least as real as anything else comes a tendency to view the similarity of one everyday object to another with respect to color, shape, and so on as the "literal" or "straightforward" kind of similarity.

But to the extent one is able to view physical objects as images of Forms one can view their kinship to their models as the primary kind of likeness, and "common" likeness (the only type *hoi polloi* recognize) as derivative. For if it is only by virtue of participation in F (by imitating or imaging F) that a worldly individual a is F, then it is only by virtue of both a and b participating in F (being akin to it by being F in the way open to worldly participants) that they are symmetrically and commonly similar to one another with respect to being F. From the Platonic point of view this will be true even if a or b is a perfect or unqualified or standard or paradigm case of being F. Indeed if the very being F of any visible participant is dependent on participation in the Form F, then the likeness of participant to Form is literally the *essential* kind of *homoiotēs*. It is the basis of a and b *being F*s at all, and is thus the basis of their being commonly similar.

The image analogy effectively reinforces the point. When we say that a certain portrait in a museum is correctly labeled "Napoleon" we do not mean that the portrait is another real Napoleon, nor do we necessarily mean that it has the same color and profile as Napoleon; a portrait may depart from both and still be a Napoleon (cf. *Cratylus* 432). Consider then pairs of correctly labeled images, starting with two portraits very much alike in color and spatial composition. Although we might associate the two as similar to one another simply on the basis of their similar visual properties, *those* properties do not necessarily make both, or either, of them Napoleons; one or both might be portraits of Napoleon's father. To get at the parallel with participants we must consider them both to be *Napoleons* (images of *F* where "*F*" stands for Napoleon) regardless of how much or little their visual properties coincide. The importance of this fact about proper handling of the analogy may be shown, ironically, by a disanalogy between some sorts of images and participants. Two paintings could be images of different originals even if one were an exact double of the other with respect to all pictorial properties. Contrariwise, if some implement (shuttle or bed) or living thing were the exact double of another, both would participate in the same Forms. (In the case of implements this holds if we assume that the maker's intention is not relevant to the classification of the product. An apprentice potter might intend to fashion a cup but botch the job and produce only a loom weight. If, following *Republic* 353a, we classify the implement purely on the basis of function, ignoring the intention of the apprentice, we shall have to classify the object as a loom weight.) Thus, from any two or more implements' or animals' being exactly alike one could argue to some common Form(s) over them, but from several paintings' being exactly alike one could not reason to a common original of which they were all images.[22]

This is not disturbing, but only helps bring out the fact that the parallel of image with participant holds only at the level at which we sort pictures, statues, reflections, and so on *as* image *F*s or image *G*s. Obviously we cannot count on grouping them correctly according to their close similarity to one another. Nor on the other hand could we conclude, on grounds that several portraits differed radically from one another in their pictorial properties, that they were of different models. "Nothing would necessarily tell one that each member of the class of Joan-of-Arc representations – from broadsides preserved at Domremy to Bastien-Lepage's remarkable 'Vision of Joan of Arc' at the Metropolitan Museum – are of the same person, so little do they resemble one another."[23] A variety of factors will determine which images – paintings, statues, dreams, *logoi*, shadows – are *F*s or *G*s; this will be a matter of deciding which models these images are images *of*, regardless of how much or little they resemble one another. But once they are classified (as when one encounters a series of portraits all labeled "Napoleon"), one can see the parallel with the Platonic one-over-many principle, and with the primacy of participation in a Form over the "straight similarity" of two cases of *F* to one another.

The point is made slightly more vivid by considering various kinds of images of Napoleon. A painting, a statue, a drawing, a reflection in a mirror, and a stage impersonation may all be correctly called "Napoleon" even though their visual properties vary greatly. The extreme case is that in which one image, such as a dream image, is not similar in any relevant ways to another, such as a portrait. The dream image existing in an incorporeal soul will not be colored or shaped at all in the same sense as the portrait. Yet they are both image Napoleons, and therefore similar to one another with respect to being (image or imitation) Napoleons, because they are both images of Napoleon.

So it is with participants. Their common similarity to one another with respect to being F is due to their all imaging the same Form, where the manner in which the imaging takes place may vary greatly. Moreover, just as one finds widely divergent sorts of images of the same visible model (paintings, dreams, reflections), so one finds widely divergent types of participants in such Forms as the Just, the Good, or the Equal. The various properties underlying their goodness or equality need not be shared by all the various equals or goods. They need not all share properties of weight, age, speed, or size with some other equal; nor, as good things, must they share an ability with other particulars to separate threads, play music, prune trees, or think. Nor, of course, do they share these properties with the abstract nature of the Good or the Equal itself. Nonetheless they can all be grouped together as worldly equals or goods, and grouped with the Form of Good or Equal rather than with some other Form, because they all, in various ways, exemplify or participate in the nature of the Good or the Equal.

E. The Regress of Similarities

If the basic conclusions of this chapter are correct, it follows that the regress of similarities of the *Parmenides* has no force against Plato's paradigmatism but is best viewed, like the other arguments given there, as bringing out the disastrous consequences of one possible (and in this case very tempting) misinterpretation of participation.

Socrates' final and most hopeful attempt to characterize participation in a way satisfactory to "Parmenides" is as follows:

The most likely view seems to me this: the *eidē* are like *paradeigmata*
fixed in the nature of things [or "in nature"; *hestanai en tēi physei*]
and other things are like them and are likenesses [*eoikenai kai einai
homoiōmata*] of them, and participation [*methexis*] of these in the *eidē*
is nothing other than their being like them [*eikasthēnai autois*].
But if, he [Parmenides] said, it is like the *eidos*, can the *eidos* fail
to be like [*homoion*] its likeness [*tōi eikasthenti*], to the extent that that
is like it [*kath' hoson aphōmoiōthē*]? . . .
No.
And must not like things necessarily participate [*metechein*] in one
and the same *eidos*?
Necessarily.
And that in which like things participate by which they are like, will
that not be the *eidos* itself?
Certainly.
Thus nothing can be like [*homoion*] the *eidos*, nor it like anything
else. Otherwise a new *eidos* will always appear besides the first one,
and if that one is similar [*homoios*] to something, then another *eidos*
will appear, and the generation of new *eidē* will never end, if the *eidos*
is similar to its participants. (132d1-133a3)

For a fourth time Socrates' one *eidos* has become many: It had been
"separated from itself " by being present as a whole to each participant
(131a8-b2), parceled out piece-by-piece among its participants (b3-c11),
and now, as in the immediately preceeding so-called Third Man regress
(132a1-b2), it is multiplied to infinity.[24] Dramatically this is especially
crushing because the suggestion had been Socrates' best hope (132d1). The
image/model distinction might well have seemed an effective counter to
the first regress argument, which had capitalized on genuinely Platonic
thought and language and on the ambiguity of '*to mega*' ('the large'), while
discreetly neglecting Plato's strong distinction in type between Form and
sensible. The argument works in part, as Ackrill saw, by leaving talk of
"the large" unanalyzed.[25] The image theory apparently provides a saving
analysis by distinguishing between that *F* which is a model or original, and
all *F*s that are images or likenesses of the model. Surely, one might suppose, there is no need for a second model by virtue of which something
may be a likeness of a first model.
    It will be useful to have before us a no-frills reconstruction of the regress
by which Parmenides frustrates Socrates' last, most promising attempt:
    (1) Each Form *F* is a *paradeigma*, an intelligible model, and other

things participate in the Form just to the extent they resemble F with respect to being F.

(2) If one thing resembles another to some extent with respect to being F, then the other thing also resembles the first to that same extent, in that same respect.

(3) Therefore each participant in a Form F will symmetrically resemble that Form with respect to being F.

(4) Any two things resembling one another in respect F must participate in one and the same distinct Form, by virtue of which they are similar with respect to being F.

(5) Therefore each participant in a Form F, and that Form itself, must participate in some distinct Form (call it F') by virtue of which they are similar to one another with respect to being F.

(6) That new Form is a *paradeigma* (and so on).

This formulation, like Parmenides', leaves many questions open. We who labor in this particular vineyard have spent many hours weeding out less viable reconstructions while nurturing and pruning favorite varieties. It must be admitted, however, that much of this activity is undertaken solely for fun, or for exercise. I shall try to confine myself here to logical points bearing on the main issues of this study.

Curiously, there is some doubt about what sort of Form is being multiplied. So far as Parmenides' words go, the argument could be regarded as producing a series either of Forms of Similarity, or of Fs where "F" is the *onoma* of whatever Form was the original *paradeigma*. The former alternative is suggested by 131a1: "similars will be similar by participation in Similarity, larges will be large by Largeness. . . ." As the first regress was a regress of Larges, the second would be a regress of Similarities. Alternately, we may have a series of Forms of F, each similar to its participants in respect F and thus calling for a new Form of F, where the F might be Largeness again, or Equal, or some other Form. This is the way almost everyone seems to take the argument (correctly, I think). It is naturally suggested by the argument's express occupation with paradigmatism, according to which Form and participant are in each case homonymous and the participant is "like" the Form in the respect signified by their common *onoma*.

Assuming now that we have on our hands a series of distinct Forms of F we must consider the validity of the argument—*and* what difference validity or invalidity makes here.

One attempt to clip the regress just above the first Form of F depends precisely on an assertion of fallaciousness. Cherniss considers the argument fallacious on grounds that, given the argument's premises, various sets of things will be similar to one another in the same respect by virtue of participating in different *eidē*, whereas all sets of things similar in some one respect were supposed to be similar by virtue of participating in one and the same *eidos*.[26] Thus there will already be an inconsistency in the premises of the argument—or at least, there will be an inconsistency as soon as one has two Forms over any given F.[27]

Now the superficial reply to Cherniss would be that inconsistent premises do not render the argument fallacious in a logical sense, but in fact guarantee its validity. This is superficial because while true (given the contemporary conception of validity derived from material implication) it would be far-fetched to interpret the argument according to a contemporary standard of validity. If one assumes a much more likely intuitive use of "relevant entailment" which, among other things, does not allow cases of validity through necessary falsehood of the premises taken conjointly, then Cherniss' point must still be faced.[28]

But I do not believe his solution will work, if only because the argument can be constructed so as to preserve both Parmenides' intentions *and* the consistency of the premises. The key idea to be preserved is that for each plurality of Fs there is exactly one Form by which they are all similar to one another, so that if we then add that one Form to the plurality of Fs, producing a new set or plurality, we will have to move up one notch to a new Form. Formally this "rachet technique" can be captured precisely, and without logical contradiction, through the notion of a Form's being *immediately over* some plurality of similar things.

This last notion is adopted from S. Marc Cohen's reconstruction of the Third Man Argument.[29] It seems however, that Cohen's formal treatment of this concept is unnecessarily complex. The same result can be achieved more simply by assuming a Form F is *over* a plurality P if and only if
- (a) F is not a member of P and
- (b) Every member of P participates in F. (Or, all members of P are called after F, or all members of P have the *eidos* of F.)

A Form F will then be *immediately over* a plurality P if and only if
- (a) F is over P and
- (b) there is no Form G such that every member of P is F by participation in G and G participates in F.

This is the simplest way I know to capture formally and fairly, using only familiar Platonic notions, the structure of Parmenides' informally stated argument. This notion can be incorporated into the argument stated earlier so as to give a consistent set of premises.

A second and much more common attempt to block the regress appeals to the asymmetry of the imaging relation. While similarity is, as Parmenides states, symmetrical (premise 2), young Socrates had appealed not to mere similarity, but to imaging, which is not symmetrical (if *a* is an image or likeness of *b* it does not follow that *b* is a likeness of *a*). So if one substitutes "is a likeness of" for "resembles" in premise 2, the premise is false. Put another way, Parmenides has illegitimately substituted *being like* for *being a likeness of*.[30]

The counterargument lies close at hand, however. *If* imaging so much as *includes* (entails) symmetrical resemblance, then Parmenides will have only to insert an appropriate additional premise to that effect.[31] That is, he can start with imaging, infer symmetrical resemblance, then proceed as before. The argument will go through even though imaging may include other factors (besides resemblance) that render the imaging relation as a whole asymmetrical.

But this reply is a bit too quick also. Logically speaking, one could use the asymmetry of "being a likeness of" to block both regresses *even while admitting common property sharing with respect to being F* between likeness and original *F*. One could simply adopt the following definition of a "Many":

> A group of things similar to one another with respect to being *F* is a Many (or a plurality of *F*s) just in case there is no one member of the group of which all the rest are likenesses in respect *F* (or after which all the rest are called "*F*").

The One-Many principle would then be:

> For every Many (or plurality of *F*s) there is a unique, distinct One — the Form *F* — immediately over that Many.

It is easily verified that on these principles the regresses will be blocked at the appropriate point. Thus those commentators who say the arguments can be blocked by appeal to the asymmetry of likeness to original are correct. Even the baldest version of self-exemplification can be saved from a regress by such means, since all that is needed is to formulate *some* difference in kind, no matter how weak, between the Form F and all sensible Fs. However that difference in kind is defined — as a difference between perfect and imperfect F, standard and non-standard F, qualified and unqualified F — the definition of a Many, and a One-Many principle, can be formulated accordingly so as to forestall Parmenides' regress arguments.

Nevertheless, no solution which allows that imaging entails or includes resemblance in respect F between image F and model F can be regarded as a satisfactory account of *Plato's* response. First, it would conflict with all the evidence showing that on the relevant use of "image," image F and model F do not share the property of being F. Second, it would conflict with Plato's general description of Forms as non-sensible, non-spatial objects, since for many Forms *any* exemplification would have to be spatial and sensible, so that any Form similar in relevant respects to any such exemplification would itself have to be spatial and sensible. It would not only abandon an important observation about imaging Plato had used to good effect in metaphysical and other contexts, but also destroy Plato's Platonism in order to save it. It would have the effect of making him a nominalist of the sort recognizing paradigm cases, non-paradigm cases, and the relation of similarity as his relation of predication.[32]

A third reply to the regress turns on an idea noted in chapter 2. Even if a paradigm or standard F shares the property of being F with its non-paradigm kin (as when the latter are roughly equal to the paradigm case in length or weight), the *grounds* for the standard's being F, and for our knowing it to be F, are quite different. This has been expressed in various ways: The standard is necessarily rather than contingently a yard long; the standard is a yard long no matter what its length; the length of one yard is predicated only analogously of the standard and its non-standard duplicates or approximations.[33] Again, one's principles relating Forms to pluralities of participants can be arranged so as to avoid the infinite embarrassments of the *Parmenides*. But all these ways of answering Parmenides carry the liabilities cited against the solution *via* asymmetry of imaging: They abandon Plato's own treatment of images and even his Platonistic metaphysics. (The Form of F becomes, for example, that which is necessarily F, rather than the abstract nature of F.)

Still others have been tempted to *restrict* the image analogy to participation of sensibles in Forms, so that no Form will be an image of any other. Some advocates of all three positions so far canvassed have suggested this fourth type of reply, apparently as an underlying rationale for the use of asymmetry, analogous predication, or the like, to block the regress. But such use of asymmetry is not the same as, and does not entail, restricting the image analogy to participation of sensibles in Forms. One might use either the asymmetry of imaging or a theory of analogous predication to block a regress within the world of Forms – starting, say, from Man, Ox, and Animal – *without* placing any this-worldly limit on the scope of the image analogy.

Nevertheless, this approach enjoys excellent textual credentials. More, its basic claim is correct. Plato never likens participation of one Form in another to imaging: Where the analogy comes into play, it applies, explicitly or implicitly, only to participation of sensibles in Forms. Philosophically this is only reasonable since there ought to be some significant difference, even if there is also some significant similarity, between one Form's instantiating another and a sensible object's instantiating a Form. Within Plato's theory a principal mark of this difference, introduced expressly in terms of the image analogy, is that images all require a medium in which they come to be. But the only medium introduced into the general metaphysical theory is the "receptacle" of the *Timaeus* (48e-52d), which serves as the place *sensible* images of Forms may come-to-be. By contrast, Forms are explicitly said not to be in any place or to enter into anything else anywhere. These points will be amplified in chapter 5, concerning the inferiority of sensibles. For the present observe that this fourth approach is very far from *ad hoc*; it is quite natural and correct, as far as it goes.

Nevertheless, it does not go far enough as a Platonic reply to the problem at hand. First, it simply leaves open the issue of resemblance between Form and sensible. Although it blocks the regress, it fails to address the very problem the regress seems designed to identify. It offers a temporary avenue of retreat but no real engagement with (much less a clear cut victory over) the forces marshalled by Parmenides.

Second, it fails to utilize the evidence, developed in this chapter, that the correct response would be a frontal assault on Parmenides' assumption that the image of F must resemble F with respect to being F.

There is no need to review this evidence, presented so recently in detail. But it is worthwhile to observe the strategy, worthy of an Odysseus, whereby Parmenides prevails over young Socrates. His procedure consists essentially in shifting unobtrusively from *homoiōmata* "likened to" (*eoikenai*, 132d3; *eikasthēnai*, d4; *aphōmoiōthē*, d6) their models, to images that are "like" (*homoion*, d6, d7, 133a3) their models. These idioms are all ambiguous; each can bear a sense which applies legitimately to images and models. But '*homoios*' is interpreted by Parmenides, as I believe all commentators agree, in a sense ("common" similarity) which correctly applies to paradigm and non-paradigm specimens of F (to a model and its *copies* or *duplicates*) but not to image F and model F as that contrast has been explained *here*. He is not, however, merely exploiting a linguistic ambiguity; he is trading also on a common understanding of imaging—one that appears in both the *Cratylus* and the *Sophist*. Socrates, like Cratylus and young Theaetetus, fails to see the crucial point: The image F must "fall short" to the extent that it fails to be another genuine F, if it is to be merely a *homoiōma* of F. (Recall that *all* examples of *homoiōmata* in the dialogues are images such as paintings or statues.) Socrates enlightens Theaetetus and Cratylus; Parmenides now has a lesson in mind for Socrates. Bluntly put, Socrates is too inexperienced in dialectic either to defend, or to persuade another of, a correct theory of *eidē* (135a-d). Once the more experienced Parmenides gains possession of his key weapon (the "common" similarity interpretation of likeness), he uses it unsparingly: The *homoios* terminology (as opposed to forms of *eikasthēnai* or *aphomoiōthē*) occurs exclusively from d7 on and is repeated ten times from that point to 133a3. But here, just as before, Parmenides' argument is one that "an able man could answer" (for this phrase see *Parmenides* 135a-b). Thus he eventually concludes his sharp interrogation not by rejecting Forms but by stressing the indispensibility of *eidē*, the difficulty of convincing others of their existence, and, again, the pressing need for Socrates to obtain training in dialectic. There is no textual or philosophical reason for thinking he has in mind some reformed *eidē* no longer serving as *paradeigmata*.[34]

It may be useful to consider briefly two possible rejoinders to this treatment of the regress, both to emphasize certain implications of the interpretation of imaging argued for above and to forestall any impression that some loophole has been left open. Suppose Parmenides were to respond that his second regress might be glossed as follows. If f is an image of Form F, then f must be like F in some respect. What respect? Well, say that f is a rather dim image of F, and embodies F's features to some measurable degree, say 60 percent. Now, F itself is not just 60 percent but 100 percent F. However, to the extent that (*kath hoson*, *Parmenides* 132d6) f resembles F, F will reciprocate by resembling f: in the respect, obviously, of being 60-percent-or-more-F. And if both F itself and f fall under that description they will have a "common" symmetrical similarity in that respect, even if they are in some sense different kinds of thing, and so will fall under some such Form as the *60-percent-or-more-F* itself. But if they fall under it by imaging it (in the sense of resembling it to some extent) then they will be symmetrically like it, being, say, 60-percent-or-more *60-percent-or-more-F*. Thus they all participate in a further Form, *60-percent-or-more-60-percent-or-more-F*, and so on.[35]

Socrates might justly object that he is not committed to Forms such as the *60-percent-or-more-F*, but only to Forms for "natural" kinds of things, or divisions embedded "in *nature*" (132d2). If so, however, Parmenides could do without the *60-percent-or-more-F* itself, stipulating that any image embodying, say, 60 percent or more of the properties of *F* itself *is an F*, even if an imperfect one, so that image and model will be symmetrically similar with respect to being *F*. This is perfectly reasonable, and probably what the approximation interpretations of participation presuppose anyway. For example, a chariot falling short of the Standard Chariot by having a bent axle or wheels too small in diameter is still sufficiently like the standard to qualify as a chariot. No matter; the problem with this argument can be seen if one keeps firmly in mind that similar things are always similar in some definite respect, then considers those respects in which the argument claims similarity. Specifically, from the fact that an image *F* embodies 60 percent or more of *F*'s properties, or embodies *F*'s properties to some sufficient degree, the argument moves fallaciously to the image's being 60 percent or more *F* (or to its being *F*, only imperfectly so).

To illustrate, suppose a sketch of a horse embodies 60 percent of its model's properties, a colored painting 70 percent, a painted statue 80 percent. It does not follow that the first is *60 percent a horse*, or *a 60 percent horse*, or that it is a horse at all, even an imperfect one. Nor is the statue a better, although imperfect, horse than the painting or the sketch. None of these is a (real) horse at all. All any of them really is, as far as horseness goes, is an image or imitation horse, a phantasm or *eidōlon* of a horse. Of course one may be a *better image* of a horse than the others; but each is only an *eikōn* or *eidōlon* of a horse, and so must lack at least some properties necessary for being a horse (e.g., being herbivorous, or solid-hoofed).

Analogously, among real horses an old gray mare and a god-like steed of Aeneas might be better or worse images of Horse itself because one is a better horse than another. But no matter how good a horse one selects, that horse will not be an intelligible, immutable Nature *at all*; so far as horseness goes, it will be only a sensible, mutable embodiment of the Nature of Horse itself, an image of the Form as intelligible model. Again, the crucial point is the *respect* in which any resemblance is supposed to hold. In Plato's image analogy, even if image F and model F show common similarity in some, or even many, respects, the image F is simply not a real F — not even a qualified one or a more-or-less-imperfect one — so long as it is an image F.

A second rejoinder does take into account Plato's point that the image F fails to resemble its model in respect F, but maintains that imaging — and by analogy, participation — must involve resemblance in *some* respects other than F between image and model. A decoy duck must be similar to real ducks in some relevant respects if it is to be a decoy duck; imitation leather must have some things in common with real leather, and so on. Likewise, one might argue, there must be some relevant similarity between sensible and intelligible F.[36]

This second response seems even less plausible than the first. Although Plato often speaks of resemblance in respects other than F between, say, paintings or statues and their models, as when a painter gets the colors of the model right, one finds no evidence whatever that sensible Fs are in general supposed to resemble the Form of F in (relevant) respects other than F. That is, even supposing for a moment that Plato believed imaging would essentially involve some relevant (common) resemblance, it does not follow, and there is no reason to suppose, that he intended this particular point to find a direct analogue in participation. Again, the only general kind of likeness he recognizes between sensible and intelligible F has to do with their kinship as one sort of F or another (the sort of association discussed in section D, above). This new argument, then, abandons not only the standard Third Man theme popular since antiquity, but with it any claim to direct textual support.

There are more specific reasons not to import resemblance in this way. Consider that in many cases the sort of properties other than F which might be relevant to participation in F plainly *cannot* be shared by sensible and intelligible F. In all cases where participation in a Form requires possession of phenomenal properties (as it will for all plants, animals, corporeal artifacts, and anything compounded of phenomenal opposites) we have Plato's repeated, emphatic assertion that Forms have no phenomenal properties. In a great range of cases, this simply leaves no plausible candidate for a relevant respect other than F in which Plato might have thought sensible Fs resemble the Form of F.

Finally, it is very doubtful that Plato believed imaging as such requires resemblance, even in relevant respects other than F. On one of Plato's frequent examples – the dream image – image and model will ordinarily not share any of the properties appearing in the dream. The dream image of a horse is neither a second horse, nor is it itself a brown thing, or suitable for riding into battle, or fond of oats, or anything else it may appear to be in the dream.

Of course a dream is something; in Plato's view it is one sort of *pathos* of the soul. According to the *Timaeus* visual images arise when motions, transmitted from the perceived object to the body by the visual stream, reach the soul (45c-d; cf. 43c). Dreams occur when sufficiently strong motions remain within after one goes to sleep, images being engendered according to the number and region of the motions (46a). But if dreams are in the soul they are incorporeal, so cannot have the colors or spatial dimensions of their models, as paintings or statues do. Nor can they speak, sing, dance, and gesture as poets or actors do in creating their imitations. In short, dream images need not actually have any properties which their models have and which appear in the dream.

These are not the only serious problems afflicting the attempt to resuscitate the "second Third Man," but they are fatal. The point about dreams amounts to overkill, but it is worth introducing as a check against premature assumptions about what imaging must include or entail, or about what Plato was committed to by use of the image analogy.

We noted at the outset of this study that Plato's image analogy has been variously approached as empty metaphor, as mere metaphor, as the reflection a great philosophical blunder, or as a serviceable, if limited, illustration of his hierarchical vision of reality. I have argued for something like the last of these approaches, and although my main concern has been to provide solid *reasons*, textual and philosophical, for adopting an interpretation of Plato's image analogy, that analogy should now appear much less limited than one might have expected. Several important points of parallel have now emerged; they may be listed as follows.

(a) There is a difference in type between image (sensible) F and model (Form of) F such that the two are not commonly similar with respect to being F.

(b) There is a positive link between image and model, in that the image is *of* the model (the sensible participates in a Form).

(c) The image's (sensible's) being what it is—an image (sensible) *F*—depends upon this link.

(d) In Platonic craft, the "real *F*" takes the role of model for the making of image (sensible) *F*s.

(e) Even a set of highly diverse images (sensibles) can form a natural plurality if its members are images of (participate in) a common model (Form).

(f) The kinship or likeness between image *F* and model *F* has priority over the common similarity of two image *F*s (sensible *F*s) with respect to being *F*.

If one began by wondering whether it really made much sense, even for a Platonist, to speak of the visible cosmos and its contents as images of abstract intelligible realities, these points should establish that it does. Even so, there are many points which have thus far received only brief attention, and which will be properly developed in later chapters. These points include the Form's unqualified claim to the *onoma* "*F*," the calling of a sensible after a Form, the separateness of Forms, the manner in which sensibles are and are not *F*, and the celebrated notion of time as a moving image of eternity. Beyond these points of metaphysics and Platonic semantics lies the matter of the Forms' role as standards by which sensibles (images) are evaluated; this matter is taken up in chapter 5 under the rubric of the inferiority of sensibles. Beyond this lie half a dozen or more significant parallels with Plato's epistemology. These last will be surveyed in the conclusion, after preparation by the metaphysical discussion. The most immediate task is to extend the analysis of Plato's image analogy. In doing this, the next two chapters address a series of questions about the philosophical motivation and viability of any version of extreme Platonism—postulating separate, or independently existing abstract Natures—including Plato's.

4

Predicates, Perfection, and *Paradeigmata*

The characteristics distinguishing Forms from other sorts of things are familiar, if not always well understood. Forms are invisible, intangible, wholly insensible, and accessible in their purity to pure reason alone (*Phaedo* 65d9-66a7, *Phaedrus* 247c6-9, *Timaeus* 27d-28a). They are immutable, not subject even in principle to any sort of becoming or change whatever (*Phaedo* 78d-79a, *Symposium* 211a, *Timaeus* 27d-28a); they do not even grow older with the passage of time (*Timaeus* 38a). Forms are not in any place at all, and so are not divisible into spatial parts (*Timaeus* 52a-b, cf. *Phaedo* 78c, 80b-c). Each is incorporeal and pure (*eilikrines, katharon*) of admixture with any sensible or any opposite it may have (*Phaedo* 66a, 74 b-c *Symposium* 211a, *Republic* 477-480, *Philebus* 59c).

And each Form is in some sense "single-natured" (*monoeides*) rather than "multiform" (*polyeides*; see *Phaedo* 78d5, 80b, *Symposium* 211b1).

Some of these attributes will be discussed in detail as we proceed, and some of the more important relationships among them will have emerged by the end of the next chapter. The focus of this chapter will be, first, the fundamental Platonic contention that each form "has its own nature," as Plato puts it at *Sophist* 258b9-10 (the phrase *tēn hautou physin echōn* being applied first to what-is-not, then by implication to the Large and to other *eidē*; see 258b9-c4); second, the complementary notion that each Form *F* is itself *F*; and third, Plato's insistence on the perfection of Forms.

It will be the task of section A to interpret the first of these persistently troublesome ideas, then to show how the claim that each Form *F* has its own nature harmonizes with and expresses an important feature of Plato's extreme Platonism. A more general result will be the explication of one sense in which such claims are true on *any* Platonistic theory of real, abstract natures which are distinct from one another and from concrete particulars.

Sections B and C address issues in what one might call Platonic semantics, considering, respectively, what is involved in *predicating* "*F*" of the Form of *F* as opposed to properly *naming* it "*F*"—where I believe the answer is not so obvious as is usually supposed—and the various grounds on which in Plato's view a given object might be justly or rightly called (*onomadzein, prosagoreuein*) "*F*," or on which one thing might be called after (*eponomadzein*) another. The results here are entirely in keeping with the interpretation of Forms as separate abstract natures whose *onomata* are borne also by their sensible participants. Again a more general conclusion will emerge, this time a rather surprising one concerning the relationship between a platonistic theory's recognition of different kinds of objects and its complementary theory of predication. Section D takes a close look at some Forms that do exemplify themselves (Sameness, Difference, Beauty, and others), assessing the implications for Plato's "Two World" ontology and for the more semantical conclusions of the two preceeding sections. Finally, Diotima's oracular deliverances on the Form of Beauty are interpreted more prosaically in section E. She reveals several ways in which Beauty is superior to its earthly participants. Playing "spokesman" (in the sense given *prophetēs* at *Timaeus* 72b) to her *mania*, I will try to explain how these apply to Forms considered as abstract natures.

A. On Forms' Having Their Own Nature

Let us begin with the non-controversial observation that both sensibles and the Forms in which they participate can be called by the same *onoma*. The *onoma* "beauty" applies to sensible beauties as well as to Beauty itself (*Phaedo* 100c, *Symposium* 209-212); "equal" applies to sticks and stones, "equal" and "equality" to the Equal itself (*auto to ison*) or Equality itself (*hē isotēs, Phaedo* ;74-75); "large" and "not-large" apply to appropriately sized corporeal objects as well as to the Large itself and the Not-Large itself (*Sophist* 258b-c), and so on. As Plato sometimes put it, sensible participants are "called after" Forms (*eponomian echein, Phaedo* 102b2, 102c10; *Parmenides* 130e10). Forms and their participants are thus homonymous, which for Plato means simply that they are rightly called by the same *onoma*.[1]

Application of the *onoma* "*F*" to the Form *F* produces rather striking statements: "the Large itself is large," and "the Equal is equal," or "*to kalon esti kalon*," and the like. These statements have provoked widely diverging responses. Some take the "is" of such statements as an "is" of predication (as opposed to an "is" of identity and an existential "is"), predication being construed as a relation between attributes and individual things having attributes. Among these are paradigm-case interpreters, who would argue that "*F* itself is *F*" follows from Plato's belief, as they understand Plato, that the Form *F* is the perfect specimen, or alternately, the sole unqualified exemplar, of the attribute *F*.[2]

Others seem to agree that any *predicative* reading of the "is" leaves Plato liable to a Third Man regress, but take the *onoma* in its application to the Form as, in effect, a proper name denoting but not describing *F* itself, and the "is" as an "is" of identity. Thus "*F* is *F*" becomes either the innocuous and trivially true statement (trivial, that is, if there are Forms) that *F* itself is identical to *F* itself, or the more informative claim that *F* itself is (identical to) the intelligible nature that "makes" all sensible *F*s *F*.[3]

Whether either sort of reading is appropriate for any given occurrence depends very much on the immediate context Plato provides. I will attempt to steer between the Scylla of regress-prone self-predication and the Charybdis of simple self-identity, arguing that a predicative reading is probably correct in certain key passages, but that (a) the predicative/identificatory contrast frames the issue too narrowly to capture all that Plato intends, and (b) a predicative reading can fit perfectly well with a consistent theory of Forms as intelligible abstract natures—*pace* the apparently universal consensus of both friends and foes of the Forms. Establishing these points will involve offering two fresh approaches to Platonic predication.

In recent decades there has accumulated a veritable rogues' gallery of "self-predicational passages" in Plato. The intelligible Animal, with its Uniqueness and Completeness, I have discussed in an earlier essay.[4] We encountered *Euthyphro* 6e in chapter 2. The special cases of Sameness, Being, Difference, and Beauty will enter later in this chapter; the "equals" of *Phaedo* 73-75 are discussed in appendix 1. *Protagoras* 330c (justice itself is just, holiness holy), sometimes the star attraction of this gathering, will not play a central role here simply because there is serious doubt whether it concerns Forms at all, and whether, even if it does apply to Forms, the dramatic context allows us to infer anything about Plato's metaphysics.[5]

It seems best to turn to two passages that are clearly concerned with Forms and that will illustrate the manner in which a Form has its own nature: *Sophist* 258b8-c5 and *Phaedo* 100c. We shall begin with the *Sophist* passage:

> Is it [Not-Being] no more bereft of reality than any of the others, and mustn't we now make bold to say that not-being [*to mē on*] definitely is, having its own nature [*tēn hautou physin echon*], just as the Large was seen to be large and the Beautiful beautiful, and so too with the Not-Large and the Not-Beautiful, in the same way Not-Being was seen to be and is Not-Being [*esti mē on*], numbered as one Form [*eidos*] among the many realities? Or have we any doubts about that, Theaetetus?
> None.[6]

The conclusion referred to for the case of the Not-Large and the Not-Beautiful was that they were just as real as the Large itself and the Beautiful itself (there is such a thing as the Not-Beautiful; *einai tis . . . to mē kalon*, etc., 257e-258a). Accordingly, one point of the Stranger's conclusion about Not-Being, a conclusion violating the prohibition of father Parmenides (258c-d), is that Not-Being *is* something. So in this context the statement "*F is F*" is meant to assert, in part, the reality of the Form *F*; it is, in part, what we would call an existence claim.[7]

Still, the phrase "having its own nature" at 258b9-10 raises the question whether "*F* is *F*" might carry what we would call predicative import. Given the context, this reading would be a mistake. If the argument just given is supposed to support the Stranger's conclusion, as presumably it is, then the clause "having its own nature" should be taken in apposition to the claim that Not-Being "is no more unreal than any of the others" and the claim that "Not-Being definitely is." The whole aim of the argument has been to establish that there is such a thing as that-which-is-not (in the sense of that-which-is-different), right along with the Large, the Not-Large, and so on. True, the Stranger points out that Not-Being applies to all the Forms, including itself (since each is different from many things). But that is only one step in the attempt to demonstrate that what-is-not *is* (taken not as the opposite of being, utter Not-Being, but as what-is-different). What-is-not definitely is, having its own nature. To remark *here* that it is predicated of itself would be odd; taken in apposition to the preceeding phrase it is perfectly apt as one way of framing the agreed upon conclusion.

Phaedo 100c gives us something much more plausibly read as a predicative statement:

> If anything is beautiful besides Beauty itself (*ei ti estin allo kalon plēn auto to kalon*) it is due to nothing other than participation in that Beauty (*dioti metechei ekeinou tou kalou*).

Here the "is beautiful" of the first line cannot be taken as "is identical with Beauty itself" (on either of the two identity readings mentioned earlier), for then Socrates would be made to say that other things can be identical with Beauty itself by participation in it. The parallel between other things' being *kalon* and Beauty's being *kalon* suggests, at least at first sight, that Socrates is attributing beauty in the same way both to Beauty itself and to its participants.[8]

On the other hand, in view of the radical distinction in kind between Forms and sensibles on which Socrates insists in this same dialogue, one must beware of concluding prematurely that Beauty itself is one beautiful thing among many, even if of surpassing or unqualified beauty, rather than the essence or nature of Beauty itself. One may find instead that the beauty of Beauty itself is entirely consistent with its status as intelligible nature of Beauty. On the alternative defended here, the Form *F* is in general the abstract nature or essence of *F* itself. This is certainly compatible with the view that Beauty is itself beautiful, but it is incompatible with *every* Form's being an example of itself.

Our starting point in determining the sense in which every Form *F* may be said to be *F* is the simple fact that Plato believed each Form to be real, and different from every other Form, as he had the Stranger prove for several specific cases in the *Sophist*: each one is what it is, and not another thing. In that sense it is appropriate to say that each Form "has its own nature." At the same time it must be remembered that Forms do not have (*echein*) or share in (*metechein*) other Forms in the same manner that sensibles have or share in Forms. Forms are not images of other Forms. Plato consistently uses the image analogy to illustrate the relation between sensible participants and Forms, not a relation between one Form and another. He uses the generic terms "participation" (*metechein*) and "association" (*koinōnia*) to cover both sorts of relationship (actually they cover more than one kind of relation within the realm of Forms), but the image analogy glosses only the relation of things in this world to homonymous Forms of the intelligible realm. Thus in the *Phaedo*, *Republic*, *Symposium*, *Phaedrus*, and *Timaeus* the image analogy illustrates the relationship of things in this world, and this world itself taken as a whole, to Forms. In fact the philosophical problems concerning participation of sensible *F*s in *F* itself could be resolved without resolving many of the issues concerning relations among Forms, and *vice versa*.[9]

To put the philosophical point into more familiar language, the relation between one Form and another Form which is true of it (Large, Different) — or the relation between an abstract sub-type and a more general superordinate type (Man, Animal) — is quite different from that between a sensible exemplification or embodiment of some abstract nature and the nature it embodies. In Plato's theory the difference is such that, for reasons he indicates (e.g., the scatteredness and divisibility of sensibles, the Form's role in production of its participants), imaging is a suitable illustration for one but not for the other. (*Some* aspects of certain relationships among Forms could be illustrated by imaging. But one can see why Plato wants to avoid introducing imaging there, given his extensive deployment of the analogy to illustrate the manifold distinction between two sorts of being.)

The implication of these observations is that each Form really is something, and is something distinct from every other Form, so that it does in that sense have its *own* nature. But each Form does not have itself or other Forms as attributes after the manner of sensibles. Its being an abstract, intelligible instance of some other Form (or of itself, as in the cases of Sameness, Being, and others discussed below) is a matter different from its imaging a Form. This is what one would expect if Forms are abstract natures, and a different type of *F* than their sensible participants. And this in turn is what one would expect given the standard list of differences between Form and sensible cited at the beginning of this chapter. Similar statements would apply equally well to universals, attributes, types, and many other Platonistic entities. Each "has its own nature" since each, considered as an intelligible abstract object, is real and distinct from every other thing. Each is imaged, in some of the same ways discussed above for Plato, by particulars; each has some universals or attributes predicated of it, but in such a way that the image analogy is less appropriate than for the case of universals in their application to worldly particulars.

B. Predicating "*F*" of *F* itself

The conclusion just stated may seem disappointingly pedestrian; but when combined with certain other equally humdrum observations, it yields the unexpected result that one can say predicatively of *F* itself that it is *F*. That such a statement does not involve a "category mistake," but is a reasonable thing to say about *any* Form, and not just of those that happen to be abstract exemplifications of themselves, can be seen in various ways. One way is to notice that given Plato's theory of three different kinds of *F*, as in *Republic* X, the "*F*" in "x is *F*" will always expand in one of three ways also indicated in *Republic* X: to "nature or *eidos F* itself," to "image of *F* itself," or to "image of image of *F* itself." Thus one may truly say "This is a horse" (pointing to Bucephalus) and "That is a horse" (pointing to a picture of Bucephalus). But it may be added, if one should be accused of asserting that the two are similar to one another with respect to being horses on grounds that one has "straightforwardly called them both horses,"[10] that such statements could be explicated in different ways if necessary, without changing the meaning of "horse," in order to remove such misunderstanding.[11] The first horse is the sort a living knight could ride and that eats grain (in Platonic terms, one which would participate in Horse itself), while the second is only a picture of a horse of the first sort. The second sort of horse could no more carry a living knight into battle than could a picture of a couch or a shuttle.[12]

The basic idea, then, is that what *we* would describe as *the* predicate or general term "F" is in fact always an ellipsis for one or another of several general terms incorporating "F": "nature of F itself" (or "F-in-nature," "What-is-F"); "image of F itself"; "image of image of F itself."[13] One might want to say that "F" is "systematically ambiguous," or to classify Plato's three "types" of F as a case of Aristotelian *pros hen legomena.* What one decides does not, however, make any difference to the metaphysical theory, so long as one preserves the appropriate relations of priority in naming among Form, sensible participant, and image of sensible — something that would *not* be preserved if "F" were applied in these three cases through bare equivocation. On the Platonic view, if we cast the point in the terminology of predication, each object said predicatively to "be (a) horse" is rightly described just in case it is either a living horse, or an image of a living horse, or a nature or essence of Horse itself—that is, only if one or another of those non-elliptical predicates applies to it. Thus, if we analyze a Platonic statement that x is F predicatively, and want to determine its truth value as applied to a particular subject, it is first necessary to determine what non-elliptical predicate is being asserted of what subject. When the subject is the Form F itself and the predicate is "is an essence or nature F itself," then the statement is true. In this case it is possible to go further. Since the nature or essence F itself is demonstrably unique (*Republic* 597c), one can say that F itself is *the* (one and only) essence F itself—that a certain definite description truly applies to it. (Notice that in the *Republic* argument, "F-in-nature" is used at the outset as a general term; the burden of the passage is to prove that the term can have at most one referent. Linguistically the phrase is like "prime number greater than six and less than eight.")

On the other hand, if the subject is the Form F and the predicate is, say, "is a living, flesh-and-blood F" (an image of the Form of F), then the statement is obviously false. Hence if one says, as at *Phaedo* 100c, that anything other than F itself is F just in case it participates in F itself, and if a worldly F's participating in F is, in the respects documented in chapter 3, like imaging a model or original, then one will be pointing out first, that while F itself and its corporeal participants arc F, they are different types of F (the corporeal F is not another intelligible, eternal, nature of F at all) and, second, the participant's being F in the way open to it is dependent on and related to that of the Form in specific ways.

Plato's use of neuter adjectival terms to refer to Forms has long appeared to some commentators the reflection of a regress-prone, self-exemplificational theory of Forms, or, perhaps, the result of an attempt to have it both ways, assigning to Forms in some contexts the philosophical role and categorical properties of abstract natures, but in others the role of paradigm cases or perfect particulars. I have just described one way in which Forms could be viewed as emphatically self-predicational—in the sense of having their own *onomata* predicated of them—even though they are conceived as abstract natures rather than paradigm cases. But it is also important, and more interesting, to see that Plato's use of adjectival grammatical forms to refer to intelligible Forms is not only safe, but also serves for him a positive polemical and, in the end, philosophical purpose. It is not the result of his inheriting a limited philosophical vocabulary. (This last point is already indicated by Plato's occasional use of abstract singular terms for Forms, such as *isotēs*, "equality," at *Phaedo* 74c1.) His insistence on applying the term "F" (usually reserved for worldly objects by all language users of sound mind) to invisible Forms located nowhere at all is the linguistic arm of Plato's attack on the received view of reality. Plato applies "F" to the Form aggressively (as in "What-is-F," or "the F itself") for the same reason that he compares sensible objects to images and Forms to models or "real things themselves." His aim is not only to establish the reality of intelligible objects as an addition to the already familiar furniture of the world, but also to radically transform our view of the status of worldly things *vis a vis* these intelligible realities. For this reason he would not have been happy to refer to the Form only as "the abstract nature of F" or as "F-ness". That way of speaking would not have been incorrect, but it remains a terminology more appropriate to a moderate Platonism of immanent universals than to an extreme Platonism of separate Forms to which sensibles owe their very being. As the model F is the real F and the imitation F is called "F" only by virtue of being an image of a real F, so the familiar objects generally thought of as real Fs are not only not intelligible natures of F; they are Fs only in that they participate in (exemplify, embody, are cases of) the nature of F itself. Correctly understood, Plato's calling the Form of F "What-is-F," or the "really real F," is a pointed expression of the ontological priority of separate abstract Forms over their worldly participants.

C. Earning *Onomata*

The argument of the last few pages shows how the term "*F*" would truly apply to or describe, rather than just denote, the nature of *F* itself. But as noted earlier, Plato does not formulate a theory of proper names as opposed to definite descriptions or predicates in general. He uses the term *onoma* freely to cover what we would call names, predicates, even demonstratives. Within that broader framework Plato himself would typically ask whether a given thing is rightly (*orthōs, dikaiōs*) called by (*onomadzein, prosagoreuein*) some *onoma*, or whether some subject deserves (*axiousthai*) a certain *onoma*. At the general level a statement of the sort "*a* is *F*" is true just in case *a* is correctly called by or deserves the *onoma* "*F*."

Thus, whereas Platonists in general, including Plato, might say that when several things resemble one another in some respect there is some one nature they all have in common, Plato could equally well speak of "hypothesizing a single Form when the same *onoma* is applied to several things" (*Republic* 596a6-8); or of "calling the same thing, whether large or small, by the same name" (435a); or of something's deserving the same name as the city because it has the same characteristics (435c); or of the propriety of giving distinct names to different kinds of learning (428e, 438d-e, 470b). (Cf. *Phaedrus* 238a: *Hybris* has many names, as it has many forms or parts; similarly 266a-b, *Symposium* 205a ff.)[14] So, too, Plato phrases the important and much-debated question of *Timaeus* 49d-50a — whatever exactly the question may be — as a matter of what is to be called (*prosagoreuein*) what, or of what *onomata* (or *rhēmata*) are to be used of what. Thus 50a1-2: "call only that [the recepticle] by the terms [*onomata*] 'this' [*touto*] and 'that' [*tode*]." (Notice the reference to demonstrative pronouns as *onomata*.) Similarly, where we might speak of one thing having several properties, Plato speaks also of calling one thing by several *onomata*. Thus *Sophist* 251a5-b3: "we call a man many things [*poll' atta eponomadzontes*] applying to him colors and shapes and sizes and vices and virtues." This very small sampling will illustrate the point; further examples may be found in virtually any Platonic dialogue.[15]

Now on Plato's view both the Form *F* and its sensible participants are rightly called "*F*," the latter being called after (*eponomadzein*) the former. Citation of eponymy here in the sense of "naming after" brings out again the Form *F*'s special and primary claim to the *onoma* "*F*" but does not really get us farther than that, since the notion of eponymy does not in itself determine *why* the sensible is called after the Form. One thing may be called after another for any number of different reasons, both in classical Greek usage generally and in Plato.[16] To say that the basis of eponymy in which we are here interested is participation or imaging is correct, but only brings us back to the main issues of this study.

Plato's practice shows that in his view the Form of *F*, sensible *F*s, and reflections, paintings, and dream images of sensible *F*s, have some claim to the *onoma* "*F*." If we then consider all the appropriately related things Plato regards as rightly called by a given *onoma* "*F*" (putting aside, that is, other items that may be called "*F*" by bare equivocation), the crucial issue becomes one of determining what sort of claim a given subject has to the *onoma* "*F*," or why a given object is justly or correctly called by that *onoma*. To apply Plato's general approach to a concrete example, one kind of shuttle is rightly called "shuttle" because it has a shape, size, and texture suiting it to separate threads on a loom. Another is rightly called "shuttle" despite its not being equipped to do that job at all. Although the mirror reflection of a shuttle is no good whatever for separating threads, it too is rightly called "shuttle" rather than "chariot" or "bed" because it is a reflection of a shuttle rather than of something else. A third kind of thing rightly called "shuttle" is equally unfit for separating worldly threads, since it is intangible, invisible, and not in any place at all. It deserves the *onoma* "shuttle" because it happens to be the nature or essence of Shuttle itself, and not the nature of Beauty itself or Equality itself. Thus there are three sorts of things to which the *onoma* "shuttle" rightly applies, even though none of these can be said to "literally" resemble either of the others in its manner of being a shuttle. The lowest member of this family tree is called after the middle one because it (the lowest) is an image of the middle sort of shuttle; the middle one in turn is called after the uppermost because it (the middle one) is a worldly embodiment or exemplification of that particular abstract nature. In this way the relation of imaging suitably illustrates a positive semantic link between two levels of a Platonic hierarchy of being; the doctrines of Form-sensible homonymy and eponymy simply follow the metaphysical facts of life.

For our purposes as exegetes it is of some importance that the description of Platonic practice in terms of justifying a claim to an *onoma* can avoid the virtually unavoidable and potentially misleading suggestions of talk about predication. As we have seen, it can look like an obvious category mistake, or at least a very odd business, to *predicate* "*F*" of the Form of *F*. (Section B above thus had laboriously to *show* why this was not after all a mistake, or even an oddity, judged from the perspective of Plato's larger aims.) By contrast, an account in terms of the various sorts of claim different subjects may have on an *onoma* — one sort being primary, another derivative, a third doubly derivative — should not strike us as an odd, deviant or muddle-headed way of talking about predication; we should not, at least, have to overcome strongly ingrained habits of speech and thought in order to see what Plato might have intended by applying "*F*" or its expansions to various subjects.

D. Self-exemplifying Forms

This account must be supplemented if it is to deal with Forms that *are* examples of themselves. Some exemplify themselves simply because everything must exemplify them: Sameness, Being, and Difference, for example. Others, like Beauty, exemplify themselves for less global reasons. All such Forms will earn the *onoma* "*F*" and be rightly described as *F* not only because each is the nature of some *F* itself, but also because it is an example of being *F*. As others have noted, it only makes good sense, and is quite harmless, that these Forms should be self-exemplifying.[17] And yet if Forms and sensibles are in these cases to be *F* in the same way — if they are here to share the property *F*, resemble one another with respect to being *F* — it is not immediately obvious why the Third Man should not now rear his ugly head. Apparently sharing these doubts, one commentator who denies Plato believed in any general self-exemplification for Forms has argued in these special cases Plato is nonetheless liable to a regress argument.[18]

If there is a problem about these cases, however, it cannot be limited to them, for if one admits the damaging sort of self-predication in the case of Being (if one admits Being has the same sort of being as sensibles), one will have similar trouble across the board. If, that is, the distinction between kinds of being is collapsed, there is no obvious reason why the being shuttle of a wooden shuttle would not be the same as the being shuttle of Shuttle itself. Collapsing the general distinction between indivisible, nonspatial, intelligible being, and scattered, divisible being would make either wooden shuttles into abstract objects or the Form Shuttle into a particular shuttle fit for separating wooden threads — something like the golden shuttle of Kalypso, perhaps.

A response on Plato's behalf might fall into two parts. First, Platonistic theories in general need have no fear the basic distinction between two (or more) sorts of being will be jeopardized in these cases. The universals or concepts or Forms of different Platonistic ontologies will *be* (something), be *the same* (as something), be *different* (from something), and be *one* (something), without thereby becoming particulars or concrete objects or worldly participants. However a given theory defines the general difference in type between universals and particulars, concepts and objects, or Forms and sensibles, that distinction will, if it has been properly formulated, obtain just as much in these cases as in any others. Self-exemplification only makes these natures abstract examples of themselves; it does not turn them into non-abstract tokens or concrete particulars.

Second, Plato's writings themselves show that he thought of being, sameness, and difference as dividing into two basic varieties. (A third, intermediate, variety is concocted by combining the basic two at *Timaeus* 35a.) Moreover he regarded the type distinction in these cases as exactly parallel to that for all other cases, and just as suitably illustrated by the image analogy. Here is Timaeus' description of the two sorts of sameness, being, and difference is as follows:

> The things of which he composed the soul and the manner of its composition were as follows. Between the *indivisible* Being [*ousia*] that is ever the same and the *divisible being that arises in bodies*, he compounded a third kind of being composed of both. Again, in the case of sameness and in that of difference, he also on the same principle made a compound intermediate between that kind of them which is *indivisible* and the kind that is *divisible in bodies*. (*Timaeus* 35a, trans. after Cornford)

The reference to divisible *vs.* indivisible being links these cases to Timaeus' theory of the receptacle: All sense objects are extended in the receptacle ("scattered") and thus divisible. Three especially important cases are here said to show exactly the same division into two fundamentally different and mutually exclusive varieties. The connection to Timaeus' image analogy is apparent also, since the receptacle is introduced with the explanation that it is the place in which all corporeal images of Forms must come to be (48e-52). The upshot, put non-imagistically, would be that the three natures, Sameness, Being, and Difference, would differ categorically from sensible participants in all the usual ways; and the sameness of Sameness (with itself or with any other Form in a given respect), the difference of Difference (from any other Form), the being this or that of Being (where this is a matter of various relations to other Forms), would all be quite as immutable, non-locatable, and intelligible as the very natures of the Forms themselves. By contrast, corporeal beings and unities, along with their corporeal or phenomenal samenesses and differences, would inevitably be perishable, locatable, and divisible rather than indivisible and intelligible.

Similar remarks apply to the beauty of Beauty itself, which is assuredly most beautiful, as are many other Forms. If this particular case poses a special problem it is in part that of appreciating the beauty of abstract objects, especially for those of us whose souls are not fully purified.[19] But Diotima could hardly have asserted more forcefully or in greater detail, at the climax of the celebrated ascent passage of the *Symposium*, that Beauty itself is a type of object different from any of its worldly participants. Her convictions about Beauty are entirely consistent with the two-world ontology of the middle (and other) dialogues, which claims a strict dichotomy between abstract natures and worldly participants.

The cases of Sameness and Difference, Similarity and Dissimilarity, raise one more interesting issue internal to Plato's theory. Socrates of the *Parmenides* had been confident that the compresence of opposites in sensibles posed no theoretical problem: Sensibles can perfectly well partake of both Similarity and Dissimilarity, Unity and Plurality. But he says he would be amazed if these Forms themselves, as well as Rest, Motion, and all the others, could combine with one another (129a-130a). We have just considered the sort of intermingling of opposite Forms—Forms exemplifying both of two opposites, including, in some cases, their own opposites— that is officially acknowledged in the *Sophist*. While this constitutes an important extension of the theory of Forms, and is important for Plato's arrival at a completely general conception of participation,[20] it does not conflict with the exclusion of opposites stressed in the *Phaedo*, *Symposium*, and elsewhere. Even as Sameness and Difference, for example, will each be characterized by themselves and by one another, they will still *exclude* one another in that neither can earn the *onoma* of the other by being a nature (or *the* nature) of its opposite. More generally, no Form "*F*" can earn the *onoma* "un*F*" by being the nature of un*F*, even if it does earn the *onoma* by participating in the un*F*. *This* exclusion of opposites Socrates (Plato) must hold onto, even as he recognizes a sense in which some Forms and their opposites must intermingle.

E. The Perfection of Forms

The perfection of Forms, though a more purely metaphysical topic, is closely related to Plato's views on the Forms' claim to their *onomata*. This section approaches the former, and more basic, topic first, then shows why the nature of Forms as abstract intelligible objects gives them an unqualified claim to their *onomata*. We may begin by expanding on some of those epithets listed at the beginning of the chapter – in particular, a Form's being *pantelōs on, eilikrinōs on, ontōs on*. All three phrases have both a broader and a narrower translation. They might be read broadly as "completely (or perfectly) real," "purely real," and "really real"; or more narrowly, supplying an understood, completing reference to some Form or other, as "being purely *F*," "being perfectly (or completely) *F*," and "being really *F*." It is not always obvious in context which reading is preferable. The former would seem intended to express the categorical characteristics of Forms: All Forms are by nature eternal, indivisible, and intelligible, so to be perfectly real (really real, purely real) is to enjoy the kind of being – *eidos ousias* (*Timaeus* 35a) – enjoyed by all Forms as such. There appears to be no suppressed variable "*F*" in that *Timaeus* phrase (as if we had something like "way of being *F*" rather than just "kind of being") because Timaeus speaks of kinds of being (*ousia*) as opposed to kinds of sameness and difference, and of the indivisible kind of being the demiurge mixed with the divisible kind found in bodily things. If so, to have that superior kind of being is to be a member of that kind of beings (*eidos tōn ontōn, Phaedo* 79a) showing no admixture of corporeality, no instability, no dissolubility, a being utterly immutable and imperishable, the proper object of pure reason. When read this way, as indicating the kind of being enjoyed by Forms, the three phrases tend to signify the same things – namely, the indivisibility, intelligibility, and so on, of all Forms as such.

Supplying "*F*" one gets the second group of readings: "being purely *F*," "being really *F*," and the like. Where *F* has an opposite (un*F*) there are two interpretations of "being purely *F*": first, that the Form's being *F* contains no admixture of anything worldly. This seems to be implied also by the phrases "purely real" and "really real" as one feature of the kind of being enjoyed by all Forms. Second, the Form F is in no way un$F$. This was not such a clear implication of the phrase "purely real" considered by itself—but is an important part of the theory of Forms as expressed from the *Phaedo* on. One finds both ways of being purely F applied to Beauty itself at *Symposium* 211a-b:

> Beauty always is, and neither comes to be nor perishes, neither waxes nor wanes; moreover [*epeita*] neither is it in one way beautiful, another ugly, nor beautiful at one time, ugly at another, nor beautiful here, ugly there, nor beautiful in the eyes of some, ugly for others. Nor, either [*oud' au*], will it appear to the beholder as a face or hands or anything else corporeal, nor as words or knowledge, nor as in anything else, as in an animal or in earth or heaven or something else, but in and of itself alone, of a single form, always being [*aei on*], whereas the rest [*ta de alla*] partake of it in such a manner that while they come to be and perish, it neither grows any greater or less nor is affected at all.

This important passage has been quoted frequently (at least in part) but not always considered point by point with the care it deserves. Diotima lists an important array of properties of Beauty itself. One may naturally divide her enumeration into four parts: The first (up to the transitional "*epeita*" of a2) recalls the general conception of a kind of being common to Forms, here expressed in terms of simply *being*, as opposed to becoming and perishing, waxing and waning. The second (down to the "*oud' au*" of a5) lists several ways in which Beauty itself cannot be both *kalon* and *aischron* or, generally speaking, ways in which a Form cannot be F and un$F$. The third (down to "*to de alla*" of 211b2) resembles *Timaeus* 52b in denying that the Form is *in* anything at all. It resembles the *Phaedo*, *Timaeus*, and *Republic* in affirming that the Form exists in and of itself and that it appears to the ultimate beholder in and of itself. The "*aei on*" of 211b2, then, brings us full circle (cf. *aei on*, 211a1) before Diotima turns briefly to our world to note, fourth, the imperviousness of Beauty to the comings and goings of its worldly participants.

Here one finds both sorts of purity of the Form: Not being in anything else at all it is free of contamination or admixture with any worldly thing; being in no way un$F$, it is also entirely free of its opposite. These remarks on the exclusion of opposites fit with, and are routinely cited in support of, an unqualified exemplar reading of Forms. However, even putting aside problems about self-predication and infinite regresses, this interpretation already lands many important Forms in serious difficulty. Forms for relative notions, including comparatives, are made to be examples of Sameness, Equality, Largeness, and Similarity without being large or similar in comparison to or in relation to anything.[21]

We have already considered objections to that interpretation of Forms. Even if those objections are sound it is necessary to explain how Diotima's remarks on being F and un$F$ (as well as her other observations about Beauty) can apply to Forms considered as abstract natures. Beginning, then, with Diotima's first point: Forms are, on everyone's account, eternal and immutable, hence in no way subject to generation or perishing, waxing or waning. Eternality is in itself an elusive concept, and is sketched in more detail in the *Timaeus*. (We shall return to this aspect of Forms in chapter 5 on the inferiority of sensibles, where reasons are given for taking the eternality of Forms in a very strong sense—something like timeless being rather than just everlasting stability.) It would be in place to observe here that Diotima's being/becoming contrast suggests yet a third interpretation for statements of the form "F itself is F" (in addition to "F itself is an, even *the*, intelligible nature of F" and "F itself is rightly labeled 'F' "). One could also say "is" has two uses, one paraphrasable in the language of becoming (as Timaeus recommends, sensibles only become, have become, will become, *Timaeus* 38a-b), and introducing all the characteristics that becoming inevitably "attaches to the changing objects of sense" (*Timaeus* 38a6). The other use, expressed as a matter of being as opposed to becoming, would be explicated primarily in terms of eternality and probably all the other components of perfect or real being. If so, one "is" in statements of the Form "a is F" may be considered an unqualified "is" applying without temporal, relational, or aspectual indices; it would be appropriate in the case of each and every Form F, since each has an unqualified claim to the *anoma* 'F.' The "is" of becoming would in every occurrence be implicitly indexed as to time and, where appropriate, relation, context, or respect. The important related point is that being F in an unqualified sense, and having an unqualified claim to the *onoma* "F," does not require non-relative relatives, but accords quite well with an abstract nature reading of Forms.

Taking "being" in a liberal sense, so that it covers not just eternality (the aspect emphasized at *Timaeus* 37c-38b) but other marks of pure or perfect being as well, we have an answer to the question of how the exclusion of opposites will apply to Forms as abstract natures (the second part of Diotima's description). Part of the answer was provided at the close of section C above: The Form of F, where F is an opposite, cannot also be a (or *the*) abstract nature of un$F$. Put another way, the Form cannot be un$F$ in the way in which it is F; or again, it cannot possibly earn the *onoma* "un$F$" or be truly described as an un$F$ in the way it earns the *onoma* "F": by being the Form of F rather than of G or H. By contrast, just as sensibles earn the *onoma* "F" by satisfying a given definition in a certain respect or context or relation, and at certain time, so they also deserve the *onoma* "un$F$" in the exactly corresponding way: by satisfying the definition of "un$F$" in some respect. There is a clear difference, with respect to exclusion of opposites, between the Form of any opposite and any of its sensible participants. To bring these arguments into line with the precise form of Diotima's *logos*: The Form, being immutable as well as eternal, is not F at one time, un$F$ at another. Nor is it F in comparison to one thing but un$F$ in comparison to another. Its being the sort of F it is depends not on any comparisons, but rather on the Form's being an (and, of course, *the*) intelligible nature of some opposite. Since it is not in space it has no spatial parts, so cannot be in any spatial sense F here but un$F$ there. Moreover its being F is not contextual (like the justice of particular acts of certain kinds) so it is not F in one context or situation and un$F$ in another. It will appear to be the nature of F and never of un$F$ to any "initiate," for if anything appears to the initiate with full and complete vision to be equally F and un$F$ then it cannot be the nature of F itself (this follows from the exclusion of its opposite and the veridicality of the initiate's perfect grasp of the Form). With all these ways of being F and un$F$ in mind one may say that the abstract nature of F itself is F, in the way it is F (or in the way in which it qualifies as one member of the larger family of appropriately related things rightly called "F"), *simpliciter*, without qualifications attaching to worldly manifestations.[22] Here I agree with paradigm-case interpreters in their emphasis on the importance of the Forms' exclusion of opposites, but this feature of Forms fits perfectly well with a thoroughly Platonistic reading of Forms as abstract natures or essences.

According to the third portion of the *Symposium* passage, the intelligible nature of F itself will not appear in the guise of any face, hands, knowledge, nor in any worldly thing at all. To grasp it is to comprehend a certain nature in itself, a nature that may be embodied in many ways in this world, but which does not in fact literally exist in them either as immanent formal factor, occurent property instance, or indwelling director of the flux. Therefore what the beholder "sees" is not the beauty *of* something other than Beauty, but the nature of beauty itself.

Finally, being eternal, immutable, and separate from its worldly participants and in no way dependent on them as *aitiai*, the abstract nature of F itself is entirely impervious to the fortunes of any of its namesakes subject to generation and corruption.

In sum, I have not claimed that there is only one way to read this important *Symposium* text. There do exist well-known alternatives, though they make Forms of relatives into very strange birds—birds of an impossible feather. I have offered an interpretation of the passage as a whole, and with that, an interpretation of the perfection of Forms, as part of a consistently Platonistic theory of Forms.

5

The Imperfection of the Sensible World

Each of the distinctions between Forms and sensibles discussed so far marks, in Plato's view, the inferiority of sensibles. It may seem odd that Plato even raises such an issue, let alone judges intelligible realities superior to the medium sized physical objects we all know and love. This impression of oddness wears off quickly, however, when one considers what Plato means by that evaluation, for most specific aspects of the alleged inferiority find clear analogues in more familiar theories about types and tokens, universals and particulars, or (mind independent) concepts and objects. Certainly those distinctions having to do with mutability, perishability, scatteredness and intelligibility apply in a broad range of Platonistic theories. Further, on extreme Platonistic theories such as Plato's the dependence of sensibles on separate Forms for being what they are—including their being anything of value—provides additional support for the elevated

status of intelligible objects. This last point especially (along with the correlated epistemological dependence of participants discussed in chapter 7)
shows that Plato's valuation does make sense; he did not simply harbor an
eccentric taste for the abstract and immutable.

The first section to follow examines various marks of the inferiority of
sensibles, with special attention to the unifying role of the coming-to-be
of sensibles in the "receptacle" of the *Timaeus*. Parallel to the spatial scatteredness of all things in the receptacle is their extendedness in time. The
image analogy helps bring out, in a surprisingly precise way, the sense in
which any sensible's everlastingness would be yet inferior to the Forms'
eternality, and why time itself is aptly called a "moving image of eternity."
We then look briefly at some instructive but neglected "perfect particulars"
inhabiting our sensible world. These examples of worldly perfection are
nonetheless inferior to the corresponding Forms in all the usual ways,
even in that very respect in which they are "perfect." Thus they reinforce
earlier conclusions about the type distinction between Form and sensible
and about the manner of being *F* of sensibles.

A final section explains how Forms are the standards by which all sensibles, including perfect particulars, are judged, building upon previous
results about the perfection of Forms and the inferiority of sensibles.

A. Inferiority and the Receptacle

Common to all sensibles is their scatteredness; corporeal things are necessarily *skedastē* (*Timaeus* 37a). I take the term to be a rhetorical expression for what we would call "extended." Timaeus is not asserting that sensibles are never continuous, but rather that they are spread out through
space and hence divisible in a way Forms are not. By introducing the
receptacle or place (*chōra*) in the *Timaeus* Plato explicitly links this feature
of his metaphysics to an image/model theory of reality.

> Let us make a new and broader beginning than before concerning all
> that is. For then we discerned two kinds [*eidē*], but now we must un-
> cover a third *genos*. Those two were sufficient for our earlier discus-
> sion, one posited as the *eidos* of the model [*paradeigma*], intelligible
> and always the same, a second the imitation [*mimēma*] of the model,
> generated and visible. . . . As an image [*eikōn*], since even that which

it is supposed to be does not belong to it, and it is an ever moving *phantasma* of something else, it must come to be in something else [*en heterōi prosēkei tini gignesthai*, 52c4] clinging somehow or other to being, lest it be nothing at all. (*Timaeus* 48e-49a, 52c)

The third, new *genos* is the medium of sensible images, the receptacle or place in which all sensibles come to be. Timaeus describes the nature of visible images in terms of their constitution out of primary bodies too small to be seen and explains their powers to affect and be affected by one another in terms of the geometrical properties of their constituent bodies. This geometricized analysis of corporeal images of Forms is to apply to all that is commonly called "fire" and "earth," and to everything made out of these. The analysis would thus apply to all sensible opposites, to all artifacts, living things, and to the visible heavens.

By introducing this *genos* Plato treats in an importantly new way an idea anticipated in the *Phaedo*: There are two sorts of things (*duo genē tōn ontōn*) of which the inferior, corporeal sort is characteristically compounded (*synthetos*) and divisible (*dialutos*), hence liable to change and destruction and unable to be *F* in the same way as the incorporeal, incomposite, indissoluble Form of *F* itself (78b-c, 80b). Just as the *Timaeus* attempts to explain in detail the working of the *Phaedo*'s vaguely indicated preferred "cause" (the good, and reason working for the good), so also it provides a graphic picture, involving the receptacle and the variety of primary bodies, of the compositeness and dissolubility of all corporeal things.

The *Timaeus* doctrine recalls the *Phaedo* in other ways, too. Burnet has noted Socrates' martial metaphors in the *Phaedo*'s proof of immortality based on the exclusion of opposites: Something "brings into the field some opposite" (from *epipherein*), or "takes possession of something" (from *katechein*); some item either "perishes" or "withdraws" (*apolluomai, hypechōreomai* upon the approach of a certain opposite.[1] But these are also *spatial* metaphors. One force brings another into the field and takes possession of a strategic spot (*chōrian katechein*), while another flees, evacuating some region (*hypechōpeomai*). Notice also the striking parallel to Timaeus' description of fire as a part of the receptacle that is inflamed (*Timaeus* 51b4-5); his inflamed portion of the receptacle will be the counterpart to the "ground" (*chōra*) over which the *Phaedo*'s opposites do battle and of which fire "takes possession." The military metaphors then recur in Timaeus' description of the transformations of primary bodies. One group is "overpowered" by a stronger "victorious" force, and thus transformed (see esp. 56e-57b). Accordingly some *chōra*, some portion of the receptacle, may now be dampened rather than inflamed.

The point of these remarks is not to read the doctrine of the receptacle back into the *Phaedo*, but only to suggest that certain intuitions about corporeal being as such that are clarified and officially incorporated into Plato's overall view of reality in the *Timaeus* are already present at the time of the *Phaedo*. Their explicit formulation in the *Timaeus* marks an important theoretical development.

The *Symposium* anticipates the *Timaeus'* theory in a different way when Diotima tells Socrates that, unlike worldly beauties, Beauty itself is not in something, "not in any thing else, such as an animal or in the earth or the heavens or any other thing" (211a8), but abides of itself, with itself (*auto kath hauto meth hautou*) everlasting and *monoeides* (211b1-2). Here she broaches, but does not develop, a central idea: it is left for Timaeus (52c2-5) to establish *being in something* as binding on all visible participants (images) in Forms. At the most general level, that in which all sensibles come to be is of course the receptacle or place. A sensible must come to be in something or be nothing at all, while a Form is not in any place at all, occupies no room (*Timaeus* 52b), "neither receives anything else into itself from elsewhere *nor itself enters into anything else anywhere*" (52a). Diotima's remarks do not go this far — she does not mention the receptacle. But they are in the spirit of Timaeus' demand for some medium for images. At the level of particular beautiful animals or features of the cosmos, it is natural to think of instances of beauty as being in particulars that have beauty (211a8; cf. the *F*-in-us of the *Phaedo*). Consequently it is easy enough to think of worldly occurrences of beauty along the lines of the *Timaeus*, as being in the receptacle along with the particulars in which sensible characters are found.[2]

Once more, the point is not to argue that Diotima (Plato) had the theory of the receptacle in reserve, but to emphasize the continuity of a basic intuition, more fully articulated later, that the Form is free from a general condition of spatiality, extendedness, or being *in* something, whether in a particular spatial object or in place in general. Hence it is free from one type of compositeness and liability to dissolution necessarily adhering to all sensibles as such.[3]

This is extremely important for a correct picture of the inferiority of sensibles as portrayed from the *Phaedo* on. As the *Phaedo*, *Symposium*, and *Republic* indicate, things having one property (beauty, equality) will also possess the opposite (ugliness, inequality) in some other respect, context or relation. Where applicable such facts distinguish Forms from sensibles (as at *Phaedo* 74b-c) and can be counted among the several marks of the latter's inferiority. But if one regards those various ways of being *F* and un*F* as giving a complete account of the inferiority of sensibles, one may be led to believe that sensible opposites, considered precisely in that respect in which they are *F*, do exactly resemble the Form of *F*, or that the Form of *F* is superior to sensible *F*s in that although it, too, is an exemplar of *F*, it is *F* (equal, larger, just) without need of any appropriate relatum or context. (This is the "unqualified exemplar" interpretation discussed in chapter 2.)

However, given the compositeness and divisibility of all sensibles (*Phaedo*), their inevitable "scatteredness" and divisibility (*Timaeus*), all sensible *F*s, including sensible opposites *considered strictly in that relation, respect, or context in which they are F,* are already inferior to *F* itself, already *F* in a different way than the Form, regardless of their being un*F* in some other way.

Equality itself, for example, is not *in* any stick or stone; nor is it the equality *of* any particular which would perish with the particular.[4] Equality itself is not equal in size or speed or weight to anything else. Rather it is the nature or essence that all members of all equal pairs (or n-tuples) of things have or temporarily image in some respect or other.[5] A sensible equal images the Form by having its scattered parts extended through place to at least roughly, and perhaps exactly, the same extent as those of some other sensible, by being composed of primary bodies so as to have the same "weight" as some other sensible, or by entering the receptacle at the same time, so as to occupy the same parts of time as some other sensible, and so on. These facts bring out another crucial feature of equality among sensibles: They are equal only in some respect, in relation to something, at some time. They are, in and of themselves, *incomplete* with respect to being equal.[6] This again yields a mark of inferiority that obtains *before* one even raises the question of being un*F* in some other respect: The Form is equal, in the way that entitles *it* to be called equal, in and of itself (*auto kath hauto*), while the sensible's being equal depends on some appropriate context or relation. The sensible's incompleteness is logically prior to its being F and un$F$, since incompleteness is presupposed both by being F in some respect and by being un$F$ in some other respect. The two are sometimes yoked in the secondary literature as if they were equivalent, or even identical, aspects of sensibles. However, being F and un$F$ entails, but is not entailed by, incompleteness. So it is probably best to contrast the sensibles' incompleteness with the Form's being what it is *auto kath hauto*, the former's being F and un$F$ with the Form's purity from admixture with its opposite.[7]

Similarly Justice itself is not a whole consisting of well-ordered parts like the just soul or just city of the *Republic*.[8] Nor is its being the intelligible nature it is dependent, as is the being just of any individual just act, on any particular situation or context.[9] Neither its being the kind of *dikaion* it is nor its claim to the *onoma* "*dikaion*" depends on the maintenance of any state or condition subject to alteration or dispersal. Its being rightly called "*dikaion*" is a matter of its being the immutable, intelligible nature imaged by all and only those particular souls or cities whose parts do stand in an appropriate relation to one another, or by those acts performed fittingly in a fitting context.

With Forms like Man, Animal, or Living Thing, one does not find the same incompleteness inherent in many opposites. Sensible members of kinds of living thing are not, say, men only in relation to some other sensible, or in some respect.[10] Still, any particular aspirant to the title "living thing" or "man" or "tree" has its work cut out for it just as surely as any opposite. Drawing again on the basic viewpoint underlying Timaeus' introduction of the receptacle, any earthly human will be composite and divisible, and must maintain each of various parts in proper working order and proper functional relationship if life is to be maintained. Moreover any individual human is constantly replacing old tissue, growing, decaying, ingesting, assimilating, even as the psychic basis of his perceptions, emotions, knowledge and opinions also fluctuate (see *Symposium* 207d-e; cf. *Timaeus* 42a). If, despite all this, the many parts are kept in proper adjustment so that human life is maintained, the particular thing in question will be rightly called "human" rather than "tree" or "shuttle" or "earth." The Form, of course, has no such worries. Its claim to the *onoma* is assured since it is the very nature Human itself, immutable and wholly imperishable. It is not *a* human being, striving as best it can to keep body and soul together, but the very nature all particular humans do their best to possess or image here below.

Artifacts too must earn their *onomata*. Every worldly shuttle must have its scattered parts distributed so as to provide the proper hardness, shape, size, and external smoothness for separating threads of one sort or another. There are, as Plato says, various sorts of shuttle suited for work with different sorts of threads. But each and every shuttle, of whatever particular design, must be fit to perform that particular task (*ergon*) whose performance is the *raison d'etre* of all shuttles of whatever description: separating threads (*Cratylus* 388a-b). Couches must be able to support human beings, awls must puncture leather, and knives must cut. Forms for artifacts, however, are called "Shuttle" or "Awl" or "Couch" even though they do not *do* anything at all. Being insensible and non-spatial, they cannot separate threads, puncture leather, or support corporeal bodies. But they do not have to do that sort of menial work: they are What-is-shuttle, or What-is-couch. They are the very natures that sensibles only image as best they can by having the right kinds of parts distributed in the right way in their particular portion of the receptacle.

Circularity, Triangularity, and Linearity are in a similarly enviable position. They are the intelligible and unique natures, Circle, Triangle, Line, that sensibles of whatever radius, triangularity, or length only image by virtue of a proper distribution of their spatially scattered parts. Geometrical Forms are not distributed in space in any way; having no shape they are yet unqualifiedly entitled to their *onomata* because they are the intelligible shapes possessed by sensibles.[11]

The underlying theme of compositeness, dissolubility, divisibility, and scatteredness of all things in the receptacle should be sufficiently apparent. Observe how the image analogy brings into focus a connection between the scatteredness of sensibles and the ontological dependence on Forms mentioned in chapter 3, illustrated by the of-ness of images. A sensible equal, human, or shuttle is compounded of vastly many primary solids scattered through places that can be infinitely divided. What is it, then, that makes these shifting, heterogeneous multitudes of primary particles of various shapes and sizes into *one*? Surely it is just that which makes them, for example, one *human*, where this is a matter of their having such a nature and disposition as to sustain life and carry out characteristically human life functions. Where that occurs there exists one human being, one thing that has the nature Human or participates in the Form Man. So it is with flickering shadows on the cave wall, or detailed dramatic imitations in words, music, and dance, or the play of light and dark in *skiagraphia*.

Whatever their complexity, divisibility, or motion, they are one – one (image) Cratylus or one (imitation) Xerxes – because they are images *of* some particular model.[12]

B. Time and Eternity

The temporality of sensibles, as compared with the eternality of Forms, deserves particular attention. At *Timaeus* 37c-38b, Timaeus describes the contrast between time and eternity in various ways: (a) using the language of becoming (37e-38b); (b) in terms of growing, or not growing, older or younger with the passage of time (38a); (c) in terms of abiding in unity (37d6); and (d) regarding time as a "moving image of eternity" (αἰῶνος ἰοῦσαν . . . εἰκόνα, 37d5-7). The traditional view is that Timaeus means to contrast everlastingness with (timeless) eternity, or temporality with atemporal being, or something of the sort. Merely formulating this sort of view precisely is a formidable problem, but for several reasons we may regard this general approach as correct.[13] One supporting argument can be made succinctly here, given the results of chapter 3. Plato's figure of time as a moving image of eternity is no impressionist rendering of a conclusion stated more plainly elsewhere in the passage. It supports the traditional reading in a precise way. At least, it supports it this far: The everlasting stability of the cosmos – its moving forever in a regular, repeated pattern – neither approximates (falls short of by a matter of degree) the eternity of Forms, nor duplicates it in *this* way while failing to duplicate it in some *other*. The "*F* and un*F*" view is thus adapted to the present case.) We may recall an earlier example: The *eikōn*, *eidōlon*, or *mimēma* of a flesh-and-blood horse will not itself exemplify the nature Horseness (or Two-footedness, or Living Thing for that matter) only to a lesser degree than its model; nor will it be a flesh-and-blood horse in *this* respect but not in another. It may resemble its model in many respects, but it cannot be another flesh-and-blood horse at all: it cannot resemble the model in *that* way so long as it is only an *eidōlon* or *eikōn* of a horse in paint, marble, or shadow. The analogy would imply that a Form's eternality does not consist in everlasting stability (since that *is* duplicated by the cosmos in some respects) but in something stronger – something that cannot be duplicated within the sensible realm so long as cosmic time is only an *image* of eternity.

To make a long story short (the longer version including detailed treatment of all Timaeus' remarks), the eternality of Forms consists in utter immunity to any sort of becoming whatsoever. Their sort of being – intelligible, non-spatial, indivisible – precludes the conditions necessary for motion, change, "or any of the things becoming attaches to the objects of sense" (38a6). If this is correct, then both Forms and the created cosmos do enjoy one or another sort of stability, so there is a positive link between image and model, and a basis for calling the image after the model. But the kind of stability enjoyed by the cosmos can neither duplicate nor approximate the kind of stability enjoyed by Forms. Even the most imperturbable sense object, even a visible god preserved forever without beginning or end by the demiurge, cannot be utterly immutable, *utterly* lacking in the conditions for change. (On the created gods' being everlasting, yet not *completely* indestructible and eternal, see *Timaeus* 41b). Thus Timaeus means to invoke the standard negative side of the imaging relation (we have called it a strong difference in type between image *F* and model *F*) here reflecting a difference in type between two sorts of stability.

A brief and more general look at Plato's creation story reinforces the point, and provides a better view of how the image analogy informs the larger framework of creation. The demiurge's procedure is for the most part exactly what one would expect of a Platonic craftsman or image maker of any kind. The demiurge cannot make another *F* of the same sort as the model (the Intelligible Animal), but makes the best image he can of that model. If the image cannot resemble its model *F* with respect to being *F*, it may well do so in *other* respects. Accordingly, the creator did not make another Intelligible Animal; that would have been impossible given the materials at hand. Instead, the best possible sensible animal was made (as a painter would not create a real lion, but only a lion in pigment). But Timaeus mentions three other properties the demiurge did try to duplicate in the sensible cosmos: completeness, uniqueness, and "being always." The demiurge was successful in the first two, making the world contain all created animals as the model contained all Intelligible Animals. Image and model were then alike in that each was complete, containing all the animals of its own sort, and each was unique, image being the sole created cosmos and model the sole Intelligible Animal.[14]

But with eternality there was a problem: No created thing could be truly or perfectly eternal. No created object, even if everlasting and entirely stable in some respect for all time, could attain the status of *utter* immutability. Therefore in this particular case, unlike those of uniqueness and completeness, the Demiurge had to settle for making an aspect of the world *image* an aspect of its model. This is why, within the overall image/ model framework of his creation story, Timaeus reintroduces the image analogy to deal specifically with the everlastingness of the cosmos. As a result, one may count the eternality of Forms as a further point of superiority over any (everlasting) sensible object, and even over everlasting sensibles considered strictly and solely in that respect in which they are everlastingly stable.

Nor is this result simply the reflection of a Platonic preference for the timelessly eternal. Here, as in every case of craftsmanship, inferiority partly consists in *dependence* on the intelligible realm. Such stability as the cosmos or the visible gods may enjoy presupposes various Forms' serving as models, and reason's efforts to embody certain types of good permanently in the cosmos. It appears also that absolute "abiding in unity" functions as a formal *aitia* of the everlasting "rotation according to number" of the cosmos, much as unity itself appears to be the formal *aitia* of number. If so, there is a two-fold dependence of the world's everlastingness on the strict eternality of true Being, as model for making and as formal *aitia*. Eternality in a *strong* sense is essential to the Forms' role as completely reliable, objective standards for classification and evaluation of sensibles, hence also to their role as formal *aitiai* of worldly participants in general. And it is crucial for their performance as the primary (and perhaps *sole*) objects of strict *epistēmē* or of *nous*. Judged from within Plato's theory, no sense object, even if everlastingly stable in some respect, could be qualified for these roles. On these grounds also it is reasonable to say that even in their everlasting stability, sempiternal sensibles "fall short of" or "are deficient" with respect to the eternality of Forms.

C. Perfection in the Sensible World

It seems to be generally overlooked that the *Phaedo*, *Republic*, and *Timaeus* acknowledge cases of perfection even in our own lowly world of becoming. In each case these perfect particulars are images of intelligible realities and still fall short of the corresponding intelligible realities in all the ways just discussed. They are perfect in the way open to worldly particulars, however, and this will help sharpen our conception of the inferiority of sensibles. First, the "spangled heavens" of *Republic* 529:

These lights which embroider the sky, since they are worked in the visible, are thought to be the most beautiful and exact of such [visible] things though they fall far short [*polu endein*] of true realities, namely the real speed and real slowness in true number and in all true figures in relation to one another, with respect to what they carry and contain, which are apprehended by reason and thought but not by sight. Or do you think they can be [apprehended by sight]?

In no way.

Then, I said, the heavens must be used as an embroidered model [*paradeigma*] in the study of those realities, just as if someone should chance upon exceedingly fine and painstaking diagrams drawn by Daedalus or some other craftsman. For someone knowing geometry who saw them would think them most beautifully done, but would think it ludicrous to labor over them as if he would grasp in them the truth of equals or doubles or any other ratio. (529c-530c)

Plato's point is not that one cannot learn geometry or astronomy properly from studying the stars, because they never move regularly or maintain regular proportions in their movements. It is rather that the stars and, for that matter, diagrams drawn by a god, could at best be visible models of true realities. He does point out that since visible images are not immutable (suggesting that even the heavenly bodies will some day deviate from their present courses), they are certainly not objects of the eternal truths sought by mathematicians. But it should not be inferred from this that, were the paths of stars forever regular (as in the cosmology of the *Timaeus*), their visible characteristics would be proper study for geometry or astronomy. On the contrary they would still be only visible models of invisible, intelligible realities.

Of course it is possible to arrive at true *opinions* by studying diagrams. Indeed one does not need perfectly drawn ones for that purpose; diagrams sketched in the sand may suffice, as the *Meno* shows. But judgments tied to the inspection of diagrams rather than "tied down" or "tethered" by reason can yield only true *doxa*, not genuine knowledge. This is not due to lack of precision in the diagram, so that a more nearly perfect drawing would bring us that much closer to knowledge. It is due to a limitation inherent in judgment based on visual inspection of diagrams—even perfect ones—as opposed to apprehension of those immutable realities the diagrams can only point to and help reveal. Essentially the same point is made in a more celebrated passage, *Republic* 510d-e, on the geometers who use visible images but whose true objects of study only the mind can apprehend. One can be sure Plato would censure a geometer's use even of Daedalus' diagrams if that were substituted for study of intelligible realities in and of themselves.

Equally revealing are the references to perfect sensibles in the *Timaeus*:

> For that Animal which was to encompass within itself all animals, the appropriate figure was that which encompassed in itself all figures. Whence he made it spherical, its extremes equidistant from the center, neatly rounded off, having of all figures that which is most perfect and most like itself; for he considered the like infinitely more beautiful than the unlike. (33b2-7)

The perfect sphericity of the cosmos is asserted again at 34b; the fixed stars will then be borne about in perfect circles by the motion of the "circle of the same." Consequently our own visible cosmos has the shape of a perfect sphere, molded by a divine craftsman who had reasons for choosing that shape. Yet on an approximation reading of participation there cannot be any such thing in this realm. So Gilbert Ryle wrote: "The squares and circles which we draw are not exactly square or circular. They are nearly but not quite good copies of ideal or perfect squares and circles, though these never exist in nature. At this stage, probably, philosophers failed to distinguish ideal circles from circularity and ideal squares from squareness. It was only later seen that they are or would be instances of those attributes and so are or would be particulars even though not ones existing in nature."[15] It may well be that the circles and squares drawn by human beings are never perfectly circular or square, but if it takes a god to produce a perfect circle in the sensible realm it is beyond the power even of a god to produce a duplicate of the Form within the sensible realm. The best that even a god could do would be to produce something perfectly circular in shape (as in the *Timaeus*). But that would still be only an image of Circle itself, even if a perfect image; it would still be inferior to Circle itself in the ways discussed above—still scattered, mutable, sensible, and dependent upon the non-spatial, eternal, intelligible nature in which it participates.

Nor is the cosmos exactly like Sphericity itself, even if in only one particular respect. It is not, even insofar as it is perfectly spherical, similar to the Form with respect to shape. As *Phaedrus* 247c points out, Forms have neither color nor shape. The perfectly spherical cosmos is, with respect to its sphericity, both like Sphere itself in having some legitimate claim to the *onoma* "sphere" (not "square" or "triangle"), and a dependent, inferior type of F as compared to the intelligible nature Sphere itself.

To these passages we should add *Phaedo* 73-75, which treats sensible equals (not just sensible near-equals) as inferior to the Equal itself. (A detailed discussion of this passage will be found in appendix I.) Neither the manner of Socrates' references to sensible equals (he refers to them repeatedly as "equals") nor the fact, as he points out, they can also be unequal, nor any of the marks of inferiority of sensibles cited elsewhere in the *Phaedo* give the slightest reason to suppose that their inferiority consists in part in their being only approximately equal to some *relatum*. Instead, these texts (and other considerations discussed in appendix I) illustrate the distinction between abstract nature and concrete example, or between intelligible nature of F itself and that which concretely possesses or has the nature of F itself.[16]

Such passages shed light on a side of the issue long in eclipse. The most perfect F or G possible in the visible realm sometimes may be a perfect instance of some Form. There is no threat to the superiority of the Form since even perfectly circular motions or perfect spheres within the sensible realm are only images of intelligible realities, bearing all the signs of inferiority necessarily attaching to sensibles as such. One need not introduce other respects in which a sensible F is un$F$ in order to preserve the Forms' superiority. At the same time, these passages show why a sensible's inferiority is not the result of some inevitable approximation to earthly perfection.

Being F *and* unF

I have stressed the evidence for a broad conception of the inferiority of sensibles, and so far tried to explicate in detail some of the most prominent aspects of that inferiority. We can no longer postpone a full confrontation with the view that Plato does conceive of the inferiority of sensibles (at least in the *Phaedo* and middle *Republic*) more narrowly, in terms of their being un$F$ as well as F. The view is widespread, and is decisive for one's conception of Forms.

Although there are several interpretations on which the concept of being F and un$F$ takes on central importance, these tend to share the conviction that there were initially (in the *Phaedo* and middle *Republic*) Forms only for opposites.[17] The textual grounds for this are apparent: Although Forms are never expressly limited in any precise way, the Forms mentioned in the *Phaedo* and *Republic* V-VII are all Forms of opposites (Beauty, Equality, Inequality, Justice, Injustice, Tallness, Shortness, Unity, Plurality, "and the like," as Socrates would say). One may recall also that young Socrates of the *Parmenides* is certain only about Forms of opposites such as similarity, goodness, and beauty; he is less confident about man, earth, and fire, and not at all hospitable to Forms of mud, hair and dirt (though to his credit he is nagged by doubt that there may be Forms in all these cases alike; *Parmenides* 130b-d). Now if, as Plato seems to think, worldly *F*s (where "*F*" stands for some opposite) are inevitably also un*F* in some respect, context, or relation, one can supply a philosophical motive for Plato's concern that there be Forms for opposites: Statements of the Form "this is *F*" will be no more true than false when applied to sensibles. Hence, *if* one needs, for whatever purpose—for settling disputes, for standards by which to rule a city or one's own life, for learning the use of general terms, for grounding timeless truths—an unambiguous exemplar of being *F*, something that is *F* and in no way un*F*, then one will have to look beyond the sense world for exemplars of opposites.[18] Where did Plato look? As he himself tells us, he looked to a non-sensible world, an intelligible region populated by precisely such unambiguous paradigms.[19] This extra-terrestrial colonization is not necessary where "*F*" stands for some substance sortal like "man" or "ox" or "shuttle"; worldly bearers of these predicates are not also opposites of man, ox, or shuttle. In these cases, so the account goes, there are in the early stage of Plato's theory no Forms.[20]

At least three important texts seem occupied with opposites and lend plausibility to the notion that worldly inferiority consists in being *F* and un*F* and that Forms initially exist only for opposites, in which case they serve as the sole unambiguous paradigms of being *F*. My object is not to deny that being *F* and un*F* was in Plato's mind a mark of sensibles' inferiority; I have already asserted it was. Rather, I hope to show these passages are not meant at all either to limit (or delimit) the population of Forms or to provide a complete picture of sensibles' inferiority. They have quite other aims in view; they focus upon opposites simply because these aims are conveniently or best met by consideration of opposites. Again, the primary significance of these passages lies in what they may imply about Plato's motivation for postulating separate Forms and so about the nature of Forms themselves.

Equals and Inferiors in the Phaedo

At *Phaedo* 74b-c Socrates briskly demonstrates for Simmias that the Equal itself (*auto to ison*) differs from all sensible equals such as sticks and stones:

> Consider the matter thus: Is it not true that sometimes equal stones and sticks, being themselves the same, are apparently equal to one thing, but not another [or, appear equal to one person, but not to another]?
> Certainly.
> But did it ever appear to you that the equal itself [or the equals themselves: *auta ta isa*] were unequal(s), or that equality [*isotēs*] was inequality [*anisotēs*]?
> Not at all, Socrates.
> Then, he said, these are not the same, those equals [sticks and stones] and the equal itself [*auto to ison*].

The gist of the argument, as I see it, was indicated in passing in chapter 4. According to the *Phaedo* there are "two sorts of beings" (*duo eidē tōn ontōn*). Socrates uses the phrase at 79a, where some basic differences between the two have already been introduced: intelligibility, and a certain unexplicated purity (66a), immutability, and non-compositeness (78c-d). One sort of thing, I have argued, is an *F* or deserves the *onoma* "*F*" in that it is the abstract, eternal nature of *F*. Worldly *F*s "cannot be *F*s in that way" (74e1), but are *F*s and have a claim to the *onoma* "*F*" in that they embody or exemplify the nature of *F*. Socrates' argument, then, is that the Form of *F* is never un*F*. That is, in the way in which it is *F*, it is not also un*F*. For if it were also un*F* it would then be the nature both of *F* and of un*F*, which is impossible (74b-c: "equality is never inequality"). By contrast, a sensible *F* is also un*F*. That is, in the way in which it is *F*, it is also un*F*. As it is *F* in some respect and in some relation, so is it also un*F* in some other respect or relation. Therefore one sort of *F* must be different from the other. A sensible is un*F* in the same sort of way in which it is

F; a Form cannot be un*F* in the sort of way in which it is *F*. In the language
of *Republic* 479b, one sort of *F* will be no more *F* than un*F*, whereas the
other will be *F* rather than un*F*.

Taken by itself the passage could be read in the unqualified-paradigm
way. But the preceding remarks establish that Socrates' argument does not
require, or even lend weight to, such an interpretation; there is a simple,
plausible reading of the text which does turn on the being-*F*-and-un*F* of
sensible equals, but which issues naturally from an abstract-essence understanding of Forms.

This leaves it an open question whether the inferiority of sensibles includes other factors. Some readers would consider this a weakness of the
interpretation, maintaining the passage restricts itself to a narrow idea of
inferiority in terms of being-*F*-and-un*F*. Though the argument does turn
on this point, it is quite another matter to infer that Plato would restrict
inferiority to being-*F*-and-un*F*, either in other middle-period dialogues, in
the balance of the *Phaedo*, or even in this particular section of the *Phaedo*.

In fact Socrates' argument does not restrict inferiority of sensible equals
to the explicitly mentioned fact of their being *F* and un*F*, or even to the
fact of their incompleteness, needing a *relatum* in order to be equal. The
text does not even represent their being *F* and un*F* as an argument for
regarding sensibles as inferior, let alone as *the* basis of their inferiority.
Their being *F* and un*F* is one premise in an argument for the difference
of Equality from sensible equals which begins with *skopei de* at b7 and is
completed, with the conclusion expressly drawn, at 74c4. This conclusion
is there joined with the assertion that one recollects the Equal from sensible equals (74c7-10). Socrates remarks that the phenomenon in question
is one of recollection whether one regards sensible and intelligible Equal
as similar or dissimilar (c11-d2). Only then, after an additional transition
marked by "*ti de*" (d4) does Socrates raise the question whether, in regard
to sticks and the sort of equals just mentioned, they seem to us to be equal
in the manner of what-is-Equal, or fall short of it (*endei ti*) with respect
to being such as it. By no means is the inferiority of sensibles presented
as the conclusion of the argument concerned with being-*F*-and-un*F*.

So what relationship, if any, is here implied between inferiority and
being-*F*-and-un*F*? The theme of inferiority had been sounded earlier:
Socrates and Simmias agreed that in being *reminded* of one thing by some
different but *similar* thing, one notices the reminding thing *lacks something*
(*ti elleipei*) in its similarity to the thing it calls to mind (74a). They proceed

to prove the Equal *different* from sensible equals, and agree that the latter *remind* one of the former. Socrates says this is true whether they are similar to it or not (74c11-d2) but other indications show that equals and the Equal are in some sense *similar* with respect to their all being equals. Logically speaking, the premises concerned with being-*F*-and-un*F* yield a conclusion as to the *difference* between Equality and equals. This, in turn, serves as a premise – along with assumptions about being reminded of something by some other, similar thing – for an argument that sensible equals are inferior or *lack something* with respect to the Equal. The validity of this larger argument depends in no way on specifying how sensible equals fall short of the Equal. It rests only on premises stating their difference (proved by the *F*-and-un*F* argument) and similarity, plus a premise about a thing's "falling short" whenever it reminds one of some different, but similar, thing. When "falling short" is now reintroduced, Socrates, rather than referring back to the being-*F*-and-un*F* of sensible equals as he might easily have done, instead offers vague metaphors of sensible equals "striving" to be like the Equal, and "desiring" to be such as it (*bouletai*, 74d9; *prothumeitai*, 75b7; *oregetai*, 75b1), but falling short and failing to be equal in the same manner as the Equal itself. So this passage does nothing to show that Plato thought of being-*F*-and-un*F* as marking *the* difference between Form and sensible.

If we extricate ourselves for a moment from isolated consideration of this brief text, we may remind ourselves the *Phaedo* at large introduces other categorial differences unmistakably regarded by Plato as marking off a higher, purer, or superior sort of being from a lower or inferior kind, even if such terms as "falling short" or "deficiency" are not always used to convey the point (see 65d-66a, 78d on intelligibility, non-compositeness). This would be universally granted, but it can be overlooked in pressing too narrowly for possible implications of 74a-c.

From this wider perspective one may also see a specific counterexample to any exclusive *F*-and-un*F* approach to inferiority (at least for any version allowing Forms only for incomplete predicates). In his final proof of immortality Socrates refers to a Form of Life (*auto to tēs zōēs eidos*, 106d5-6). Like the Forms mentioned earlier in the dialogue, Life itself is an opposite. It is also a matter in which Socrates, by his own "autobiographical" account, was keenly interested from early on; it had been the crucial opposite in his earlier proof of immortality based on the "cycle of opposites." It seems to have as strong a claim on Formhood as the Equal, and I know of no one who has denied it is a Form. But Life, or Living Thing, will behave, with regard to being-*F*-and-un*F*, like a substance sortal such as "ox" or "shuttle" rather than a relative such as "equal" or "large." Life does not show the kind of incompleteness that makes possible the being-*F*-and-un*F* of sensible equals, largers, or smallers. Indeed, on the interpretation sketched at the outset of this section, there should not be a Form of Life at all. A more general moral may be noted. The approach under discussion is often framed by its proponents in terms of the modern notion of an incomplete predicate: a predicate whose applicability to a subject cannot be determined without the addition of some completing term. For example, something may be small (fish) but large (bluegill). Helen may be beautiful (compared to a monkey) but ugly (compared to Aphrodite). Now Plato speaks, in the relevant stretches of the *Phaedo* and *Republic*, of opposites. The case of Life shows the category of predicates for opposites does not coincide with that of incomplete predicates; some important Platonic opposites do not correspond to incomplete predicates. Again, this casts doubt on the attribution of certain philosophical motives for postulating Forms and an accompanying criterion for the population of Forms. It provides one more reason for not supposing Plato's Forms were, to begin with, unqualified exemplars of incomplete predicates, differing from sensibles by performing the impossible – by providing examples of largeness, equality and so on without being large or equal in relation to any *relatum*.

The case of Life poses no problem for the interpretation defended here, since any living thing will be inferior to Life itself in all the standard ways having to do with compositeness, mutability, perishability and sensibility. We shall see in chapter 6 more systematic reasons the *Phaedo* could be expected to recognize a Form of Life, along with other Forms whose participants will not be both *F* and un*F* in the incomplete predicate sense. But let us proceed to the middle books of the *Republic*.

Lovers of Spectacles and Lovers of Wisdom

The philosopher, says Socrates, is a lover of learning, undertaking any study, always eager to learn more. But then, replies Glaucon, are we to call lovers of spectacles (*philotheamenes*) philosophers, since they too delight in learning new things, scurrying from one Dionysian festival to another, never getting enough (*Republic* 475c-d)? The answer is obvious, but how is one to justify it? Socrates' solution is to show that only philosophers are lovers of wisdom, since only they pursue knowledge (*epistēmē*), while lovers of spectacles in fact love only opinion (*doxa*). To demonstrate this in a way that will be agreed to by the doxophilists themselves, he gets them to agree (in abstentia) that (a) only what fully is, is knowable, (b) what falls between full being and utter non-being is only opinable, not knowable, (c) anything that is both *F* and un*F* falls between full being and utter non-being, and (d) any sensible thing that is beautiful or just or pious will also be ugly, unjust, impious, and so on. Each will be both *F* and un*F*, hence fall between full being and non-being. Finally, (e) the sight lovers' cherished spectacles, being visible beauties, are both beautiful and ugly. Given all this it follows, as Socrates and Glaucon graciously agree on behalf of the sight lovers, that those beauties are at best only opinable. Thus is the difference between lovers of spectacles and lovers of wisdom made apparent.

Without addressing the details of this argument one can already see a serious philosophical problem threatening. *If* Plato maintains that sensible opposites cannot be known, but only opined, simply because they are un*F* in some way as well as *F*, then he would be rather easily answered. All one need do is qualify one's claims about sensibles appropriately ("that object is *F* in this respect, in relation to this relatum"). For all Plato has said, such a statement should be as knowable as any other, and cases of opposites should not require a brave new world of Forms any more than cases like man and ox: One simply disambiguates one's ambiguous exemplars. Advocates of the *F*-and-un*F* interpretation of inferiority will see this as a problem for Plato; if that was his view on knowability his Platonic heaven of knowable Forms should never have gotten off the ground. Supporters of the approach for which I have argued will see this as a problem rather for an unqualified exemplar interpretation of Forms, which attributes to Plato a defective reason for postulating separate Forms: a distinction between the opinable and the strictly knowable inadequate to motivate a theory of separate Forms. Such a reading is dubious not simply because it attributes a rather lame position to Plato, but because Plato himself shows mastery, in *Republic* IV, of just those procedures needed to disambiguate earthly participants *without* postulating separate Forms. I have in mind his "principle of opposites," instrumental to tripartition of the soul: Nothing will either do or suffer opposites in the same respect, in relation to the same thing, at the same time. (436b-c; cf. *Symposium* 211a, and the careful wording of *Phaedo* 102b-e on Socrates' being taller than Simmias, shorter than Cebes.) If the epistemological problem with sensibles were simply their ambiguity (their being F and un$F$) it is unlikely Plato would have thought it necessary to take the drastic step of postulating separately existing, non-relative relatives. He was perfectly able to eliminate the ambiguity by properly qualifying, as to time, relation, and respect, all judgment about sensible opposites.

Regarding the specific text of the *Republic*, it is true that Socrates' argument will not show men and couches to be "between full being and complete non-being" (since a man is not also the opposite of a man). As proponents of the unqualified exemplar interpretation rightly say, it would neither prove the need for a Form in any case other than the F-and-un$F$ cases, nor rule out full being, hence knowability, of human beings and oxen. But that does nothing whatever to show that other considerations would not locate men and couches between complete being and complete non-being, along with sensible larges and the beauties of the sight lovers. More positively, the standard marks of inferiority prominent in the *Phaedo* and *Symposium* suffice to show, on the one hand, that particular men and couches are not "purely real Fs." They are not of the same sort as the Form F; one can adduce their compositeness, mutability, sensibility. On the other hand, they are not nothing (*medamōs on*), but Fs of an ontological type lower than Forms. The middle books of the *Republic* point toward such a view also, treating *all* sensibles as non-intelligible, so that the lower section of the divided line stands for the sense world as a whole, and so that all *plants, animals, and artifacts* are called objects of *pistis*, or conviction.

Moreover, as the gentle reader has been often reminded, the image analogy (which effectively enters in the middle books of the *Republic*, not only book X) illustrates the fact that every sensible, whether man, ox, large, small, equal, or just, will "be and not be" F: Each will be an F of the inferior sort, but will not be an F of the superior, intelligible sort—just as a painted Simmias is rightly called "Simmias" rather than "Cebes" but is not a real Simmias. Recall *Sophist* 240b: The image is not a real thing of the same sort as its model, but it really is an image—a fact which according to the Eleatic Stranger produces "an intertwining of being and non-being." This is probably the point also of *Republic* 597a, where the image is *toiouton hoion to on, on de ou* ("such as that which is [F], but is not [F]"). To draw, again, a general moral: The things falling between pure or real being on the one hand, and non-being on the other, include not only sensible opposites, but also all sensible images of Forms, and may perfectly well include not only opposites, but also plants, animals, and artifacts. Why, then, does Plato choose only incomplete predicates such as "large" or "heavy" or "beautiful" to argue against the sight lovers? Because he can bring them to agree that sensible examples of light, large, and beautiful "are and are not *F*" even if they do not admit the existence of Forms. That is, one sort of "being and not being" applicable to these cases must be acknowledged even by those incapable of apprehending the one over the many. Thus, anyone who accepts the original framework of complete being, utter non-being, being and non-being (as the sight lovers do, although of course not in terms of Forms and images) can be brought to admit these beauties belong to the intermediate class and hence are objects of *doxa*. For this reason Socrates does not unveil the Forms as completely real objects of *epistēmē* until after he has clinched his point about the beauties of the sight lovers. Contrast his interchange with Simmias in the *Phaedo*: Since both Simmias and Cebes unhesitatingly affirm the existence of Forms, Socrates can freely appeal to the premise that the Equal itself is not also unequal in the course of distinguishing it from sensible equals.

It is unwarranted to see in this *Republic* passage any limit on the population of Forms, or any suggestion that earthly plants, animals, and artifacts are fully real, hence fully knowable in the same sense Forms are knowable. Moreover, viewing matters in that way would create for Plato a philosophical dilemma (about non-relative relatives) he is unlikely to have created for himself, and which does not arise on a fuller account of the inferiority of sensibles.

Turning Toward Forms

One can readily see why *Republic* 523b-d might seem to support an unqualified exemplar interpretation of Forms. There Socrates considers sight adequate for judging fingers, but not for judging various properties that occur together in fingers with their opposites: long, short, thick, or thin. In the latter case, but not the former, the intellect may be stimulated to look beyond sensible appearances because the senses deliver up apparently conflicting judgments like "this (some finger, or perhaps the length of

some finger) is long and short." The senses do not give paradoxical signals
in the case of a finger—they simply tell us that this is a finger and stimulate
no further investigation.

Here another serious problem presents itself. According to the exclusive
F-and-un$F$ approach, (a) Plato appreciated that there could not be non-
relative bearers of relative predicates (long, short, thick, thin), as opposed
to sortal predicates (finger), in this world; (b) he desired, for one or another reason mentioned above, non-relative exemplars of relative properties. Therefore (c) he created a realm of other-worldly, non-relative
relatives. Plato had a sufficient grasp of what we might nowadays call
the "logic of opposites" to see that every *worldly* case of thinness, being
greater than, and being double *must* be thin compared to something, longer
than something, and double some half (and I believe he did)—if he did see
the impossibility of non-relative relatives or non-comparative comparatives in this world, it would then seem brazenly arbitrary of him, to say
the least, to solve his problem by creating a world in which non-relative
relatives could live happily ever after. Again, some will say this is another
of Plato's blunders; it seems to me another implausible consequence of one
account as to why Plato initially postulated separate, non-sensible Forms.

Turning now to the details of the passage, it should be noted first of all
that whatever it does or does not show about the population of Forms, the
purpose of *Republic* 523-525 is not to argue for Forms, or to give, even
in an informal way, a reason for postulating Forms. The passage openly
and emphatically *assumes* there are Forms.[21] The question at issue is not
whether there are Forms, or what sorts of Forms there are, but "how do
we turn men's minds toward the Forms?" To get this process underway
certain properties are more useful than others. Most people are not stimulated to inquire into the nature of a finger. For some properties, however,
such as hardness, softness, unity, or plurality, the senses deliver "opposite
judgments," and so invite reflection upon the nature of those properties.
The immediate purpose of the passage, then, is to single out properties of
a kind likely to stimulate an initial turning toward non-sensible reality.

Moreover, one cannot easily find here a principle by which to guage the
population of Forms. It does not follow, without the additional assumption
that there are Forms only for predicates inviting study in the manner of
"large" and "small," that there are Forms only for opposites. One must
show, in cases of non-opposites, that there is no reason to look beyond
what the senses tell us. In fact, the passage gives no reason to think the

study of a finger or man or carpentry or living thing as such, or the whole of nature, cannot be approached in a philosophic way which carries one beyond the realm of the sensible. Socrates does not specify the purpose for which sight is "adequate" (*hikanos*) in the case of fingers and the like. It would seem to be adequate for non-problematic *identification* of fingers as fingers. By contrast, sight seems to tell us (so Socrates says here) this same thing—this finger, or perhaps the length of this finger—is both long and short. So sight's identification of things as long and short, even if correct, is problematic, because apparently contradictory. Now there is nothing in this to suggest sight is adequate for understanding, rather than just identifying, either fingers or things long or short.

What Socrates explicitly says is that the souls of "the many" (*tōn pollōn hē psuchē*) are not led to inquire into the nature of a finger in itself (523d4). Coming from Plato this hardly shows he considered the non-enquirers to possess an account of the nature of a finger, as opposed to the ability to recognize fingers or to apply the predicate "finger" correctly. It has, indeed, been claimed Plato here *overlooks* the fact that understanding the nature of a finger requires considering the function (and perhaps unobservable structure) of a finger, that he here mistakenly concedes that the pronouncements of the senses are adequate for giving an account of, as well as identifying, fingers, and that he corrects this mistake later, in the *Timaeus*.[22] But consider the important discussion of function in *Republic* I, where Socrates discusses the function and coordinate excellence of horses, eyes, and the soul; recall the emphasis of *Republic* X on the use or function for which "every living thing, artifact, and action is made or by nature suited"; review the discussions throughout the *Republic* of the natural functions of different segments of the *polis*, and of different cognitive capacities of the human soul. It is difficult to believe that in *Republic* VII Plato forgets the nature of fingers must be understood in terms of the function for which they are suited by nature. Herein lies the reason why the few, if not the many, may want to look beyond mere *phainomena*, even in the case of a finger.

Moreover if one considers the whole of the passage, not just the portion about fingers, it seems compresence of opposites cannot in any case be a criterion for judging when a Form is to be postulated. In its larger context, *Republic* 523-5 reflects Socrates' concern with finding studies appropriate for guardians. He is looking for studies which will both elevate the mind and train it in abstract thought, studies which will prepare minds for higher realms of dialectic and ultimate apprehension of the Good, as well as enable the guardian to do his work within society. Arithmetic is one such study: It is necessary for generalship and for every other branch of art or science; moreover, numerical predicates are among the "stimulating" ones (525a) and the challenges of higher arithmetic can strengthen the mind. Geometry is taken up next; it, too, will be included. Circularity, traingularity, and linearity are not, however, said to appear together with their opposites. They *could*, perhaps, by some stretch of the imagination, be regarded in this way, but Plato does not show any concern about that. Geometry is included because it is another challenging study, and thus conducive ultimately to apprehension of the Good (526e). (Recall 510d-e: Even those geometers who use sensible images must in fact be thinking about non-sensible things.) Nor will Socrates be concerned with the compresence of opposites in solid geometry or mathematical astronomy (527). So while the passage opens with cases of being-*F*-and-un*F* as likely to stimulate inquiry beyond the sensible realm, it proceeds to further objects of abstract thought with not so much as a glance at any criterion of being-*F*-and-un*F*. So the passage yields no general principle for generating separate Forms or for census taking among Forms, nor does it exclude Forms corresponding to complete predicates.

Essentialism in the Phaedo?

A final allied, but significantly different, reading links being-*F*-and-un*F* to an alleged Platonic essentialism. This interpretation assumes that Plato considered opposite characteristics of *sensibles* to be only accidental properties of them; their essential properties—being human, being an animal— are among those not co-present with any opposite, for they have no opposite. By contrast *Forms* of opposites do possess themselves, as it were, essentially, and not in conjunction with their own opposites.[23] Textually, this approach relies heavily upon Socrates' distinction between Simmias' being Simmias and Simmias' having a certain height:

> For Simmias does not in the nature of things overtop by this, by being Simmias, but by the height he has [τῷ μεγέθει ὃ τυγχάνει ἔχων]. Nor does he overtop Socrates because Socrates is Socrates, but because Socrates has smallness relative to the largeness of Simmias [ὅτι σμικρότητα ἔχει . . . πρὸς τὸ ἐκείνου μέγεθος] (*Phaedo*. 102c1-4)

Much has been made of the phrase "ὃ τυχάνει ἔχων" as if Socrates' point were to contrast the height Simmias "happens to have" (accidentally has) with the characters, here unnamed, Simmias has essentially. (Cf. 102e: Socrates can admit shortness or tallness without ceasing to be the very same person.) But that phrase in itself carries no such connotation. It is often used by Plato of properties that are, on most any essence/accident distinction, essential.[24]

It is equally wrong to argue[25] that the "ἔχει" of 102c4 suggests accidental possession of a character. Only a very short time later (103e4-5) Socrates uses the same term of properties that would clearly include all (but not, perhaps, only) the essential properties of a thing: "Not only does the *eidos* itself always deserve its own *onoma*, but also any other thing that is not that *eidos*, but always has the form of that *eidos*, whenever it exists [ἔχει δὲ τὴν ἐκείνου μορφὴν ἀεί, ὅτανπερ ᾖ]." So neither of these phrases supports the claim of an essence/accident distinction in *Phaedo* 102c.

More important, Socrates' concern is not to distinguish properties Simmias has accidentally from any he has essentially, but to state correctly *why* Simmias is both tall and short. Socrates wants the *aitia* to be tallness rather than anything else. That this is his concern is shown by the larger context. The general point at stake is that for any Form *F*, a sensible *F* will be *F* by participating in *F* itself. Or, in the *Phaedo*'s tripartite ontology, the sensible is *F* on account of nothing other than the *F*-in-it (102a-b; cf. 100c). (*F*-being-in a thing is equivalent to that thing's participating in *F*.) In the present example Socrates suggests the statement "Simmias is taller than Socrates" does not, strictly speaking, "convey the facts" (102b8). His own view is that strictly speaking Simmias' tallness (or, the tallness that is in Simmias) overtops Socrates' shortness, and that is why Simmias has the *eponoma* "tall." This more meticulous description does bring out the true *aitia* of Simmias' being tall. But this insistence on the proper form of the explanation has nothing to do with any question of whether tallness is an essential or accidental property of Simmias. Socrates could just as well have made the same point using the statement "That white thing is taller than that blue thing." (Assume *white* and *blue* are accidental properties of the things in question.) It is not by being white it overtops the blue thing, nor by the blue thing's being blue. The original statement does not, strictly speaking, convey the facts. The white thing is tall because of the tallness it has relative to the shortness of the blue thing. The point is exactly the same and has nothing to do with a distinction between a thing's essential and accidental properties. It is rather a matter of properly expressing the *aitia* of something's being *F*.

Socrates' later remark (103e) about things that not only have their own *onoma*, but also always have the *morphē* of a certain other thing, so long as they may be (ὅτανπερ ᾖ), might at first sight have the look of essentialism about it: A thing's essential predicates are just those it cannot *be* without. But this passage is no more essentialist than Quine's example of the cycling mathematician. Metaphysical essentialism claims a distinction between essential and accidental predicates in some absolute sense—or as it is sometimes put, a distinction independent of how an object is described. Socrates' example implies only that if a thing is, say, three-numbered, it is always odd, so long as it may be (three-numbered). Thus threes (*ta tria*) or trios will perish or undergo anything else whatever before they endure to become even while being still three (*eti tria onta*, 104c); the general point will hold whether or not "three"refers to a Form of Three. Nothing need be assumed about *three* being an essential predicate of trios. Surely, in fact, it would not be an essential property of all trios, either of their individual members or of their members taken collectively. Granted it is necessarily true that all three-membered clutches of rabbits are trios and vice-versa, still, being a trio, or being a member of a trio, is not an essential trait of any individual rabbit or of the three rabbits taken together. One would have to posit an appropriate abstract object distinct from the rabbits themselves (a group or a plurality; a set would not be adequate, I think) to find a subject for *being three* as an essential property.

The most plausible way of finding essentialism here would be to regard the opposite-in-us (the equal-in-us, tallness-in-us, etc.) as a sort of substance essentially characterized equal, tall, or whatever. (I do not consider this very plausible, but let that pass.) But this assumption would be self-defeating for the view under consideration. One would then no longer need separate Forms to serve as essential bearers of opposite predicates, since items in our own world (the opposites-in-us) already fill the bill quite nicely.

Having now addressed various attempts to circumscribe rather narrowly the inferiority of sensibles, we return to our earlier discussion of the multifarious perfection of Forms and the correspondingly complex inferiority of sensibles. We will consider not only their incompleteness and being-*F*-and-un*F* (where applicable), but also their scatteredness, divisibility, temporality, and opacity to pure reason. These properties are meant, I believe, to mark off sensible embodiments from the abstract natures they embody – be they natures of opposites or of substantial kinds. If so, Forms are not paradigm cases resembling their non-paradigmatic bretheren. We have looked into several implications of this claim. Clearly, it will have a bearing on the matter of Forms as standards.

D. Forms as Standards

Forms not only constitute an order of being higher than sensibles, they are also standards providing the criteria by which their sensible namesakes are judged better or worse specimens of their specific kinds. This much is clear already from the *Cratylus* and *Republic*, both of which emphasize that only he who has knowledge of the appropriate Form is a proper judge of the quality of a given artifact made in its image (*Cratylus* 390b, *Republic* 601-2). Some sensibles are better than others since some craftsmen produce better products than others (*Cratylus* 429a). All sorts of actions may be performed in a better or worse manner; some men, horses, trees, or circles are better specimens of their kinds than others (whatever being better or worse amounts to in a given case).

These two basic points – that Forms are somehow the standards by which one judges particulars and that particulars are, at least in a broad range of cases, comparable to one another in degree of excellence – must be supplemented by the fact that in many instances a given Form must serve as standard for different varieties of sensible *F*. The Equal itself must serve as standard for all the different ways of being equal, Beauty for all the many ways of being beautiful, Shuttle for all the different sorts of shuttle.

In such cases an interpretation of Forms as highly specific abstract structures, designs, or patterns of perfection (or, of course, as paradigm cases) runs into difficulty: No single specific pattern or design will do for all varieties of shuttle, couch, tree, equal, or beauty. Such cases harmonize well, however, with the view that what Plato requires as a standard is an abstract intelligible nature or essence which can be exemplified in various ways while providing a criterion of excellence for any and all of its sensible namesakes. Thus the Form of Equal itself has no shape, weight, size, speed or age, but is participated in by various sorts of equals; accordingly, understanding the nature of equality is the central precondition for judging

degrees of earthly equality in speed, age, volume, or length. Similar remarks apply to the Greater and Less, to Forms for kinds of living things,
shapes, artifacts, and so on. We have seen also that the Form allows one
to rate certain particulars as both perfect (as when two sticks are exactly
equal in length, or two fixed stars move with exactly equal velocity) and,
at the time, as deficient (since the perfect sensible is still necessarily inferior, with respect to its manner of being F, to the intelligible Form of F).

It is not difficult, finally, to see how this view of Forms as standards contributes to Plato's image/model vision of reality. The key points follow
easily from the results of chapter 3. Like sensible participants, images are
a type of F different from their models or originals; and, like sensible Fs,
image Fs may be of different varieties (paintings, reflections, dramatiza-
tions, dreams). Yet their single original is the standard by which the
faithfulness or correctness (*orthotēs*) of all those many varieties of images
is judged.

The Correctness of Images

The parallel does not depend on saying more exactly *how* correctness
of images is to be assessed, and Socrates takes a clearer position on what
such correctness is not than on what it is. But several dialogues, including
the *Cratylus*, contain important positive suggestions. (It would be surprising if the *Cratylus* had nothing at all to say on the matter, given its occupation with correctness of *logoi* and with the concept of *logoi* as images.)
It will be worthwhile to seek out these suggestions, both for their intrinsic
interest and for their bearing on the role of Forms as standards. In general,
however, the topic is more interesting for what it reveals about Plato's attitude toward art — specifically, toward what is nowadays called the "autonomy" of art — and for what it contributes to a general theory of imaging
than for any new information it conveys about Platonic metaphysics. At
least three initially plausible suggestions find some support in the dialogues.

(1) Given that some image is an image of a particular model, the correctness of the image lies in its *being like* its model, perhaps in weighted
respects — always with the proviso, of course, that the image not become
another real F. One thinks especially of *Cratylus* 431c where a good portrait is one getting the shape and colors of the original just right, and of
Socrates' remark (432e) that at a minimum the "general character" (*typos*)

of the thing is to be perserved in its (linguistic) image; but it is not clear this suggestion could or should be generalized to all images. The *Cratylus* discussion dealt with corporeal images (gestures, sounds, portraits) regarded as imitating (in part) by duplicating certain properties of their models (see 423a1-b2). The discussion does not consider deliberate departures from resemblance (such as the monumental sculpture of *Sophist* 236 which must systematically depart from the proportions of their originals to look right). Nor, of course, does it consider incorporeal images arising in the soul (dreams, for example). Also, by this criterion even the most realistic and deceptive of dream images would rate no higher in correctness than the murkiest shadows, since dream images typically do not resemble their originals in any of the respects in which they appear to do so.

(2) The image *F*, while not a real *F*, must nonetheless look like, sound like, or in general *appear* like its model *F*. This suggestion ties in well with the important theme of appearance *vs.* reality: The good image has the look of the real thing and is called after it, but isn't the real McCoy at all. The suggestion also allows for the often highly faithful dream image, as well as the monumental statues of *Sophist* 236a. It allows, too, of course, for images that look like their models because they are like their models in some respects. So this is an attractive and plausible suggestion, even if not one enjoying direct textual support. But notice that if *logoi* are images, and if their being images of their subject matter does not *in general* require either actual or apparent similarity to it (granting that many *logoi* imitate through *onomatopoeia*) this second proposal will also be unacceptable.

(3) Probably the most interesting positive suggestion in the dialogues, and the one providing the most satisfactory link to participation, has also the best textual credentials. It occurs, among other places, in the same work in which the criterion of correctness as duplication is rejected, the *Cratylus*: The correct image depicts its original accurately, or truthfully. This criterion would apply to paintings, sculpture, mirror reflections, and dream images. Some of these would depict their models as of such-and-such a nature by (in part) actually being like them in some respects, others by merely looking like them, and others, perhaps, without even looking like their models.

This third suggestion appeals largely to a philosophically important parallel between *logoi* and images. For one thing, both images and *logoi* are *about* something.[26] The primary *logoi* of *Sophist* 262e are about something, as are the *doxai* of *Republic* 478b which are imaged in *logoi*. Moreover, images purport to reveal something about their models, just as *logoi* say something about their subject. This gives rise to the *Cratylus'* discussion of learning about things through their images, and the extreme danger of basing one's convictions about real things solely on examination of their images. Above all, the suggestion relies on Plato's explicit parallel between truth of *logoi* (or more precisely, of names analyzed as descriptive *logoi*) and correctness of images:

> Would you allow that the name [*onōma*] is an imitation [*mimēma*] of the thing?
> Certainly.
> And would you also say that pictures are imitations of things, only in some other way?
> Yes.
> Are not both to be allotted and assigned to the things of which they are imitations?
> Yes.
> First then consider this: One may assign the image [*eikona*] of a man to the man and of a woman to the woman . . . or vice versa . . . The right [*orthōs*] way . . . is that which assigns to each that which belongs to it [*to prosēkon*] and is like [*homoios*] it.[27] That one, whether in paintings or names, I call "correct" [*orthos*] while in the case of names I call it "true" as well as "correct." The other, which gives and assigns what is unlike, I call "incorrect," and in the case of names "false" as well. (430a10-d7)

The general idea is that images in their own way tell us something about their models, the image being correct or incorrect depending on whether what it tells us is true or false. This in turn would make it quite natural for Plato to extend the terms "true" and "false" to images, and this is precisely what occurs in the *Philebus*:

> Would you say that very often when someone sees objects from a distance, and not at all clearly, he wishes to decide what it is he sees? . . . And he would say to himself, if he got it right, that it is a man . . . or if he went astray and thought that what he saw was something made by shepherds, he might call it a statue [*agalma*]. . . . It seems to me that at such times our soul is like a book . . . that the concurrence of memory with sensations, together with the feelings attendant upon these, may be said to write words in our souls. . . . Then please

accept a second artist in our souls at such a time . . . a painter, who comes after the scribe and paints in the soul pictures of these assertions [τῶν λεγομένων εἰκόνας ἐν τῇ ψυχῇ τούτων γράφει]. . . . Then are the pictures of the true *doxai* and *logoi* true, and those of the false, false? Undoubtedly. (38c-39c)

By introducing a distant and indistinct object of perception Plato has in effect portrayed the psychological sequence in slow motion. A man wonders what it is he is seeing; after some reflection (38c-d) he makes up his mind (the scribe writes in his soul), then pictures the distant object to himself as whatever it was he judged it to be. The true *eikōn* is that which illustrates a true *logos* or *doxa*: As the true *logos* states things as they are, so the true picture pictures things as they are.

The Goodness of Images

Thus despite important differences between his views on imaging and modern theories of representation Plato seems to favor a notion of *correctness* that has more recently had a liberating effect on the study of representation, freeing it from unreflective servitude to similarity,[28] directing attention instead to the quality of information conveyed by the image. Nonetheless Plato's insistence in the *Republic* that art correctly portray *appropriate* subjects imposes conditions that today are generally less well received. Plato's attitude toward art is an enormous subject in its own right.

My justification for raising the matter here is that the general study of Plato's remarks on imaging can contribute to a fuller understanding of his views on art in ways not ordinarily recognized; the points about correctness (above) would make one such contribution, the distinction of correctness from goodness of an image (below) another. Moreover, both the correctness and goodness of images, as Plato conceives them, have natural analogues in his image metaphysics.

First, how is goodness different from correctness of an image? That there is some difference appears from the fact that although *Republic* 601d brought together beauty, excellence, and correctness of plants, animals, and artifacts in a way suggesting their equivalence, a correct or excellent specimen of injustice or depravity is hardly a thing of beauty or goodness. Glaucon's just and unjust men of *Republic* II are each with equal zest "polished off for the competition . . . as if it were a statue" (361d). As examples of human types each is a pure and excellent aid to discussion; as types of life to be lived, one is by nature admirable, the other, repellant. The difference is not a matter of correctness since both are quite correct or faithful; it lies rather in the fact that only one is a correct image *of a good or worthy model*. The best or most beautiful image is not simply the most correct image, or the one most (artfully) pleasing, but a *correct image of a good or worthy model*. This condition imposes severe limits on the autonomy of the arts. For painters or poets to survive in Plato's *kallipolis* they must be "most politic" artists whose productions are strictly limited to those promoting proper *paideia*. When Socrates says the ultimate aim of education is inculcation of a love of beauty (403c) he does not have in mind the admiration of pretty pictures, any more than enjoyment of conventionally pleasing Athenian drama. Since the gods and their semi-divine heroic offspring are good, and should provide good examples for youth, Socrates makes it imperative the poets set to work imitating truthfully (377d, 378a) these good models. At the time, they were said to imitate poorly (*eikadzein kakōs*), even going so far as to represent the gods as sources of evil, the heroes as rapacious and cowardly. As for imitations of human subjects, only those *accurately* representing a good man in his better moments could be approved (396c-d, 399a-c).

The Athenian Stranger of the *Laws* would impose on *musikē* in general the same complimentary pair of conditions:

> If someone says that in music pleasure is the standard of judgment, we should least of all accept his statement. It is not this type of music, if indeed there could be such, which we should seriously pursue, but that other which bears a likeness to the image of the noble [ὁμοιότητα τῷ τοῦ καλοῦ μιμήματι]. (668a9-b2)

The *Laws* reveals more of Plato the art critic than does the *Republic*, especially through the Stranger's treatment, in this same context, of "beautiful execution" in art. This he judges in such terms as the appropriateness of various combinations of words, rhythm, melody, and posture (implicit in the *Republic*'s discussion of licentious, soft, or manly rhythms, melodies, or words). He seems to regard certain results as not only dangerous but plain bad art ("senseless and complicated confusion," "the worst of bad taste," or "unmusical legerdemain" in Taylor's spirited translation). Even so, the noblest song or *kallistē odē* (668b) is not simply one combining the compatible modes in a skillful way, but a correct image, beautifully executed, of a noble model (668a-b).

The single most important application of all this to metaphysics would be the whole of Plato's account of creation in the *Timaeus*. Timaeus' story manifestly incorporates the distinct factors of correctness or faithfulness of the image and goodness of the model. According to this "most likely tale," the divine craftsman, being good and without jealousy, wished to fashion, from a primeval disorderly motion, as good a cosmos as possible (29d-30b). To this end he created the *most faithful likeness* he could of the *best possible model* (30c-31b, 37c).

The application to statecraft is (almost) too obvious to mention. Perhaps the two factors distinguished here will now stand out more sharply in the *Republic*. The philosopher would fashion an image using the *divine model* (τῷ θείῳ παραδείγματι χρώμενοι, 500e3). Starting with a clean slate (501a), then looking often to the Just, Beautiful, Temperate, and the like in nature, the philosopher would blend and mix just the right hues, erasing and repainting if necessary, until the human character most pleasing to God is achieved (501b-c). This would be the most faithful, hence most revealing, image of the Good and Just obtainable in the medium of human bodies and souls. As Adeimantus observes, "this would be the most beautiful of paintings" (*kallistē an hē graphē genoito*, 501c3).

6

Models, the Good, and Participation

The separation of Forms from sensible participants places Plato's theory among strong versions of Platonism, as opposed to those whose abstract entities depend for existence on things that exemplify or instantiate them. Plato goes still further in insisting that sensible participants depend for their being upon the separate Forms in which they participate. Forms, in Plato's version, are ontologically prior to their sensible participants.

There are two ways in which sensibles depend upon Forms, neither of which makes Forms into efficient causes. The first applies to all purposeful production of images of Forms by craftsmen human or divine. In such cases Forms are *aitiai* of the generation of sensibles in the way an artist's model is one *aitia* of a finished portrait. The Form as model for making is roughly comparable to a final cause, insofar as the creator's aim is to bring forth an image of the Form.

The second is most clearly expressed at *Phaedo* 100c:

> If anything else is beautiful besides Beauty itself [*auto to kalon*], it is beautiful for no other reason than that it participates in that Beauty [*dioti metechei ekeinou tou kalou*]; and likewise in all cases. Do you agree that it is for this reason [*tēi toiāide aitiāi*]?[1]

Here is Plato's characteristic expression of the dependence: It is because of participation in *F* itself that any participant is *F*. This is not to ascribe efficient causality to the Forms, or to anything else. Rather, Socrates seems to claim for Forms a role as formal *aitiai* of sensibles such that where "*F*" stands for a Form, any worldly thing is *F* because it participates in *F*. The claim is not trivial, since it implies that there are Forms and that it is by participation in Forms particulars are *F*. Given that there are Forms, however – and all parties to the *Phaedo* discussion emphatically agree there are – the statement becomes considerably less controversial. So Socrates refers to Forms as his "simple" (with the intended connotation of "simple minded") but "safe" *aitiai*.

Notice this second aitiological role is quite general, in that it applies whenever any sensible participates in a Form. By contrast, the role of model for making applies only when a participant is brought into being by productive activity appropriately guided by apprehension of the relevant Form. A pair of wood chips produced "accidentally" in the production of a cult statue or shuttle might participate in the Form of Two, and each in Forms for Same, Different, and so on, even though not deliberately made as images of those Forms. Where intelligent production has taken place, *both* aitiological roles of the Form are fulfilled and are distinguishable at least in *logos*. We shall observe in a moment the analogues of the two roles on the side of worldly models and their images.

The safety of Socrates' safe *aitiai* has been called into question by many critics, including Platonists of a more moderate stripe; two main difficulties are said to follow upon separating Forms in this way. First, critics have charged, this "reifies" them, making them into individuals or particulars having the nature *F*, rather than common characteristics or shared natures. Second, separating Forms from sensibles, so that they are neither in sensibles in any way, nor located where sensibles are, and not dependent upon sensibles for their being, seems to obviate their role as formal *aitiai*. They can serve neither as particular property instances ("unit properties" or "abstract particulars") nor as Aristotelian forms informing matter (however Aristotelian forms are interpreted). They are no longer the repeatable universals of Aquinas and many others (including, perhaps, Aristotle), which exist in indifferently many individuals, nor the scattered individuals of Goodman, composed of sensible *F*s. Far less are they Anaxagorean "bits" mixed into the composition of things. How *can* sensible objects participate in these Platonic Forms, so separate and aloof?

This line of criticism is as old as Aristotle, and applies not only to Plato but to all other Platonists who separate their Platonic entities from worldly individuals. A recent critic expresses it concisely:

> The greatest difficulty of extreme realism is [to explain] how essences, entities independent of the actual world, can ever enter the actual world as characters of things.[2]

Sir David Ross, having asserted "Anyone who writes about the theory of Ideas is bound to state as precisely as he can what Plato's conception of the relation of Ideas to particulars really was,"[3] discusses the topic of "transcendence *vs.* immanence" of Forms without asking how either sort of Form would be participated in by sensibles. He thus discusses an important preliminary issue, but leaves off just where our problem arises.

Others have proposed that Forms *are* the natures that sensibles *have*. Commentators as disparate as Harold Cherniss, G.E.L. Owen, and Gregory Vlastos agree this is a good statement of what Plato's theory either was (Cherniss) or should have been (Owen, Vlastos).[4] Accepting this as a correct characterization of the classical theory of Forms would not answer the question, however; the problem only re-emerges as one of how sensibles have separate Forms as natures.

Nor should we be content with the observation that "participation" is a primitive term of the theory. That, too, is true enough, but does not imply the nature of participation is clear, or that one need not try to understand it, even if (one might say, *especially* if) it is not to be defined.

The principal aim of this chapter will be to develop one suggestion as to how Plato conceived of participation. This notion cannot be attributed to Plato with complete confidence, partly because he is notoriously reticent on the subject, and because it involves claims about several other large and difficult issues of interpretation. In particular it relies on a specific reading of the separateness of Forms, on some key assertions about the relation of the Good to Forms in general, and on a broad census-taking among Forms.

It may be easiest to begin with the image analogy. We have already
noted that the counterpart to a sensible's participating in *F* itself is the image *F*'s being an image of some real *F*. For purposes of illustration the
analogy works well: The model (Napoleon himself) is independent of its
many images. They are indebted to it both as the model or original to
which their creator looked, and as a kind of formal *aitia* in that their being
images of Napoleon is what makes them (imitation or image) Napoleons,
thereby entitling them to the label "Napoleon" rather than "Wellington."
There are *two* ways in which a Form might be an *aitia paradeigmatikē* (an
aitia or "cause" in the manner of a model) of its worldly participants' being
what they are. The role of model for making is perhaps the more obvious,
but the formal role is crucial: It is the analogue to Plato's general notion
of participation. Notice that in neither case is the model an efficient cause
of the portrait—except sometimes "accidentally," Aristotle would say, as
in a self-portrait. (Some originals are causal factors in this way when they
cast a shadow or a reflection; but this feature, unlike the of-ness of images,
is not generalizable to all Plato's images.)[5] In addition, because any image,
whether painting, statue, reflection, or dream, must come to be in some
appropriate medium, the *Timaeus* stresses a dependence of sensibles both
upwards and downwards: The image (sensible *F*) is a phantasm *of* something else (the Form *F*) and must come to be *in* something else (the receptacle; 52c 2-5). Without a medium it could not even "cling precariously
to being" (52c4-5); without being *of* the original or "real" *F* it would not
be an imitation or image *F*.

The analogy even captures the "simple-mindedness" of Socrates' simple
aitiai. To say that a certain drawing in a dictionary, picture book, or
museum is a Napoleon because it is an image of Napoleon is, in one way,
quite trivial. But it is not trivial insofar as it assumes there is or was a
Napoleon and these ink marks or pigments constitute a drawing or painting
of him. Considered in this light, an image's being *of* its model illustrates
a strongly Platonistic metaphysics in which a sensible *F*'s "participation
in" a separate, intelligible *F* makes it what it is—a (sensible) *F*.

A. Formal *Aitiai* and The Being *F* of Sensibles

There is a genuine problem here regarding the nature of the *relata* said
to be related as model to image: separate, immutable objects on the one
hand, and sensible, spatial, mutable objects on the other. While the anal-

ogy illustrates several important things Plato wants to say about participation, it is not at all obvious the metaphysical claims illustrated are jointly coherent.

It must be kept in mind, in trying to say how Plato thought of participation in separate Forms, that one need not *define* "participation." As the term is probably best treated as primitive, it is not explicitly definable in other terms of the theory. This is not to say Plato had a distinction between primitive and defined terms (though some things he says, especially in the *Theaetetus*, suggest he did). It means only that he did not explicitly define "participation" and the term should in fact be regarded as primitive, like "instantiation" or "falling under" in other versions of Platonism.

How, then, to convey this primitive? Lesniewski is said to have resorted to pounding on the table to convey the primitive ε ("is") of his system of ontology. My own approach will be less Khrushchevian, involving, as a first step, an analogy suggested by Socrates' discussion of the just city in the *Republic*. The analogy is drawn to a system of city government in which various sorts of people and their functions, along with various political offices, their perquisites, responsibilities, and interrelations, are defined in a comprehensive charter. The various sorts of status groups, offices, official acts, and so on defined in the charter may then be regarded in the abstract as so many governmental types or kinds. These include the offices of mayor, dogcatcher, policeman, and such kinds of official acts as appointing deputy mayors, making arrests, performing marriages, and so on.

This description admits of a strongly Platonistic interpretation, since these governmental kinds are in one clear way independent of the people, thoughts, or actions that hold, perform, or realize them. There may be no dogcatcher or justice of the peace, though one or both offices exist, vacant, in a given town; no marriages, though the appropriate type of performance is established in the charter. Even if the town never has a dog-catcher but always has a mayor, the former office still exists just as surely as that of mayor, since it is equally provided for in the city charter. One might say that in establishing the office and describing the duties of dog-catcher the charter "provides the being and essence" (*Republic* 509b) of the abstract governmental type. Thus the office itself is *separate* in that it depends not at all for its being what it is on any worldly mayors or dog-catchers, only on the charter. (To clinch the point, suppose the charter itself is independent of worldly conditions, having been handed down by a god.)[6] Why, then, is the mayor of the town mayor? Or, what "makes" the mayor mayor? One might cite an efficient cause—his or her having been elected mayor by the officially eligible voters, or appointed by the town council.

This leaves out what is more important for present purposes, and which normally goes without saying: One is mayor because one holds the office of mayor. More generally, worldly mayors are mayors for no other reason than that they hold the office of mayor. This is simpleminded in the same way as Socrates' safe *aitiai*. But it is non-trivial in the same way, too, for it presupposes there is an office of mayor and that people are mayors because they officially hold that office. If the office itself were eliminated, one could no longer be mayor, no matter how mayoral one's demeanor. Likewise, if there were no such action type as the performance of a marriage, certain actions and utterances ("I do," or "I now pronounce you . . .") could under no circumstances effect a marriage. The ontological priority of the abstract type should be clear: The type is presupposed by its particular participants, not *vice versa*.

Simple as this is, I believe it marks some progress. Already it shows directly that a separate abstract type *F* can function as a formal *aitia* of worldly things' being *F*. The examples show the coherence of the claim that participation in *separate* abstract types or natures can be an *aitia* of worldly things being what they are, in some respects at least, without those natures being made into efficient causes of any sort or perfect examples of themselves, and without their inhabiting sensibles or entering the world as the immanent characters of things. To see this is already to remove what has been for many a stumbling block to serious consideration of Plato's separate Forms.

Still, these examples may not seem to go far enough. For while one is made to be mayor by holding that office, one is also many other things: human, pale, musical, equal (in age, to the Justice of the Peace), just. There is no obvious way in which one is made to be these things by some counterpart to holding political office. The person exists already, as it were; the separate abstract object is presupposed only when one happens to take on some official, but metaphysically accidental, role in society. By contrast, Plato seems to want a much more thoroughgoing ontological dependence of sensibles on Forms. It is not that sensibles already exist with a variety of properties, then take on some further character—much less only come to be *seen* in a different light—by participating in a Form.[7] Plato seems to believe a sensible could not be anything at all without participating in various Forms. (This formulation is ambiguous, but it will serve as a first approximation.) Nonetheless, with the help of certain key Platonic assumptions about the Good and its relation to other Forms, the examples do provide an accurate and fully generalizable model for participation in separate Forms. This can hardly be seen clearly or rendered plausible until those subsidary issues have been considered; I postpone for the moment a summary statement of the interpretation.

Raising the topic of the Good is something like opening Pandora's box. I hope to clamp the lid down on all but three related propositions. The first will be agreed to by virtually everybody (and is also, I think, true); the second is somewhat controversial, but has strong textual support; the third is, again, largely uncontroversial.

First, the Good is separate from all sensible things. It is not located where they are, not contaminated by any admixture with them, nor dependent on them for being what it is. Independence, especially, seems to be intended by Socrates' analogy to the sun in *Republic* VI, where the sun provides for the generation of living things but does not depend for its being on them. I will for the moment assume this first point without further comment, though we shall soon encounter one basic reason for Plato's thinking the Good — and all other Forms — separate.

Second, Plato's Forms constitute a realm of *natural* essences restricted in population. Not every *onoma*, or every property of things, or every grouping of worldly things corresponds to a Form: Some are only arbitrary aspects or parts of the world rather than natural ones. At other times and places this point would not need documentation, but nowadays one encounters resistance even to the idea that Forms are closely associated with what is "natural" or "by nature." So a review of the principal evidence should be useful in securing agreement here, before we turn to participation itself. Such a review is called for in any case, since there *are* some apparently recalcitrant passages to be faced. Moreover, even a consensus about the "naturalness" of Forms would not explain how the concept can apply to *all* sorts of Forms, including not only those for basic opposites and for living things, but also mathematical Forms, vowel Forms such as Sameness and Difference, and others.

Plato has Socrates attest explicitly that Forms are "in nature," though not, of course, in the sensible world, to which some *physikoi* restrict the realm of nature. Forms of important opposites are located "in nature" at

Phaedo 103b, where Socrates distinguishes the *F*-in-nature from the *F*-in-us and from the things that have *F*.

Key Forms (the Just, the Good) are again placed "in nature" (*physei*) at *Republic* 501b. For this reason the just city founded by the philosopher with an eye to the Good and Just in nature is constructed "in accordance with nature" (*kata physin*, 428e9) and ruled by the wisdom of a group which is "by nature" (*physei*, 428e9) its smallest part. More specifically, the justice of the city depends on various people performing those essential tasks, and only those, for which they are by nature suited (456a, ff.). This sort of legislation is not impossible of realization because it is *kata physin*, in contrast to the actually prevailing law, which is *para physin* (456b12-c2). Bodily health as well depends on relevant elements ruling and being ruled *kata physin* (444d3-4); disease arises when these are related contrary to nature (*para physin*, 444d5-6). Analogously, justice or injustice come about in the soul as a result of relevant elements dominating and being dominated in accordance with, or contrary to, nature (*kata physin, para physin*, 444d8-11).

The theme of naturalness is equally prominent in *Republic* X, where the Form of Couch is "in nature" (*en tei physei*, 597b, 598a; see 597d: God made only one couch *in nature*). Notice in this last passage the use of *phyō* ("beget," 597d3; cf. c4-5) as a variant for *poiein* ("make, create"). God is thus the Form's "natural begettor" (*phytourgon*, 597d5), since it is by or in nature (*physei*) that he made this Form and all the rest (d7). As has been often noted, this passage is unique in speaking of Forms as *produced*; Socrates' language is nonetheless useful. The biological connotations of *phyō* and *phytourgon* fit well with the joint notions that the Good of *Republic* VI supports a realm of *natural* essences and that the god of Book X is a stand-in for the Good. Plato introduces precisely this stand-in not because Forms are produced by God, but because in that context it helps make several relevant points. For one, God fills out the sixfold classification within which a distinction between three types of *F* can then be highlighted by distinguishing three types of producer. Introducing a god also helps drive home the epistemological point that painters (and poets) are three removes from genuine knowledge; god naturally represents full understanding or *nous* (*Timaeus* 51e). In addition, the device adds vividness—though in a manner not logically requisite—to the uniqueness argument for what-is-couch: Even god could not have made so many as two of them (*Republic* 597c).

The *Phaedrus* and *Statesman* require, in their discussion and exercise of Platonic division, that the Forms in proper division correspond to natural kinds of things or natural distinctions among things. One must not hack off pieces of reality like a clumsy butcher, but carve along the joints (*Phaedrus* 265e); one must always divide off a part which is a genuine kind—an *eidos* as opposed to a mere *meros* (*Statesman* 262b ff). At *Phaedrus* 266b Socrates declares himself a lover of collections and divisions, saying that where someone is able "to discern a natural unity and plurality" (*hen kai epi polla pephykoth' horan*) he follows that person "as a god."

Similarly, the notion of many Forms, at least, as natural kinds (animals, metals, "primary elements") to be exemplified in the visible cosmos is central to the creation story of the *Timaeus*. Perhaps it is less widely recognized that the *Sophist's* use of a divine craftsman points in the same direction. (It does not matter for this particular point whether the creator god of either dialogue is a literary fiction, or whether the Forms of the *Sophist* are separate.) Assuming this demiurge works, like every Platonic craftsman, with an eye to some *eidos*, he will look to much the same natural kinds as the demiurge of the *Timaeus*. Such parallels to the *Timaeus* need not be *inferred*: At *Sophist* 265c the Eleatic Stranger explicitly cites, as examples of divine handiwork, animals (*Timaeus* 39e-40a), plants (*Timaeus* 77a) and inanimate bodies compacted beneath the earth, both fusible and non-fusible (*Timaeus* 58c-61c). At 266b he adds that "we ourselves . . . and all other living creatures and that from which natural things come— fire, water, and their brethren . . . are the offspring of divine craft." (On "elements" as products of divine workmanship, see *Timaeus* 53a-55c).

Further testimony concerning the naturalness of Forms could be gathered from these and other dialogues, including the *Philebus* and *Laws*. But when Socrates describes Forms as "models fixed in nature" (or "in the nature of things," *paradeigmata hestanai en tēi physei*, *Parmenides* 132d) he is only making explicit a basic connection between two thoroughly Platonic conceptions of Forms (at least as they appear in middle dialogues): one as the *paradeigmata* of which worldly participants are images, the other as *natural* essences or types.

It is sometimes contested whether Plato consistently held a theory of Forms restricted in population. *Republic* 596a might seem to postulate a Form for every (general) *onoma* and so contradict the *Phaedrus*, *Statesman*, and other dialogues—including, perhaps, itself—on this point. But

Socrates' observation "we customarily hypothesize one Form for every plurality to which we apply a common *onoma*," is, as others have pointed out, descriptive of a usual procedure which, in any controversial case, would include further considerations. No further considerations (such as of naturalness) arise in that context because the particular example there (a couch) is a thing assumed to have a clear function corresponding to natural needs of human beings. The specific example might, however, be playful: There were no couches in the "healthy city" of Book III; these were first found in the "fevered city" along with hairdressers, actors, and other such riff-raff. Socrates' choice of example would be apt: Glaucon is the respondent at this point in Book X; it was he who objected to the first city as a "city of pigs," and couches were the first thing he mentioned when asked what more he would like (372d). Still, some things that enter the fevered city *do* survive the subsequent purge, including proper furniture, embroidery, and painting (with 373a compare 401ab). But, in any case, even the "healthy city" (in which, notice, there is not yet any philosophy) contains numerous types of *artifacts*, a class of which the couches of Book X may be taken as representative.[8]

Parmenides' remark that in time young Socrates will cease to worry about what people might think and recognize Forms even for undignified kinds of things like mud (*Parmenides*, 130c-e) does not imply Socrates will eventually acknowledge a Form for every predicate or every group of worldly items. Parmenides' prediction is entirely in harmony with a restricted population of Forms because the kinds mentioned, though they lack the glamour of Beauty itself, are natural kinds. The natural function of hair appears at *Timaeus* 76c-d; dirt is a type of thing essential in many ways to the operation of the cosmos, and mud (or perhaps clay, *pēlos*) will be useful for brickmaking, doll making, pot making, and other things. (The *Theaetetus* lists these uses for varieties of *pēlos* and supplies their common *logos*, 147a-c.) The moral Parmenides has in mind is that, in time, Socrates will give due recognition to every naturally deserving kind, regardless of its standing in public opinion.

The Stranger's comments in the *Sophist* on the bathman's art and on the "motley" of business hagglings carry the same suggestion. The former deserves the dialectician's notice, who cares not at all that it may be undignified but seeks only to discern the kinship or lack of kinship among the arts, for the sake of true understanding (*nous*, 227a-b; see 224b). The latter is a class (*eidos*) distinguishable by *logos*, but does not form any unified art, so will not be given a name by dialectic in its division of arts (225c).[9] This passage also illustrates the Platonic dialectician's policy of bestowing names upon only natural types of things.[10] One consequence of such a policy would be that, on any correct general scheme of *onomata* (correct in revealing the natural articulation of reality), individual terms must correspond to genuine (natural) Forms—which is why the true name-giver will be the dialectician.[11]

Negative Forms may appear to raise a problem because (a) Plato seems, above all in the *Sophist*, emphatically to acknowledge such Forms (Not-being, Not-large, Not-beautiful), and (b) such Forms apparently correspond not to natural groupings of things, but in each case to vast miscellanies of worldly items.[12] So has he not here, at least, allowed a One for every worldly plurality, no matter how motley? Some commentators contend he has, and that he changed his mind about the population of Forms. Different explanations have been suggested. Perhaps Plato now wants a Form for every predicate, to serve as that which is attributed to subjects in *logoi*, or to serve as meanings of predicates; or perhaps he now recognizes only immanent Forms, or repeatable universals, and sees that "arbitrary" universals are still universals. Perhaps he still recognizes some separate Forms but does not intend various parts of the Different to be separate Forms, only non-separate ones.

The main cause of this concern is a mistaken assumption that the Not-large, Not-beautiful, and the rest cannot correspond to natural essences. To see why "carving nature at the joints" yields the Not-large as well as the Large it would he helpful first of all to think in terms of "parts of the Different" rather than of "negative Forms," and to regard the Stranger as showing the natural way of dividing the Different, considered strictly as such. Given the realm of Forms up to, but not including, those introduced as parts of the Different, the natural parts of the Different are then marked out by the contrast (*antithesis*) between any designated Form F and the rest of the Forms (*onta*, 258a-b). One immediate result is that the articulation of Difference must exactly parallel that of Being itself. Granted, further, the key notion of a contrast with something points to the very nature of difference as such, it follows the Different-from-F, for any Form F, constitutes a natural part of the Different as such, and hence a real, natural kind. Each part will "have its own nature" just as much as the F itself (258b-c).[13]

This points up an important general moral about Platonic division. In determining whether a given *onoma* corresponds to a Form one cannot be guided simply by consideration of whether the bearers of that *onoma* are, in some absolute sense, too motley to form a natural kind. The worldly participants in the Not-large are as diverse a group as one is likely to meet, but they can receive Formhood *from above* as it were, since they correspond to a natural part of the Different as such. Where there is no salvation from on high, a motley can fail to correspond to a Form—as with the business hagglers of 225c.

One might imagine that once Forms become the predicables introduced in a *prōtos logos* one will need a distinct Form for every predicate (or, more moderately, for every non-compound predicate). In itself this is a *non sequitur*, but one could respond that given Plato's views on the composition of the soul in the *Timaeus* there is no need for an unlimited population of Forms to explain human ability to ascribe any number of natural and non-natural predicates to various subjects. The soul is compounded of "intermediate" sameness, being, and difference; its various circles are marked off at harmonic intervals such that it can discern samenesses and differences among both sensibles and intelligibles (*Timaeus* 35a-37c). Presumably this basis of our capacity to see sameness and difference generally among things will establish a capacity for dividing reality into arbitrary parts or natural ones—and thence for assigning predicates that may or may not be the *onomata* of any Form. One would like more details about the basis of the soul's capacity to perceive differences and similarities, but Plato need not assume a distinct Form to account for the use of each and every distinct (non-compound) predicate.

So there would seem to be no good reason to question the limitation of Forms in the *Phaedrus, Statesman,* and elsewhere to natural distinctions among things, or to suppose that Plato vacillated or changed his mind on the matter. Thus Aristotle commends Plato by name (*Metaphysics* 1070A 18-19) for postulating Forms for "natural" sorts of things (which is not to say he agrees with Plato on the scope of the "natural"), and Xenocrates, in a phrase reminiscent of *Parmenides* 132c-d, describes the Platonic Form as an *aitia paradeigmatikē tōn kata physin aei synestotōn* (fragment 30).[14]

Finally, if the realm of Forms is restricted, its population is determined in some manner by the Good itself. The only alternative is to suppose either that something other than the Good accomplishes this, or that nothing at all does (perhaps it is just a matter of chance). For Plato the latter alternative is out of the question. And in light of his expressed view in the *Republic* that the Good provides the being and essence of other Forms (*kai to einai te kai tēn ousian hup' ekeinou autois proseinai*, 509b7-8) one must conclude the population of Forms is determined by the Good rather than by something else.

This much is common ground to numerous interpreters, though there is disagreement over how the relationship should be conceived. The two main lines of interpretation have been that (a) the Good is itself a distinct nature, only somehow presupposed by all the rest, and (b) the Good is not a distinct nature, but is identical to the overall scheme of Forms. With the former, one encounters different opinions as to *how* the Good is presupposed (neo-Platonic views being the most colorful among these); on both, *what* sort of intelligible realm the Good establishes. It is worth remarking that the rather modest point I require is only the common denominator of most of these views: There are these Forms, related in these ways to one another, because it is good that it be so. Historically, disputes arise only when the time comes to explicate this "because." (I am not convinced it is warranted or fruitful to seek beyond the general claim, but that is another issue.)

Let us review briefly the three points just established.

(1) The Good is separate from all sensible things. It is not located where they are, not contaminated by any admixture with them, nor dependent on them for being what it is.

(2) Plato's Forms constitute a realm of *natural* essences restricted in population.

(3) The population of the realm of Forms is determined in some manner by the Good itself.

From these three points we can draw some interesting results. If the Good is the sole provider and guarantor of the existence and nature of a realm of Forms, and is separate from sensibles, then all Forms will be independent of sensible participants. They will owe their existence to the Good itself rather than to any events in the sensible world, as our abstract governmental types owed their existence and nature to the divine city charter rather than to the activities of worldly citizens or office holders. Or again, sensibles will not be *aitiai* of the Forms in which they participate.[15]

The independence here claimed for Forms is consistent with the fact, usually overlooked but recently given proper emphasis, that some Forms must be instantiated at least some of the time. According to the *Timaeus*, Goodness itself requires the cosmos contain representatives of all the kinds of living things (39e). So, in some sense of "cannot," some Forms cannot be permanently empty. Thus the familiar characterization of separateness in terms of "possible permanent emptiness" must be appropriately hedged.[16] But this in no way entails that the Form depends upon its sensible participants, or that they are *aitiai* of it. In such cases participants depend on *F* itself *and* on the Good (along with other, worldly, factors), while *F* itself depends ultimately only on the Good for its being. Similarly it may be necessary that, at a certain hour on a sunny day, Socrates will cast a shadow—that one *cannot* have Socrates without a shadow. Still, the shadow depends on Socrates and on the sun, while Socrates depends on the sun for his continued existence (as in Plato's example in *Republic* VI) but not at all on his shadow.

Plato's depiction of a cosmos created in the image of an intelligible model makes possible a worm's eye view of the separateness of Forms. Because the relevant Forms are separate, one could say it would be good to have a cosmos containing *these* kinds of things (these animals, plants, fusible metals) even if, *per impossibile*, the actual cosmos lacked members of some of these kinds. The kinds it is good to have in a cosmos is determined eternally, independently of the actual state of any sensible realm. Viewed in this way, the separateness of Forms, often debated as an issue in metaphysics, or metaphysics-*cum*-epistemology, is a consequence of a strong view about the objectivity of Goodness and its intelligible articulation.

This interpretation has implications for another longstanding controversy. Making Forms separate from the created world does not, *pace* Aristotle and many others, turn them into "things" as opposed to abstract natures.[17] It is perfectly coherent to hold that the Good itself determines and anchors a realm of abstract natures independently of any orderly or disorderly events in the receptacle. This reason for separateness gives no grounds for supposing that in separating Forms Plato was thinking of them as paradigm cases or perfect particulars. In this regard it would be useful to think of Plato's kinship with Augustine, Aquinas, Cudworth, and other philosophers who conceive of God as creating the universe according to a divine plan specifying the kinds of things a good cosmos must contain, the sort of shape best for a universe, and so on.[18] It does not matter here whether these *kinds* are taken to be immutable archetypes existing eternally in the mind of God (as in Augustine and Aquinas), or as intelligible natures existing independently of God and apprehended by him (as in Plato). The point is that either God (or the Good) guarantees the being of these abstract intelligible kinds, independently of the existence of a created universe — and on some versions, before any worldly instantiation of these natures.

Similar remarks apply, on Plato's view, to the nature and separateness of the objectively determined excellence of cities and the natural virtues of individual human beings.[19] Each of these three sorts of thing — cosmos, city, and individual soul — has its own natural virtues and vices, the character of such excellence and its natural corruptions being objectively and immutably determined by the Good itself rather than by anything happening here below.[20]

These points about the Good and the separateness of Forms can help explain how participation in separate abstract natures is the formal *aitia* of sensible participants' being what they are. To state the point very generally: To participate in a Form is always to exemplify some nature having a place in the intelligible order determined by the Good, where that order includes not only Justice and Beauty, but (at some point in the development of the theory) Man and Ox, Equal, Greater and Less, Odd and Even, Same and Different, and other Forms whose connection to the Good may not be immediately apparent. This is not circular; it is not intended as a definition. Nor is it simply a conjunction of the claims that sensibles exemplify Forms and that Forms are separate and natural. It is perfectly possible to accept both claims and still deny that invoking participation does anything to show how *separate* Forms can be the (formal) *aitiai* of sensibles. As we have noted, there is a long and still strong tradition that holds the theory is impossible; another that its workings must remain a mystery. The force and plausibility of the general account is best shown by specific applications. To these we now turn.

Forms of artifacts, though *perhaps* not included in the initial realm of Forms, illustrate especially clearly some general principles.[21] With regard to the pruning knives of *Republic* I, if there is a nature Vine itself there will be natural kinds of actions (such as pruning) pertaining to the proper care and nurture of vines, and natural kinds of artifacts suited to do such jobs. Under those conditions an appropriately shaped piece of metal is a pruning knife rather than just a piece of scrap metal. To put a finer point on it: The fact that the intelligible realm determined by the Good includes a functionally defined Form of Pruning Knife entails that to *be* a worldly pruning knife is to be something suited to serve a specific function having a place in the natural order. A sensible object can be this only if (a) there is that natural type of work or function to be performed, and (b) the object's (corporeal) parts are so constituted and distributed that it is suited to perform that work. When these two conditions are met, the piece of metal participates in the separate, intelligible Form of Pruning Knife "fixed in the nature of things."

This is not simply to claim that where there is a certain functionally defined abstract type, a worldly thing is of that type just in case it is suited to perform that function. That is true (and a truism) so far as it goes, but the crucial and elusive goal is to explain why the worldly object's being what it is should depend essentially on a *separate* Form as simple *aitia* (or even how it *could* depend in that way on a separate Form). The answer is that the pruning knife is not merely something suitable for pruning trees, but is an implement serving a type of function provided for in the natural order. If there were, objectively speaking, no particular point to pruning trees—if irrespective of what people were inclined to think, tree pruning were not a type of function grounded in the immutably determined good order of things—then even if someone made an object suitable for pruning trees and someone else was fool enough to buy it, the object in question would not *be* a thing performing a specific natural function. While this claim may seem trivial, it is no more trivial, and no less important for understanding Plato, than the claim there are certain kinds or essences (here natural sorts of needs or purposes) anchored by eternal, immutable considerations of Goodness. We may contrast Plato's position with those "godless" philosophers according to which blind operations of physical causes give rise to worlds and to animate things such as trees or vines. In such worlds it may be true that in order to maximize the longevity and productivity of fruit-bearing trees, one should prune them in a certain way at a certain time of year; and that such pruning is best done with an instrument of such-and-such composition and design. Even granting all this, it does not follow there is any ultimate, eternally fixed good to be served by pruning this sort of tree with this sort of instrument. Nor does it follow there is any naturally determined good to be served even by the existence of fruit trees. Another "spontaneously generated" world might lack fruit trees altogether, but contain its own unique life forms for whose care and feeding unique sorts of instruments are best suited. At the cosmic level, as at the level of individual or city, there is an issue of relativity. Are natural ends and excellences of artifacts nothing more than the ends cast up, as it were, by whatever course the history of some world or other happens to take? Plato's answer is a resounding *no*; there is an eternal, independently existing specification for the best sort of cosmos (a cosmos for which the *Timaeus* gives many details) so that certain sorts of things, certain aims and excellence *do* have an objective place in the order of things, a genuine "point," while others do not. Which activities and artifacts serve a natural purpose (in Plato's sense) depends not on how the world happens to be or what people happen to think, but ultimately on the Good through its determination of the best sort of cosmos or city.

Returning to our government analogy, one might now add that even if many people were to write a name on a piece of paper and, on the second Tuesday in November, place it in a large wooden box in the town hall, these activities would not *be* acts of voting, and the papers deposited would not *be* votes, if the city charter did not "establish the being and essence" of votes and of certain types of voting procedures. What "makes" these motions acts of voting and these pieces of paper votes, is the fact that (a) there *are* such *types* of things as voting and votes, and (b) these particular events and objects fit the requirements laid down in the charter. In this way the abstract, separate governmental types serve as formal *aitiai* of particular votes and acts of voting. Notice that, like many Forms, they also serve as a kind of final *aitia*, in the sense that they specify a type of aim or goal; it is most unlikely that the citizens would go through this ritual every four years if they did not have in view the goal of exercising their right to vote.

Analogously a pruning knife, cloak, or shuttle will *be* a thing of a sort answering to natural human needs only because there *are* such types of natural needs and these particular items do answer to them (formal *aitiai*). Such artifacts normally come into being only because someone has it in mind to provide for some need. This is not to deny that humans, being human, will devise other sorts of artifacts answering to no natural needs. But no fondness on our part for any shiny gizmo, no misguided assignment to it of great value, can make it actually *be* a thing of use or benefit or value in the sense of answering to a need or purpose eternally established in the natural order of things.

Plato's own just city will be an especially important human artifact, should conditions ever allow it arise. As we know from the *Republic*, the various types of offices, stations in life, or roles essential to its goodness are all immutably determined whether or not any earthly city measures up to perfection, or even includes members of all the kinds that must be represented in a good city. Various members of any actual just community are then what they are – guardian, shepherd, carpenter – because their abilities and actions are such as to fulfill some role represented in the natural order. As their contribution is essential for a good city, so they, considered as guardians or carpenters, essentially *are* makers of some specific contribution essential to the life of any naturally good *polis*: A guardian simply is a maker of *this* sort of contribution, a craftsman the maker of *that*, and so on. *Being* a guardian or farmer or craftsman is not simply a matter of engaging in a certain type of activity, but of embodying one naturally ordained way of contributing to an objectively good *polis*. Again, there can be makers of such a contribution only if, in the natural order of things, there is such a contribution to be made. Individual humans actually become makers of such contributions, become guardians, herders, and so forth, only if they have the skills and training to perform the job in question.

It is against this sort of background that some residents of the city appear from the Platonic point of view to be drones, even as they occupy positions of prestige and apparent power. Plato's sustained drone imagery of *Republic* VIII is little short of spectacular, with subdivisions into flying and walking drones, spirited and dispirited, with and without stingers. In a democracy the fiercest class of these takes over, making speeches and transacting business, while the rest swarm about the podium buzzing loudly, permitting no dissent (*Republic* 564d). If there were no Form or Forms determining the basic organization of a naturally good *polis* there could be no ultimate, objective separation of drones from genuine citizens. Socrates could not *rightly and wisely* aspire to be a citizen in that "heavenly city," practicing its politics alone (*Republic* 592b) even as he finds himself in a city overrun by drones. Nor could he rightly claim (as he had at *Gorgias* 521d) to be the only true politician of Athens, or deny Themistocles and Pericles were genuine politicians. They did hold offices ordained by the Athenian *polis*; they did function as right-thinking Athenians believed politicians should – but they did not perform the true function of leaders of the city. (Whether Plato, at the time of composing the *Gorgias*, had as yet inferred an independent ontological status for such functions and virtues is a question I leave entirely open.)

With these relatively clear examples in hand, two general points of contrast will sharpen the picture of participation offered here. First, a Platonic Form is not an immanent universal, but neither is it a separate universal, a separated one over many. Certainly a legislator might dream up any number of governmental universals or types. But to instantiate such a universal, whether separate or immanent, is not necessarily to participate in a Platonic Form. Again, it is not just any functionary or so-called statesman who functions or contributes in a way essential to a good *polis*. Similarly, even if one wishes to say that the hairdresser and the business haggler are what they are only insofar as they instantiate certain social types or universals, nevertheless instantiating those particular universals cannot *make* them contributors of a type essential to a good city, because hairdressing and haggling are not types of activity having a place in the natural (good) order of things. Such types will show up in purely descriptive treatments of some worldly societies, and perhaps in someone else's normative theory of society; their human exemplifications may even occupy positions of status or importance in existing societies. But they have no place in the realm of natural essences anchored by Plato's Good.

Second, one must distinguish Plato's theory of participation from more purely ontological (or "logical") theories of inherence, instantiation, or exemplification familiar from textbook accounts of traditional Platonism. For the sake of contrast, one might say Plato's is a teleological as well as ontological theory of participation, in that, for Plato, participants are not simply things exemplifying universals or having attributes but things exemplifying types, or natures having a place in an intelligible realm founded on the Good. It would not stretch the point intolerably to say the theory is ontological because teleological in a very strong sense; it is the teleological component, the faith in an eternal, independent specification of individual, political and cosmic ends (the specification being accessible to reason) that ultimately gives force to Plato's theory of *separate* Forms as both formal and, where pertinent, final *aitiai* of sensibles' being what they are. (We shall see there are a variety of ways in which Forms earn their place in such a scheme, but this does not affect the broader issue.)

In general, then, one may suppose the kinds of artifacts (beds, tables, knives, shoes, houses, cloaks, shuttles, awls) and kinds of activities (weaving, ruling, piloting, building) answering to natural needs of living things of natural kinds are represented in the world of Forms, their own particular excellence determined, as Socrates remarks (*Republic* 601d), by the purpose or use for which they are produced or undertaken.

Kinds of living things, too, have their place in the natural order. (Certain kinds of artifacts and actions have their place because they correspond to needs of living things.) Accordingly, to understand the natural order of things—and to understand nature even in the narrow sense of "phenomenal realm"—one must recognize *this* particular compaction of flesh, bones, and sinew as an embodiment of a kind, or essence, having a place in the natural order. By contrast, another fleshly creature must be recognized as a monstrosity not embodying any type included in the Intelligible Model on which the demiurge modeled the best possible sensible cosmos. Of course any mooncalf will be something, if only a mass of bones, flesh, hair, and sinew, or only a composite of earth, air, fire, and water. To say there is no Form of Mooncalf is not to say that mooncalves do not exist. Nor does the Eleatic Stranger's denial of a Form of Barbarian Human imply there are no *barbaroi*. It is to say, rather, that mooncalves as such do not embody any nature having a place in the intelligible scheme for a good cosmos—just as *barbaroi* will not be found, under that description, in the demiurge's cosmic blueprint.

It is easy to see how this approach extends to more elementary levels of worldly organization. Bones, flesh, hair, and sinew will be natural kinds, if there are Forms for men or dogs or things of which they are functional parts. Thus *Timaeus* 73e-74b treats bone, flesh, and sinew as handiwork of god, each having its own natural function to fulfill. If so, the mooncalf must participate in some Forms to be what it is. True, from the point of view of mother nature it is nothing more than a freakish arrangement of organs of certain kinds. Nonetheless its various organs participate in diverse, functionally defined Forms because its parts perform kinds of functions (locomotion, digestion, perception) necessarily performed by inhabitants of any best cosmos. The eternal model calls for organs of the sorts it possesses, but not for organisms *put together* like it. This would be true even if several such things arose and were all called by the common *onoma* "mooncalf," and even if one acknowledged an immanent universal *mooncalf* inhering in these monsters.[22]

Descending further, the various bodily organs of mooncalves, as of oxen, bees, horses, and humans, will necessarily be composed in an appropriate way of earth, air, fire, and water—elements assuredly having their place in the natural order. A good deal of planning and coordination is required to produce a sensible cosmos that will maintain a complex harmony of parts and an overall equilibrium while recycling itself for all time. To manage this, according to Timaeus, requires there be four basic kinds of element, that they occur in proper proportion to one another, come in a variety of sizes to provide for the various metals, liquids, and the like needed for the cosmos' overall economy and stability, that they be capable of undergoing transformations into one another (with one exception!) and, of course, that they be beautiful. As Timaeus realizes, microscopic regular solids responsible for the powers (*dynameis*) of sensible earth, air, fire, and water are just right for the job. Fire, for example, plays a multiplicity of roles in the turning of the seasons, the nurture of living things, and the power of sight in animals. In this light the primary bodies are like artifacts and living things in that they occupy a well-defined place in the life of the cosmos, as the bearers or embodiments of kinds of powers called for in the demiurge's model for an everlasting, fair cosmos. Even if they are not required in quite so direct a way as living things, and though their definitions are not overtly functional, they are still required as the best types of building materials for construction of living things (including the cosmic organism as a whole) and as the best means for obtaining a variety of further goods. By the same token the basic geometrical Forms such as Line, Plane, Solid, Triangle, Cube, and Pyramid required for construction of the primary bodies must have a place in the intelligible world; the Sphere, which "contains within itself all shapes," enters because it is the kind of shape fitting for an all-inclusive cosmos (*Timaeus* 33b). In each of these cases, too, the demiurge grasps the nature of each intelligible Form, and purposely creates corporeal embodiments of it because these are needed to make the best possible sensible cosmos. Described one way, there are important places to be filled by things of these sorts in the economy of the created world; put another way, these sorts or kinds, these properties of things, distinctions and relations among things, appear in the demiurge's immutable plan for the best possible cosmos.

Having followed this line of thought even to the level of basic shapes and elementary regular solids, we may observe the further consequence that *every* sensible thing must participate in *some* Forms in order to rise above the level of disorderly motion. Even if it does not, under all its descriptions, participate in a Form (not *all* predicates true of a sensible thing, such as a mooncalf, correlate with Forms) it must participate in earth, air, fire or water (or its microscopic parts must participate in determinate shape Forms) if it is to be anything corporeal. Non-corporeal souls, too, insofar as they are determinate and different from other things, showing regular motion in those respects required for bringing life, must participate in relevant Forms. Beneath the level of participation lies only the receptacle itself.

The geometrical cases show again a Form's definition need not be framed directly in terms of some natural work or function in order for it to have a place in the realm of nature. They also raise a question about use of the term "natural kinds" in speaking of Platonic Forms. Nowadays one is accustomed to thinking of natural kinds as those corresponding to the "kind predicates" of a given science (something like those predicates "whose terms are the bound variables of its proper laws"[23]). A tacit assumption in most contexts is that the science is empirical, as opposed to mathematical, science. Here I use the term in a more Platonic sense, so that natural kinds correspond to whatever sorts or kinds have a place in the natural order (or are "fixed in the nature of things"); this includes at least all those sorts of properties, distinctions, divisions, relationships, and objects essential to a good cosmos. Nonetheless Forms have at least one important affinity to our natural kinds: Both correspond to select predicates (or, they are select properties), rather than to any and all predicates one might use or define. Further, they correspond to predicates playing a part in our genuine understanding of the world rather than those reflecting an unexamined or arbitrary conception of the way things are.[24]

Given this important similarity, what exactly is the difference between Plato's Forms "in nature" and contemporary natural kinds?

Plato's Forms, remember, encompass kinds or types not included in the kind predicates of empirical sciences: mathematical Forms, Justice, Beauty, Piety, Forms for artifacts, "vowel Forms" such as Sameness, Being, and Difference. The Platonic dialectician must have a very broad range indeed. Moreover, a view of Forms as our sort of natural kinds gives no inkling of the ontological basis of separateness, since there is ordinarily no reason to regard natural kinds as abstract objects existing separately from the physical world. This does leave room for an epistemological argument for separateness, but it misses the fact that the Good "provides the being and essence" of all the (other) Forms, and with it a demonstration that Forms are what they are independently of the created world.[25] Finally, the contemporary natural kinds appoach presumes a conception of *how* we understand the world that Plato emphatically rejects. For if certain features of our world obtain because it is good that they obtain (or because they are the sorts of things called for in the divine Model for the best cosmos), then anyone who would properly understand the phenomenal realm of nature must recognize certain of its aspects *as* tokens of natural, immutable types anchored by the Good, and must acknowledge the role of reason in any theory of their genesis. Empirical investigation may (or may not) suggest such a conclusion, but viewing fire, oxen, shuttles, or city organizations in a Platonic way is not entailed by a view of them as individuals falling under the general terms of some physical or social science. Even supposing some modern science freely acknowledges, and frames explanatory laws for, teleological systems, the existence of the teleological systems it recognizes will not ultimately have a teleological explanation—at least, not one framed in terms of goodness. By contrast, for Plato the Good is an explanatory first principle; it provides the key to true understanding of both the sensible and the intelligible realms.

Plato is severely critical of self-styled *physikoi* who have no inkling their supposedly "automatic" works of nature (which may well result in what we call "teleological systems"), along with the works of human arts and sciences, are alike "products of mind in accordance with right reason" (*nou . . . gennēmata kata logon orthon, Laws* X, 890d7).[26] They fail to comprehend that certain things, and the ratios, proportions, equalities, and inequalities among things do participate in separate abstract Forms fixed in the nature of things as their formal *aitiai*, and that in many cases these worldly participants come into being because reason in some guise created them thinking it was good to make things of this kind. Such *physikoi* do not comprehend that many features of the sensible realm are as they are through the handiwork of god (*Timaeus, Sophist*), through the guidance of mind and wisdom (*Philebus, Laws*), or through goodness and the right binding things together (*Phaedo*). As Socrates puts it in the *Philebus* (59a-b), "they consider themselves students of nature [*peri physeōs hegeitai . . . zētein*], yet have nothing to do with what always is [*ta onta aei*] but only with what has become, is becoming, and will become." Such *physikoi*, even if they should be numbered among the award-winning cave dwellers with surpassing knowledge of conjunctions and sequences of the passing shadows (*Republic* 516c-d), are still ignorant of the most fundamental facts of cosmology, as their counterparts in "ethics" or politics are ignorant of, or even deny, the most basic aspects of those domains. First, they deny there are immutable, independently existing criteria of goodness, beauty, and justice for the cosmos, for cities, and for individual souls. Second, they deny a true art of world-making or statecraft or education must derive from knowledge of these otherworldly guides.[27]

Our customary distinction between fact and value, on which the kind predicates of natural sciences are construed as factual rather than evaluative, must from Plato's point of view be put aside. For him, many kinds of things that seem to us non-evaluative will be essentially normative. Kinds of animals and plants, types of metals, and more elementary kinds of components of the corporeal world already must be understood with reference to their place in the natural order. For Plato, "fire" is not merely the name for something having a certain geometrically describable micro-structure – or better, for something that really, or essentially, is just stuff having a certain structure, but which also happens to be naturally suited for a complex of roles in the making of an optimal cosmos. Rather, fire has an essentially functional nature, given by its capacity to affect and be affected by other things.

Here one must go beyond "functionalism" in the contemporary, not necessarily evaluative sense of the term. There are kinds of *dynameis* essential to the beauty and economy of the best possible created world, and fire is that stuff which provides certain of those *dynameis*. Perhaps some particular substructure is required for possession of that complex of *dynameis*; but to define "fire" exclusively in those terms would be to ignore part of what it is to be fire – and to overlook the reason there *is* fire in our created cosmos.

We have dealt so far with Forms enjoying a straightforward connection to the Good; each is associated with a distinctive excellence (whether that be a state of health or of fitness to perform some job well), or, taking matters one step further, each is a sort of thing needed to bring about certain sorts of excellence. We approach now several of the most fundamental and most frequently mentioned Forms of the *Phaedo, Republic, Symposium,* and *Phaedrus*, some of which have a clear and essential connection to the Good, but others of which seem at first to have no such connection. The group consists of Forms for crucial opposites: Greater, Less, Slow(er), Fast(er), Equal, Unequal, Unity, Plurality, Justice, Beauty, Similarity, Dissimilarity.

An important step toward bringing these cases into line with the rest, and toward a general conception of participation, is to observe the role they play in constituting the terrestrial realm of nature. Although these Forms are very far removed from a modern notion of natural kinds, we must recall that from an ancient Greek point of view basic opposites would be primary candidates for "principles of nature." In one way or another primary opposites were, as Aristotle observed, basic to every Greek's concept of nature – with allowance for considerable variation as to which opposites were basic, and how. Plato, aside from his Platonizing of kinds of opposites, was only a limited exception to the general rule. To judge not only from the *Phaedo*, but also from the more detailed claims of the *Philebus*, Plato considered a description of the phenomenal realm in terms of opposites a useful complement to his less traditional geometrical analysis of sensibles in the *Timaeus*. Both of Plato's approaches are fundamentally teleological, and they are complementary rather than contrary. (Which, if either, has priority in one respect or another will not be discussed here.)

Even so, Timaeus' divine composer of the cosmos makes extensive use of basic opposites. The relative speeds and positions of the stars may not suggest or disclose to us any intelligent purpose, but they are carefully disposed so as to distinguish and preserve the parts of time (38c), secure the cognitive capacities of the world soul (35b-37b), and bring alternation of light and dark in a way that stimulates intelligent earthly beings to a conception of number and time (47a). Similarly, Timaeus' accounts of human physiology and life activities appeal often to functional heating and cooling, depletion and replenishment, growth and diminution, relaxation and contraction, equality and inequality, roughness and smoothness.

In the *Philebus* Socrates emphasizes more broadly the role of opposites in securing a wide range of goods—bodily health, a variety of fair things found in the soul, proper turning of the seasons (through alternation of greater and less between opposites such as hot, cold, wet, dry, fast, and slow, 25c ff.), and the pains and pleasures coordinated with destruction and restoration of the natural (good) state of a living organism. To the extent that living things of the *Timaeus*, the fair weather, health, and virtue of the *Philebus*, and large segments of the whole natural realm of the *Phaedo* consist of combinations of various opposites in certain proportions, these opposites and relations between them (greater, less, equal, unequal) will be as securely "fixed in nature" as the things they constitute.[28]

Above all, opposites having to do with the natural excellence or deficiency of worldly items or features of the cosmos as a whole—their beauty, ugliness, justice, injustice, strength, weakness—will be fundamental to a theory drawing basic connections, especially explanatory ones, between Goodness and that which is in accord with nature. At bottom it will be for the sake of instantiating Goodness, Justice, Beauty, and such opposites that reason must look, in a multitude of more specific cases, to the Equal, Greater, Less, Like, Unlike, Fast, Slow, Animal, or Shuttle. Moreover, since various sorts of goodness and beauty consist in one or another sort of symmetry or harmony, one should expect a fundamental role for the Equal, Greater, and Less considered as general sorts of relationships among things (often among further opposites such as fast, slow, hot, cold, high and low pitch) that bring about beauty or its opposite. Thus various Forms of excellence and their opposites, along with prominent kinds of thing essential to excellence, figure centrally already in the *Phaedo* (and *Meno*[29]). These would secure a place in a general Platonic vision of a good, reasonable order of things even at a stage where many details of how Goodness or Beauty may be manifest in the world were yet to be worked out. A large body of further, specific Forms involving relevant opposite things or qualities, requisite ratios of opposites, opposite processes between opposite things and qualities, kinds of living things and their parts, and useful artifacts, might well come into play only in the finer articulation of such Forms as the Good, the Beautiful, and the Just.

For this reason we need not settle the issue of population growth between the *Phaedo* and *Timaeus*. Chapter 5 criticized some attempts to limit Forms in the *Phaedo* and middle *Republic* to those for disputed predicates, incomplete predicates, or opposites. However, if the view defended in this chapter is correct, questions as to whether Plato recognized Forms for species of living things only first in the *Timaeus*, or whether *Republic* X's Forms for artifacts represent a development later than *Republic* V-VII, are not important for understanding the basic principles of his two-world metaphysics. The same fundamental convictions about Goodness and reason, and their role in making the world what it is, obtain throughout. I am *inclined* to think there was no dramatic upsurge in the post-*Phaedo* population; it seems unlikely Socrates would hold (as he does in the *Phaedo*) that *nous* tries to arrange the cosmos as a whole and its individual contents (98a-b) for the best, and that life and intelligence are part of the realm of nature so disposed, without concluding that various forms of life (human life and species of living things) are also part of the intended disposition. Also, the *Meno's* examples of bees, *Republic* I's discussion of the natural function and excellence of horses, eyes, and human souls, Socrates' inclusion, in *Republic* VII, of plants, animals, and artifacts in the second section of the divided line, and *Republic* X's Forms of artifacts all strongly suggest Plato believed throughout the middle dialogues in Forms for various substance sortals, and held that their being was connected to the natural and the Good. But again, I emphasize that none of our principal claims about participation depend on postulating a stable population. The view defended here allows for diachronic unfolding of Plato's notion of Goodness, Beauty, and their opposites, and with it growth and progressive systematization of Plato's *noetic* realm.

Meanwhile, our broad survey of various sorts of *paradeigmata* fixed in the nature of things has implications for another longstanding controversy. It has often seemed, for reasons with which one can easily sympathize, that although Forms for living kinds, artifacts, actions, and moral virtues have a direct connection to the Good, in that they either are some excellence or virtue, or have a functional definition indicating their particular sort of excellence, other Forms, such as vowel Forms and mathematical Forms, do not have any particular connection to the Good.[30] Now while it is true that *some* Forms may have a connection to the Good that does not apply to other Forms, *all* Forms have one common connection to the Good, even a common dependence on the Good for their very being, for each Form is one place or position in the natural (good) order of things.[31] Considered in relation to the lower realm generally, Forms of *all* sorts are types of things needed, directly or indirectly — substantial constituents, basic phenomenal building materials, geometrical structures, harmonious ratios of materials (and the mathematical entities entailed by these) — to make the best of a rather unpromising situation. Thus it is that the Good of the *Republic* "provides the being and essence" of *all* Forms of the *noetic* realm.[32]

When all is said and done, many readers will not find the preferred picture of participation sufficiently ontological. Perhaps the interpretation simply requires some getting used to, so that initially one does not see the extent to which it is ontological (the extent to which participation in *F* itself is responsible for a sensible's being *F*). It may look as though the interpretation simply takes over the familiar furniture of the world and, without explaining how participation is responsible for things' being *that* much, accounts only for some additional evaluative properties while offering but a new way of looking at familiar things. And yet, if one fully recognizes what it is to be an ox or a shuttle, to be earth, air, fire, or water, to be odd or even, one finds this involves more than simply instantiating the appropriate universal. It is to be a thing suited to promote in some way, direct or indirect, some objectively determined good (or its opposite), or to be a thing of a sort having a place in the objectively determined order of nature. Worldly items participate in being, have a share in reality, not by being Forms or by having parts or wholes of Forms spatially present to them, but by instantiating some abstract type that itself has a place in the realm of true Being, a type that is a *paradeigma* "fixed in nature." Given this account of a worldly thing's being such-and-such, it follows trivially that participation in a *separate* Form of *F* is necessary for being such-and-such; it is what makes the worldly *F* what it is.

Why else might one object that this is not sufficiently ontological? Presumably anyone accustomed to thinking of Forms as full-blooded efficient causes will find mere formal (or final) causality a rather anemic alternative. The efficient cause account is, to borrow a Platonic metaphor, enflamed, fevered, diseased; bloodletting in such a case results not in anemia, but restoration of health. But even among readers who do not believe in separate Forms as efficient causes there may be a tendency to require participation to carry more than its share of the ontological burden. One may be tempted to speak of sensibles arising from the "interaction of Form and receptacle."[33] Perhaps the Forms' separateness will be infringed upon in other ways, even to the extent of making them somehow inhere in sensibles, in order to give participation a decisive role in making participants what they are. This reading can, although it need not, arise from a failure to keep clear the two different ways in which Forms are *aitiai* of sensibles: formal *aitiai* in every case, and Models for making where relevant. A "one step" or single-featured account of Forms as *aitiai* of sensibles can lead either to flirtation with efficient causality (even to Forms as living agents, as Zeller thought) or to terminal *aporia* about how separate Forms can be *aitiai* of sensibles, and thence to an immanent Form account.

A rather different sort of metaphysical *angst* could arise from a fear that if Plato's two worlds are, after all, separate, then something must be found to link them together, some sort of truly universal joint, and this seems not to have been provided for in the present account. It is true the reader will find here no account of participation as a copulative device over and above Forms on the one hand, worldly things on the other. There is no need for such a device. There are Forms, and there are worldly things. Insofar as worldly things have certain properties—the right size and shape, the right vital organs, or the right relation to one another—they *are* participants. No ontological bridge from this world to the other is possible, or necessary.

This in turn may seem to have all the advantages of theft over honest toil. One seems to have appealed illegitimately to the notion of sensibles' *having properties*. Doesn't this only call forth the old problem of inherence or instantiation? Will not participation in a separate Form occur if and only if there is instantiation of some immanent universal? And haven't the problems inherent in *that* notion simply been ignored? In a word, the answer is no. There need be no immanent universals in Plato's world, only individuals. He is perfectly free to adopt a strict nominalism with regard to this world. The usual objections to nominalism (e.g., that it cannot supply an adequate basis for mathematics, hence for science) are met by postulation of Forms. Plato's own attitude, where one finds it recorded in the dialogues, seems to be that either there exist separate Forms, or there exist "only what we see," meaning individual objects of sense (*Timaeus* 51c). If there are no immanent universals, there is no problem about the inherence of them in individuals.

It may be too much to hope these remarks have allayed all philosophical misgivings. I would still urge consideration of the present reading on the ground it gives Forms an indispensible, and completely general, ontological role as *aitiai* of worldly participants, while accounting for many important, closely related Platonic themes. It does this without calling into doubt, indeed it strongly motivates, the separateness of Platonic Forms.

We have considered in this chapter a series of large issues, most of which are not ordinarily raised in discussions of participation: the connection between the Good and Forms in general, the population of Forms, the ontological basis of the separateness of Forms, the relation of Plato's concept of nature or the natural to goodness and to Forms in general. If it is now tolerably clear why all these issues have a bearing on Plato's view of sensibles as participants in immutable, intelligible Forms, it would be fitting to close with a last, brief look at the image analogy. Above all, we should observe that the analogy is well designed to illustrate a Platonistic theory of abstract, separate essences and worldly exemplifications of those essences. The models imaged are exclusively natural essences, or *"paradeigmata* fixed in nature," and an image's being of its model is what "makes" it an image or imitation *F* or *G*. Given this, it makes good sense to speak of participation in a separate Form as the imaging of an abstract, eternal, intelligible Model. There could hardly be a better means of expressing in a vivid, coherent, and controlled way Plato's basic vision of reality.

7

Conclusion

The most basic conclusion of this study is not calculated to shock. It is that Plato was a Platonist. This does entail, however, that he was not a closet nominalist believing, at least in some contexts, in a realm of Forms as paradigm cases, with resemblance the relation of predication. At the same time, Plato is not a *typical* Platonist. His Forms are not Aristotelian or Thomistic universals, nor, therefore, are they universals somehow miraculously transported to a noetic Isle of the Blessed.

In this chapter I will consolidate and extend the account of Plato's separate Forms. It will be particularly helpful to draw together the various functions performed by Forms, in order both to survey what has been rightly termed the "philosophical economy" of the theory, and to take note of some important features falling outside the range of this study. To show why Plato postulated Forms—to explain the theoretical needs they satisfy — is probably the best way to show that Plato's image metaphysics, for all its diversity, is neither internally inconsistent nor a merely consistent patchwork of philosophical ideas. It is a tight-knit theory, with additions and developments over time to be sure, but with each new strand securely woven into the same basic fabric.

A second breathtaking conclusion is that a Form is what it is, and not another thing. To appreciate this truism, however, one must distinguish Forms not only from paradigm cases but also from their many Platonistic brethren. There is a striking family resemblance between Forms and some of these other entities, especially as different members of the clan often serve similar functions. It is important to see precisely how Plato's separation of Forms from the world of sense issues in a distinctive response to basic questions of ontology, epistemology, and value theory.

Plato's metaphysics is comparatively detailed, and shows a surprisingly large number of revealing parallels with the image/model relationship — as that relationship is conceived by Plato. Perhaps even more surprising than the number and importance of the parallels between participation and imaging is the general result these imply, namely, that it makes good sense to regard worldly individuals as images of abstract, intelligible models. It will make more or less sense depending on the details of the particular Platonistic theory at hand, but on any of a large number of theories involving abstract objects (universals of various kinds, objective concepts, and the like) many significant parallels will emerge. For this reason the analogy could serve a useful illustrative and integrative role in many Platonistic theories, though there will tend to be serious disanalogies with versions of Platonism weaker than Plato's, such as those whose Platonic entities are not separate from worldly embodiments, or are not ontologically prior to sensible exemplifications in the manner of Platonic Forms. On Plato's theory the analogy draws together all the basic functions of Forms and the main features of their relationship with our world.

A. Forms and Functions

As a student of what there is, Plato can be regarded as a distinguished heir to the tradition of "pre-Socratic" *physikoi*, and reckoned among those who stressed the need to look outside the sensible world for the basic principles on which that world is to be understood. Unlike Anaxagoras — at least as Plato has Socrates portray him in the *Phaedo*—Plato did not betray this basic conviction by falling back on air and winds and fire, to the neglect of reason and the Good.

For Plato nature encompassed, in the first place, the intelligible realm. By contrast, that which most people call "nature" and which most students of nature study, is only this world, the world of becoming rather than Being. The created world may be regarded as part of the entire realm of reality or of nature in a broad sense; this is unobjectionable so long as one recognizes sensible or corporeal being as dependent upon, and variously inferior to, the sort of being common to Forms, and so long as one acknowledges that any correct account of the true *aitiai* of this world and its contents must begin with the roles of reason, the Forms, and the Good itself.

This way of viewing the world, and its consequent view of "physics," derives from the Form's dual role as *aitia* of worldly participants: first, as a kind of formal *aitia*; second, as a model for the making of many terrestrial participants. Chapter 6 discussed the first, noting the close connection between Forms' relationship with worldly namesakes and their status as natural types or kinds. It is the support of the Good itself that underlies both the independence of Forms from sensible namesakes and the dependence of sensibles on Forms as formal *aitiai*, despite the fact that Forms cannot interact with anything in this world, and do not exist in any place at all.

These same abstract objects are also in many cases the models for deliberate production of sensibles. Forms serve in this capacity whenever reason, divine or human, in whatever guise, brings forth a worldly thing exemplifying some specific nature (Form) reason had in mind for it to possess. Moreover, the same abstract nature often serves as model for several varieties of sensibles, including Justice, Equality, and Shuttle—a role for which abstract intelligible natures are well suited, but for which neither highly specific patterns (whether separate or immanent) nor paradigm cases qualify.

In a third role, Forms are standards by reference to which their own participants rank as better or worse specimens of their kind—both where this involves the simple truth of the matter, regardless of anyone's opinion, and where proper assessment is made by some knowledgeable judge. Here again abstract natures, rather than specific patterns or paradigm cases, provide criteria for evaluation of worldly individuals; those other sorts of objects could not have served as standards for all the different ways of achieving such virtues as Justice, Equality, or Beauty, any more than they could have served as models for all the varieties of things falling under such Forms.

According to Plato the realm of natural kinds is knowable by the demiurge and the philosophical student of nature: Forms are the kind of thing — utterly immutable, and accessible in their purity to reason properly prepared — that can be known with a certainty and a completeness of understanding unobtainable in the case of worldly objects of cognition. As abstract, eternal objects of "unshakeable" understanding, they provide a basis for every genuine *technē* or *epistēmē*, and for the authority of every genuine *technitēs* whether in statesmanship, craftsmanship, world-making, geometry, or medicine.

At a more mundane level, Forms also provide a basis for sense perception: Some innate grasp of Forms is essential to the very ability to group many things together into a single class of a given description. Thus some grasp of Forms is needed and exercised even by those who have never heard of Forms, who would be incapable of fully grasping them explicitly, and who would take up cudgels against anyone trying to lead them up from the cave. The role of Forms as objects of strict knowledge and as the basis for everyday sense perception is easily related to roles that come fully into their own in late dialogues. Along with important developments in the theory of language (including Plato's analysis of the *"prōtos logos"* into two components, one from the category of *rhēmata*, one from *onomata*) comes an attempt to relate Forms in a corresponding way to *logos*. So, for example, when a *logos* says something of some subject, that which is said of (or attributed to, or predicated of) the subject is, in the first instance, a Form. Forms assume in the *Sophist* a role very like what some philosophers have called "predicables": They are what is said of things, or predicated of things by statements having a specified, simple structure.[1]

There is no need of a new sort of object for this purpose or for the *Sophist*'s more complex analysis of negative statements: Abstract natures or types will naturally serve as predicables, and these are precisely the sorts of objects postulated in classical paradigmatism. It is satisfying that the sort of entity presupposed by everyday sense perception of objects as *F*s should be the same as that said of subjects in discourse generally, as well as the sort of object that can be known explicitly and fully by *nous*,

"the possession of God and a small number of men." These roles harmonize well, even if the second mentioned does not clearly emerge as part
of the theory until a suitable analysis of the appropriate sort of *logos* has
been achieved.

This list of (six) roles of Forms is not definitive, since the territory could
be sectioned legitimately in different ways. Moreover, the divisions given
here could be described differently, and in some cases subdivided further.
Nor is the general approach original: Others have drawn together the roles
of Forms, though not with quite the same results.[2] The points to be emphasized in opposition to some of those who have taken this approach, are:
First, on philosophical grounds, all these diverse roles can be performed
by the same sort of abstract intelligible object; second, on textual grounds
discussed in chapters 3-6, it can be shown Plato consistently had in view
a realm of Forms consisting of just such objects.

This is not to say the entire theory sprang full-blown from the head of
Plato at about the time of the *Phaedo*, but it does have consequences for
any account on which his metaphysics takes a radical turn after the *Parmenides* on grounds that he then saw for the first time, whether face-to-
face or only through a glass, darkly, a fatal flaw in paradigmatism. It also
suggests one need not raze the metaphysics of the *Phaedo* and *Republic*
in order to gain a view of Plato's purposes and achievements in the late
dialogues. On the contrary, one should expect a large measure of continuity, such that full appreciation of some later developments, at least,
would not be possible apart from the larger perspective of classical paradigmatism.

To cite only a single, slight example (leaving the rest, for the time being,
a matter of suggestion): The opening and closing sections of the *Sophist*
dealing with images and with the sophist as image-maker need not be regarded merely as a frame for the important business of the central sections. The dialogue as a whole appears rather as the place where Plato
finally distinguishes definitively between philosopher and sophist, and,
using the concept of the image-maker, properly brands the sophist in terms
at once metaphysical, epistemological, and valuative. By the same token
this task requires an account of how not-being and falsehood *can* enter the
world; to say coherently how that is possible requires, among other things,
an analysis of Not-being and of certain sorts of discourse. As a result, one
is privileged to observe Plato bringing these more "technical" discussions,
themselves of great philosophical interest, to bear decisively on a long-

standing effort to separate the sophist from the philosopher, and to reveal their true relationship – an effort undertaken in similar terms, but at a more rudimentary level (and sometimes in emotionally charged terms) in earlier dialogues. Both aims were of philosophical importance to Plato, even if the one no longer seems urgent to us, while the other involves problems now of much concern.

In a word, the basic middle-period theory of Forms as *paradeigmata* probably underwent important development over time, and was apparently supplemented, especially in late dialogues, by treatment of related philosophical issues. In some ways it was to be supplemented by discussions to which it had nothing directly to contribute, but with which it was entirely consistent (such as the *Philebus*' four-fold account of worldly things). In others it was modified in ways fitting more closely into the general framework of paradigmatism (the *Timaeus*' theory of time as a moving image of eternity; the *Sophist*'s treatment of Forms as predicables). The basic theory is a consistent and unified, if highly ramified, Platonism, as well as a viable foundation for investigation of further issues. The question of Plato's subsequent *development* therefore turns largely on the issue of how the important new material of late dialogues clarifies, builds upon, harmonizes with, or brings about revision in – rather than replaces – the fundamental outlook of the *Phaedo* and *Republic*.

B. What Forms Are Not

There is some justification for familiar descriptions of Forms as (separate) universals, meanings, or structures, in that Platonic entities are defined largely by their theoretical roles, and the work of the Forms does overlap significantly with that of most of their metaphysical kin. To sharpen the boundaries of Plato's intelligible realm one may distinguish various grades of Platonistic commitment, from minimal to extreme.

Let us call "minimal" a Platonism recognizing abstract objects but not non-extensional ones. In its usual, set-theoretical, form, this variety is of recent origin, as is the theory of sets itself; Quine would be a well-known contemporary adherent.[3] Among numerous differences between sets and Forms, two are especially helpful for present purposes. (1) There will not be a distinct Form corresponding to every distinct group of sensibles, though there will be a distinct set in every such case. As other metaphysicians have noted, set theory is not particularly discriminating; anyone wanting an ontology of "natural" classes, one based on some principle of natural rather than arbitrary groupings of objects, must go a step beyond properties associated simply with any and all sets of particulars. Anthony Quinton's *The Nature of Things* (especially chapter 7) argues for such a discriminating version of what we are calling minimal Platonism. (2) Forms are intensional rather than extensional objects. They cannot be individuated by their worldly participants, since two Forms can (necessarily) have all the same worldly participants, as in the case of Sameness and Being, but still be different from one another.

Abstract structures or patterns (chapter 2's *paradeigmata* of type C) are closer relatives of Forms. Forms could not, however, be *immanent* structures, or structures dependent for their existence on the things that embody them. Forms owe their existence to the Good, not to things in this world, and they are not located anywhere, not even in the same place as their participants. Even if the field is narrowed to *separate* abstract structures, one must still insist Forms are not *highly determinate* structures (as described in chapter 2). Since different participants in the same form may vary in structural properties (different sorts of bee, awl, shoe, shuttle, clay, equal), the Form cannot be identified with any finely specified structure.

This does not rule out identification of Forms with some more general, separate, abstract patterns or structures, provided there actually could be some such common structural property making all bees bees, shuttles shuttles, and so on for every case. Whether or not such a claim can be made good, this is apparently not the way Plato conceived of Forms in general. While some Forms are definable in structural terms (those that *are* structures, such as Circle itself), others are defined in purely functional terms. As we saw, Plato seems to have thought that not only implements but also actions and living things were to be defined in terms other than purely structural ones. The important point is that even if there were some common general structure peculiar to each kind of thing, the non-structural definition would be essential for specifying the goodness, excellence, or utility of actions, implements, and living things. This remark raises a touchy issue about the reducibility of functions to structures, and the eliminability of functional language in favor of structural descriptions. However, for bringing out Plato's view it suffices to remember that even where some life function, say, can best be fulfilled by a uniquely determined structure (rationality, perhaps, fulfilled in souls structured as in the *Timaeus*) from the point of view of the demiurge's cosmic plan, or simply from the point of view of Goodness, priority lies with the function, or the functional description. The demiurge makes the cosmos into an intelligent animal because, other things being equal, an intelligent thing is better than an unintelligent one (*Timaeus* 30b); divisions of soul stuff into circles and elaborate demarcation of harmonic intervals along these circles (35 b-c) are to secure this particular good, among others. The psychic *structure* in question, then, appears in the created cosmos *because* it best embodies a needed type of *function*.

This point recalls also a reason given above for not identifying Forms with sets: One needs a principle of selection for Forms. There will be an infinite number of structures or patterns, whether fully specific or more general, immanent or separate. And while there will surely not be a distinct Form for every distinct structure, conceiving of Forms simply as structures provides no way at all of saying which structures correspond to Forms and which do not. It is in many cases only by considering the use of a kind of thing, wherein its beauty, goodness, and correctness lie (*Republic* 601d), that one understands why it should be considered a participant in some essence or type fixed in the nature of things, rather than simply as an embodiment of some specifiable structure. So while some Forms turn out to be abstract, separate structures or patterns, Forms cannot in general be conceived in those terms. (Even this rather cautious statement must be amended, as we shall see in distinguishing Forms from separate attributes or properties.)

Forms also bear striking resemblance to common characteristics, shared properties, attributes, or, in general, immanent universals (provided these are defined intensionally), since these objects, like Forms, *are* in some sense the natures or essences that worldly individuals only *have*. Each such theory constitutes a "moderate Platonism" recognizing abstract, intensional common natures, but not acknowledging *separate* natures or essences (ones existing independently of their instantiations). The traditional head of this tradition is, of course, Aristotle.[4] Some contemporary versions of moderate platonism could be brought closer to Plato by emphasizing (a) an ontology of *natural* kinds and (b) the epistemological role of natural kinds in our *understanding* of nature. But again, even assuming that done, Forms cannot be immanent in, dependent upon, or actually (spatially) present to their worldly participants in the manner of immanent universals. In other words, immanent universals are not ontologically prior to their exemplifications, since dependence between these sorts of items is mutual. Nor, for the same reason, could Forms be particular characters of things, which would be akin to what Plato in the *Phaedo* calls "the *F*-in-us"; nor what some philosophers call "abstract particulars" or "occurrent property instances."[5] Nor could they be Anaxagorean bits or portions mixed into the composition of sensible objects.

The *separate* properties or attributes of an "extreme Platonism" are yet more like Forms, since they can be considered eternal objects not literally existing in this world, but still entities to which worldly things stand in a very close relation (like instantiation or falling under). Such entities are sometimes described as "eternal possibilities" for different sorts of actual earthly existence. On the pure form of this approach, according to which there is no literal admixture with worldly things, one may think of possibilities as ontologically prior to their actualizations, since there *actually* being things of a given sort presupposes the *possibility* of there being such things, but not *vice versa*. Notice that separate possibilities are not the same as Aristotelian *potentialities* which are, in effect, immanent characteristics of actual things. The former entities are much more problematic than the latter; immanent potentialities at least are conditions of change whose existence, if not precise description, is uncontroversial (putting aside certain notorious eccentrics of antiquity). By contrast, there is always a serious question about the grounds for postulating a realm of separate abstract natures. Here Forms may be distinguished from separate natures in general, including eternal possibilities, by reference to Plato's particular reason for separating Forms—in a word, the eternal objectivity of Goodness and its intelligible articulation, reflected temporarily and spatially in the created world. This is not the only possible reason for a metaphysics of separate abstract natures; indeed, it is perhaps not Plato's only reason. But without some such specific ground or motivation, one misses not only an appropriate limit on one's abstract population, but also part of what is essential to the very nature of Forms.[6] For even if one held a theory of types, essences, attributes, or possibilities separate from their worldly tokens or instantiations, and *even if one's abstract objects corresponded one-to-one to homonymous Forms*, it would be the case that if those abstract objects were selected on some basis other than Plato's (if, for example, they were simply enumerated, or were selected on some sort of "scientistic" principle, as when they are said to correspond to all and only the general terms of certain sciences) they would not essentially *be* determinate places in a natural or good system of natures. (This indicates why the concluding point about abstract structures or patterns needed correction. Even Forms defined in purely structural terms cannot be simply identified with abstract, separate patterns or structures: A simple identification omits the fact that the Form in question is one place in a natural scheme of Forms.)

Historically, extreme Platonism, of which Plato's metaphysics is the primary example, has not been popular. A hybrid strain in which abstract natures exist both independently of our world and in their worldly exemplifications, has had broader appeal. There abstract natures both serve as the natures or characters actually occurring in various worldly items (so that they are, on grounds of an Aristotelian sort, immanent natures) *and* enjoy a separate existence guaranteed on epistemological, theological, or other grounds. Although the details of Whitehead's metaphysics are a matter of some dispute, his theory falls in this intermediate category combining elements of moderate and extreme Platonism. His *ideas* are eternal objects whose "metaphysical status is that of a possibility for an actuality." But they also seem to be the occurrent characters of things when they "ingress into," or "are ingredient" in things.[7] Christianizing interpretations such as those of Augustine and Aquinas yield a similar but clearly distinguishable hybrid in which Forms are both archetypes in the mind of God *and* universals immanent in worldly things.[8] (The idea of universals having two modes of being, one in things, one in intellect, is traditionally found first in Aristotle, for whom universals exist in minds as well as extra-mental things. Still, much of the Christian trend is inspired by interpretations of Plato's *Timaeus*.)

The resulting theories are in some ways close to Plato's and in other ways very remote. There may be a similar foundation for the population and separateness of a realm of abstract natures, amounting ultimately to belief in an objective goodness whose nature (whether or not in the person of a god) and articulation is eternally determined without dependence on the worldly course of events. This is not to say the abstract realms thus determined will coincide in detail, but only that at a general level they share a similar underlying principle of determination. Plato's Forms, however, exist independent of mind *and* matter, so to speak; they are apprehended by mind and imaged by worldly things, but do not exist in either. Thus Aquinas sides with Aristotle in rejecting Plato's opinion that Forms exist of themselves and not in the intellect.[9]

This is not to say, either, that Plato's theory could not be extended consistently to acknowledge existence of Forms in minds and in things. But the usual *reasons* for thinking universals must be present to their exemplifications (that otherwise they could not serve, as they are supposed to, as the common characters of things, and that in separating *eidē* one thereby transforms them into "things", rather than abstract natures) were refuted in chapter 6. Whether there would be any gain in such an extension, either for ontology or epistemology, is an enormous further question. But there are large differences of theory here, differences that bring on their own philosophical problems about the nature of exemplification, of sense perception, and knowledge.

Meanings of general terms, if construed as intensional, mind-independent concepts existing independent also of the objects falling under them, are very close relatives of Forms, and lead us again into extreme Platonism. On this approach one would naturally liken Forms to Fregean concepts — depending on one's interpretation of Frege.[10] But once again, even if these conditions are met, the lack of an essential connection to the Good must be noted. Meanings or Fregean concepts also lack a pertinent characteristic of possibilities mentioned above (note 6): Aside from questions about the Good, concepts or meanings as such need not be limited by what can exist or occur in this world. While there can be a meaning of the general term "round square," or a concept Round Square (a necessarily empty one), there can be neither such a possibility nor Form. Every Form is, at least potentially, a One over many intelligible or sensible participants. In addition, there is no obvious reason for regarding such meanings (or, for that matter, separate attributes, types, or essences) as formal *aitiai* of the objects, individuals, or tokens falling under them. With Forms it was the backing of the Good that underlay both their separateness from sensibles *and* their role as formal *aitiai* of sensibles. It is imperative that one distinguish, among extreme Platonisms, those simply embracing "two worlds" and those in which denizens of the sense world *depend* for being what they are on a separate, abstract realm.

There remains, however, an instructive parallel with meanings. One sometimes observes a distinction between the relation of meanings to the *words* that *signify* them, and the relation of objective (Fregean) concepts, or abstract types, to the *objects* that *fall under* them. This distinction does not require two different kinds of abstract object — one for the meanings of general terms, the other for the concepts under which objects fall. The meaning of some general term "*F*," that which is grasped in thought, could perfectly well be identical to the concept under which all individual *F*s fall. Plato's Forms do the work of meanings and (objective) concepts, in that they are what is grasped in thought, they are what is attributed to or said of things in *logos*, they are the objects of shared knowledge, and they are the intelligible objects under which sensibles fall.

These remarks point to an additional feature of classical paradigmatism, namely that, while one can speak of words signifying concepts and of objects falling under those same concepts, Plato's Forms are not only signified by words and fallen under by worldly objects, but also are signified by worldly objects. Recall that, in Plato's view, sensible objects can be *paradeigmata* in the sense of "illustrative examples," illustrating some more general type or principle. The image analogy underlines this function of sensibles insofar as *eikones* or *mimēmata* reveal the nature of their models. This is just to say the participation of sensibles in Forms could in one important way be seen as a kind of meaning relation. This fact lies behind Plato's insistence in the *Phaedo* and elsewhere that when one recognizes a sensible *F* as *F* one is exercising, perhaps quite subconsciously, one's innate apprehension of *F* itself. The point could be suitably adapted for use on many different theories of meaning. But from the distinctly Platonic perspective described in chapter 6, one must take the point a step further: The true student of Nature understands the realm of becoming by knowing what it is that becoming "strives" for; the student knows explicitly the Forms of which the sensible realm and its contents are supposed to be images, of which there must be images if there is to be a good cosmos. As the formal language of nature, as it were, Forms alone allow one to make true, objective sense of the otherwise unintelligible realm of phenomena—or at best, the conventional language of a blind, spontaneously generated world of generation and decay.

It is now fully justified to conclude that Forms are very hard working, performing many tasks of a number of other types of Platonic entities. However, it is only in the sense that they do the work of these other sorts of things that they could be said to be attributes, universals, meanings, possibilities, or the like. Such identifications are best resisted, since they can seriously mislead, and in some cases they obscure very basic aspects of Plato's Forms. Since each philosophical job-well-done would provide a motive for postulating Forms, the various tasks just reviewed show Plato may have had from the outset one such motive, and may have accumulated more as the theory developed and expanded. If the emphasis of Chapter 6 on Forms as the doubly objective ground of value (immutably establishing the varieties of goodness and their opposites regardless of human opinion and what happens here below) points to the central motivation, neither it nor any other single-featured account can give the whole story of why Plato believed in Forms.

C. Image, Model, and Participation

Plato's image analogy has proved useful throughout our investigation not only for illustrating points reasonably clear in themselves, but also for avoiding potential misunderstanding of the nature of Forms and their relations to worldly individuals. The analogy also brought to light peculiarly Platonic ideas that might otherwise have gone unnoticed. A review of these points will bring out the power of the analogy to organize and unify the classical theory of Forms as well as to provide for the imagination a picture, detailed and vivid, of Plato's two worlds.

(1) The Form of F is itself one type of F, or thing rightly called by the *onoma* "F" rather than "G" or "H." It is in fact the "really real" F, being unqualifiedly F in the way it is F, and enjoying an unqualified claim to the *onoma* "F." So, also, is the model or original the real F relative to its image in paint or stone, on water or a mirror.

(2) Sensible Fs are of a different type than F itself, not resembling the intelligible nature of F with respect to being F (except as both are Fs of one or another of Plato's hierarchically ordered types) just as *eidola, mimēmata, eikones,* or *phantasmata* of real Fs are not themselves Fs of the same sort as their models.

(3) Still, sensible Fs are rightly called after the Forms in which they participate, as a painting or dream image of Napoleon or of a horse is correctly labeled "Napoleon" or "horse" rather than "Wellington" or "mule."

(4) Forms are separate from and independent of their sensible participants, as a model or original or "real thing itself" is independent of its images in stone or pigment or in dreams.

(5) Sensible Fs depend for their being F on participation in the Form of F, just as the image F is of the type it is only so long as it is an image of a model or original F: Its *being of* a horse makes it an imitation horse rather than an imitation mule or just so much pigment or wood.

(6) As the similarity of two sensibles of the same sort is due to their both participating in some common Form F (their both being sensible Fs) so the kinship of various images of a model (as, say, Napoleons rather than Wellingtons) depends on their all being images of a common original. Thus the kinship or likeness of sensible F and its Form, considered as things rightly called "F," is prior to the "common" similarity of two sensible Fs with respect to being F.

(7) Sensible Fs are in many cases dependent upon F itself not only as formal *aitia* but also as model for purposeful production, just as created images depend for their coming-to-being, in part, on the model to which their creator looks.

(8) Sensibles, like images, are dependent also upon a medium, the receptacle in which all scattered (extended) things come to be.

(9) That sensibles have scattered, mutable being suggests why the term "particular" must be taken with a grain of salt. From Plato's perspective their alleged unity, their being one, becomes problematic. Scattered and mutable as bodily things may be, divisible as they are into multitudes of parts, their unity depends upon each serving some function, engaging in certain life activities, or, more generally, satisfying some *logos tēs ousias* (where the *ousia* is some Form). Similarly, that which gives *these* contrasting patches of pigment spread across a wooden surface, or *this* light playing on the surface of the water, its unity as an (imitation) horse or a shuttle is its being an image of a horse or shuttle. The *unity* of the image F qua F, like the *being* of the image F qua F (point 5 again) depends "formally" on the model F, as the unity and being F of a sensible F is a matter of participation in the Form F itself.

(10) As a sensible F "is and is not" or lies "between true being and utter not-being" (in that although it is not a really real F, an eternal, intelligible nature of F, it is yet a sensible F), so an *eidolōn* or *eikōn* is not a real F, but is in fact an imitation F. (Recall that this sense of "being and not being," which occurs at *Sophist* 240c and, in effect, at *Republic* 597a, is different from, because more general than, that expressed at *Republic* 479 and elsewhere, in which a sensible is F in one respect but un$F$ in another.)

(11) Forms serve as standards in that they provide criteria for evaluation as well as classification of their participants, just as the correctness of images or likenesses is measured against the model itself. Greater accuracy or correctness (*orthotēs*) of an image, however that accuracy is achieved, corresponds to greater excellence as a sensible F. In addition,

on both sides of the analogy a single model will serve for many sorts of images, some of which may image the model in quite different ways.

To these may be added several epistemological parallels. Although these have not been analyzed here they are important for appreciating the scope of Plato's analogy, and should be readily comprehensible given the detailed treatment of various metaphysical and evaluative parallels. In several cases they mark important parallels with Platonist metaphysics.

(12) Our ability to perceive sensible Fs as Fs depends on our apprehension, whether fully conscious or not, of F itself (*Phaedo* 75), just as the being F of a sensible is a matter of participation in F itself as a "simple" *aitia*.

(13) A grasp of one and the same Form may underlie perception of a wide variety of participants varying greatly from one another, just as F itself (Equal, Just, Good) is often participated in by various sorts of worldly individuals (recall point 6). The image analogy will illustrate both points if we picture ourselves attempting to pick out an image, or a variety of different images of some original, where we may have either a recent, clear memory of the original (or a present view of it), or only a dim and distant one. The prenatal inspection of Forms in the recollection stories of the *Phaedo* and *Phaedrus* may be likened in part to gaining acquaintance with various originals or models whose sometimes very disparate images we must later identify.

(14) Ability to assess the quality of participants depends upon apprehension of Forms and on referral of participants to Forms for evaluation, just as the objective ranking of participants independently of what anyone may judge rests upon criteria of excellence supplied by the Form (point 11). Analogously, evaluation of the correctness of an image rests on some sort of comparison to its original. (This last matter is less simple than one might suppose; some of the problems involved were raised in chapter 5.)

(15) On the other hand, some perception of sensibles is needed to jog one's memory of Forms, or to begin turning the mind toward the intelligible realm even if, having recollected some Forms, one may recollect others without needing to perceive worldly participants in each of those further Forms. On the level of everyday sense perception one does not first recognize some sensible as F and later recollect F itself. Instead one recollects F itself to some extent in the very act of perceiving some sensible as F—as one exercises the knowledge of a long-lost friend in recognizing a picture as a picture of him.

Here one encounters a disanalogy, in that one need not perceive images in order to gain access to worldly originals. One can, however, adapt the analogy to suit by imagining one has forgotten some original and has available, as stimuli to recollection, only its images. Then, too, Plato's conviction that we begin life in this world among images and ultimately, given the right aptitude and *paideia*, achieve recognition of worldly *F*s as images of an intelligible model, can be illustrated well enough if one allows the imagination a bit of play. One might imagine a group of people in a cave, chained so that they could look only straight ahead at the cave wall. Meanwhile, behind, burns a fire. . . .

(16) An image is not just of its original, but also purports to say something about it, to depict it in some way or other: the relation to its model is descriptive as well as referential. So, too, will a worldly *F* help indicate the nature of the Form(s) in which it participates. (Hence the use of sensibles as illustrative examples—*paradeigmata* in the first sense described in chapter 2.) Putting aside problems arising only in special circumstances, the success of a sensible participant in revealing the nature of its intelligible model depends in part, as with worldly images of worldly models, on how faithful or correct an image it is (how excellent a specimen it is of a given kind of thing).

(17) Although one must begin with sense perception it is possible ultimately to rise above it to apprehension of Forms alone, in their purity. Just as Forms are not in anything else, so they may in principle be grasped in themselves, dissociated from their particular images. Similarly, one may gain some conception, or perhaps dim recollection, of a man through studying images of him, but can in principle have direct access to him independently of any of his images. One emerges from the cave, or wakes from a dream, to confront the real thing itself. This gives an epistemological parallel to the ontological independence of Forms: As forms are not dependent for their being on worldly participants, so also can they be known by some few people and by god—the possessors of *nous*—in themselves and not through worldly manifestations.

This point, together with point two, implies there is an epistemological priority of Forms parallel to their ontological priority. The being *F* of sensibles depends on that of Forms, and the perception of sensibles *as F* depends on apprehension of Forms, while Forms are what they are independently of sensibles, and can be known in their purity apart from sensible imagery.

This does not exhaust the epistemological parallels, and does not address directly the philosophical problems involved with the points mentioned. But these remarks help bring out the range and power of the image analogy, and contribute significantly to an account of Plato's conviction that sensible objects are related to intelligible ones as mere images to their models.

Metaphors, analogies, similes, and miscellaneous figures of speech play many roles in philosophy, as they do in science and everyday discourse. They may try to fill (or hide) a gap in one's evidence or argument, communicate a suggestive but vaguely formed thought, or convey points of theory already formulated in other terms. They have been used to clothe some doctrine in appealing and perhaps persuasive garb, make an unfamiliar idea seem less alien, suggest new possibilities for investigation, or even create for some "transferred" term a new meaning not reducible to its old, literal meaning.

At one place or another we have seen Plato's image analogy performing most of these functions. Three should be emphasized above all. First, the analogy serves as structural metaphor, consciously and purposefully articulated, organizing the major tenets of classical paradigmatism.[11] The analogy can seem casual because the introduction of individual points is often, in their dramatic context, casual, and because the theory unfolds, dramatically and to some extent in Plato's thought, over a considerable span of time. This largely accounts for the fact that even commentators justly sympathetic to the analogy have provided only a partial view of its extent and significance.

Second, the analogy exercises an important control on the interpretation of several philosophical ideas expressed also in non-figurative language. This reverses the more common situation in which one must look for explicit, non-metaphorical, indications as to precisely which aspects of a proposed metaphor bear on the theory illustrated, and how they bear upon it. Thus, the type-distinction between eternal, non-spatial nature of F and sensible F, which can be obscured by the fact that both have a claim on the *onoma* "F," is clarified by application of the image analogy. Ironically, a misreading of the analogy has obscured, in much literature of the past twenty-four centuries, the distinction Plato wished to convey. We saw the record of Plato's concern with this misreading in the *Parmenides, Cratylus,* and *Sophist*, and examined his reaction to it in the latter two dialogues. Proper application of the analogy helped also in deciding among alterna-

tive accounts of Plato's theory of predication and, perhaps most importantly, his conception of participation—a matter about which he said very
little in a non-metaphoric vein. The analogy helped convey a primitive
term of the theory—which is perhaps what Paul Shorey had in mind long
ago by "expressing the inexpressible."

Third, the analogy represents what was then, and still is for many
readers, a radically counterintuitive philosophy. This contribution would
be considered by some to be "non-cognitive" and dismissed as mere orna-
ment, unimportant for philosophy. Much depends here on what one counts
as philosophy. The image metaphor, by conveying with great immediacy
a range of evaluative, as well as epistemological and ontological, convictions can in any case contribute to one's overall grasp of a complex theory.
It can also advance a primary aim of philosophy, as Plato saw philosophy,
the leading towards truth of those souls naturally receptive to the spirit of
classical Platonism.

Appendix 1

The Approximation Reading
of *Phaedo* 74-75

Rightly cited by Gregory Vlastos as "by far the most important of the relevant texts" for the question of "imperfect embodiment" of Forms,[1] *Phaedo* 74a-75d supports the case *against* an approximation reading of participation in general and of the inferiority of sensible equals in particular. The passage occurs during Socrates' demonstration of the prenatal existence of the soul, wherein he appeals to a theory of Forms and to a theory of recollection. Both theories are illustrated by the example of the Equal itself (*auto to ison*), which is said to be distinct from all visible equals (74b7-c5) and "brought to mind" by the perception of visible equals (74c). Several times the latter are said to be inferior to (*phauloteron*; 74e2, 75b8) or fall short of (*endeesterōs echein*; 74e3, 75a3, b2) the Equal itself; they all strive for it and wish to be like it, but cannot be such as it (*ou dynatai toiouton einai* [*ison*] *hoion ekeino*; 74e1).

It is tempting to conclude at first sight that Plato must be thinking of "inferior" equals as visible things which are approximately, but never quite exactly, equal to one another.[2] But Plato does not say sticks and stones are never exactly equal; on the contrary, he consistently refers to them simply as "equals" (74b6, b8, c4, c7, e7, 75a1, b6). These passages suggest Plato has in mind some inferiority of visible equals—be they exact or only approximate—rather than just visible near-equals.

Plato's argument for distinguishing the Equal itself from visible equals supports that suggestion (74b7-9):

> Is it not sometimes the case that equal stones and sticks, though remaining the same, appear equal to one man [or possibly "to one thing" or "in one respect"' or even "at one time," depending on the reading of "tōi" at 74b8, 9][3] but unequal to another?

Socrates points out that sensible equals can be (or, possibly, can appear to be) the opposite of what they are, whereas the Equal itself can never be (appear to be) the opposite of what it is.[4] And, as Plato says, this is a characteristic of all sensible *equals* (*isoi,* b8, and *isa,* b6). There is no textual or philosophical justification for restricting the argument to near-equals. The argument would apply to all visible equals, exact or approximate, and as stated is concerned expressly with equal sticks and stones whose (metrical) equality is not at issue.[5]

Still it may be argued that visible equals must really be only near-equals. When Plato says at 75b7 that we refer (*anoisein*) sensible equals to the Form and see that they all "want to be such as it, but are inferior to it" he must have in mind a comparison of the not-quite-equal to the perfectly equal. But in fact the passage contains definite indications Plato intends a comparison that holds for sticks and stones which do have metrically equal dimensions. He is concerned here with the recollection of likes "from likes" (*homoia*) and has previously given several examples of recollection. Looking down the list[6] one finds the "approximation" case is conspicuously absent. As others have noted, it is significant that Plato's only example of recollection "from likes" is that of recollecting Simmias on seeing a "drawn Simmias" (*Simmian gegrammenon*).[7] The fact that Plato's only such example is one of image *F* and real *F* (*Simmias autos*) indicates he is thinking of the version of the participant/Form relationship so prominent in the *Republic, Phaedrus,* and *Timaeus,* and alluded to later in the *Phaedo,*[8] that of an image or imitation *F* to its original. If so, Plato intends not approximation to a standard of perfection, but a "referring" of concrete example of equality to intelligible nature of Equality itself. We saw earlier that all the "striving" of sticks and stones, *even if* it results in dimensions metrically equal to those of some other stick or stone, will still leave their equality inferior—in its compositeness, relativity, non-intelligibility, and liability to change and destruction—to that of the nature of F itself.

Moreover, on the approximation view *some* visible things at least will come very close to perfection while others will fail by a greater margin. Yet all sensible equals are said to be "greatly lacking" with respect to the Equal itself (*polu endei*, 74d8). By contrast, on the "abstract nature" reading of Forms, the remark is fully justified and points to the many important marks of inferiority of all corporeal equals, including any exact equals.

Likewise the *'ou dynatai'* of 74e1 is unjustified on the approximation reading: "Visible equals always and *necessarily* fall short of the Equal itself." On the approximation view that claim would be at best very dubious; one would have to show Plato (mistakenly) believed it was *not possible* for two sticks or stones to be exactly equal. This may be the assumption of many commentators, and may be one reason why the approximation view can at first sight seem so attractive; it looks as if Plato is only appealing to an obvious truth. But so long as one does not confuse the impossibility of knowing for certain that two sticks are exactly equal in length by performing measurements upon them, with the possibility of there simply being two equal sticks (regardless of whether anyone has tried to make them equal or tried to measure them or even observed them at all), then one should not be tempted by the assumption that two sticks *could* not be equal in length.[9]

Once again on the image theory, which preserves an appropriate type distinction between visible equals and the Equal itself, Socrates' remark makes good sense, since for reasons cited above, even visible *equals* never *could* be equals of the same sort as What-is-equal.

In any case I do not believe anyone will deny, even in Plato's name, that sticks and stones sometimes *appear* to some people to be exactly equal, whether they really are so or not. Yet what Plato says is that in each case (*hotan*; 74d9) in which we perceive sensible equals we judge them inferior to the Equal itself (74d5-7, d9-e1, 75a1). But how, on the approximation reading, could two sticks which an observer takes to be exactly equal in length also be judged by that observer to be inferior, in that very respect, to some standard of exact equality?[10]

It is worth noting also that Plato's frequent use of *"endei"* phrases (*endei ti*, 74d6; *polu endei*, d8; *endei*, e1; *endeesterōs echei*, e3, 75a2; *endeestera estin*, b2) to describe the shortcoming of visible participants parallels the use of *"hosou endeousin"* at *Cratylus* 432d2 and *"polu endein"* at *Republic* 529d, where it is made explicit that the inferiors are images. In the former passage, Socrates emphasizes that an image "falls short" of its model at least to the extent that it not be "another *F*" — in which case it will not (*pace* the approximation view) be a more-or-less perfect *F*. In the *Republic* passage Socrates maintains that the paths of the stars, "like geometrical diagrams drawn by a Daedalus," provide the most perfect of all possible shapes and visible doubles, halves and so on. Nonetheless, even these diagrams must be used only as models of true mathematical realities and despite their perfection will, as visible things, fall far short (*polu endien*) of those realities. This case of "falling far short of" the Forms is not a matter of being a more or less imperfect *F*, but of being a visible image, even a perfect one, of immutable, intelligible entities.

Finally, there is a more general objection to construing participation in Equality along approximationist lines. It is hard to see how the Equal itself could provide a single standard to which all sorts of equals would approximate. Just how is one standard instance or perfect specimen supposed to serve for equality of length, shape, age, speed (of rotation, locomotion, alteration) and so on?[11] Even if it could do so, we would only have an Equal equal in all sorts of respects, and at all times, not Equality itself, which is never said to be equal in this respect *and* that respect or in each of many respects, but is said rather to be "Equality" (*isotēs*, 74c1) or "the Equal itself" (*auto to ison*, 74c4), that "single natured" (*monoeides*, 78d5) essence shared in or imaged in various ways by sensibles.[12]

So far we have found no firm support for an approximation reading of the *Phaedo* passage and much evidence against it, even while discussing the issue in terms of Plato's example of the Equal itself, where the approximation view enjoys its greatest initial plausibility. But such a view is not even initially plausible in the case of such Forms as the Greater and the Less. For would anyone say one stick is never quite longer or shorter than another? If that were not absurd enough in itself, it would contradict the previous assertion (of the approximation view) that no sticks are ever quite equal. Yet at 75c7-d5, Plato says the arguments of the preceding section apply not only to the Equal, but also to the Greater and the Less and "all such things."

On the other hand, if the inferiority is one of type, and the comparison in question is like that of an imitation F to a real F, then Plato's conclusions concerning the Equal will indeed apply just as well and for like reasons to the Greater, the Less, Justice, and Beauty.[13]

So a close examination of *Phaedo* 74-75, that key text for an approximation view, has led to the conclusion that even if one's first impression is favorable to an "approximation to the perfect specimen" reading, that interpretation will not bear up under critical examination. Plato's statements about the comparison of sensible participants to Forms and the inevitable judgment of inferiority upon the former make perfectly good sense if the inferiority is one of type, as it is on the "imitation" version of participation. But the same statements are sometimes puzzling, unjustified or even absurd on an approximation reading. The explanation is that the type distinction between Forms and participants which Plato emphasizes so strongly elsewhere in the *Phaedo* is not collapsed, but is presupposed throughout *Phaedo* 74-75.

Appendix 2

Allen and Lee on the Image Analogy

R.E. Allen's well-known paper, "Participation and Predication in Plato's Middle Dialogues" (*SPM*, 43-60), addresses a large number of issues in a brief space. Some of the strengths and weaknesses of his views, as I see them, have been discussed in chapters 3, 4, and 6. Regarding interpretation of the image analogy, Allen has correctly seen several important points: the difference in type between image F (sensible F) and model F (Form of F); the role of the model as a One over a many; the ontological priority of model to image (though he does not explain how one is to understand participation in separate Forms); and the role of model as standard or paradigm by reference to which we judge the faithfulness of its images. With all these claims I have agreed, while trying to show Plato's use of the analogy goes substantially beyond these items.

One important difficulty with Allen's treatment of the image analogy emerged in chapter 3: His attempt to "assimilate" other sorts of images to the nature of mirror reflection is gratuitous, since *all* Plato's various sorts of images will illustrate his basic views about the model's (Form's) ontological priority to its sensible participants. Here I would like to address directly Allen's principle argument for his assimilation view.

Allen's argument is central to his reply to those who would allege "accidental" resemblance between image *F* and model *F* (what I called "resemblance in respects other than *F*"), then infer some corresponding resemblance between sensible and Form. Allen makes no pretense of having provided a textual basis for his interpretation; his paper is more in the nature of a broadside attack (Gregory Vlastos has called it a "delightful diatribe against the 'self-predicationists.'") Nonetheless, Allen's discussion has the virtue of beginning with a consideration of the sorts of images Plato had in mind: paintings, statues, reflections, shadows. His basic strategy, however, is to assimilate all other sorts of images to reflections in water or in mirrors. More precisely, he argues that "resemblances of" are only "quasi-substantial"; they "stand to their originals as the dependent to the independent, as the less real to the more real" (50-51). Comparison to the case of reflections clarifies the point. "The very being of a reflection is relational, wholly dependent upon what is other than itself: the original and the reflecting medium. . . . The reflection does not *resemble* the original; rather, it is a *resemblance* of the original" (50). By contrast, paintings or statues may appear more than "quasi-substantial." They may in fact seem plainly to have a substantial existence of their own and to resemble their models in a variety of relevant respects. But if, Allen continues, we consider Plato's theory of art, we learn that the picture "as an art object . . . no longer retains its independent character; it is assimilated to that of a reflection, which is to say that its full meaning is relational, dependent upon the nature of its original" (51,n.1). Likewise, sensible participants are really only "quasi-substantial . . . relational entities," and are not to be regarded as having a life of their own, as it were, which would enable them to resemble Forms. Thus on Allen's view "Plato's metaphor of imitation brilliantly expresses a community between different orders of objects, different levels of reality" (51) without importing resemblance into participation.

Allen's position requires argument at two points at least: (1) He must show that reflections are on Plato's view "quasi-substantial . . . relational entities" – that although they are resemblances of their models they do not resemble their models – and (2) he must show that other sorts of images are, on Plato's theory of art, to be assimilated in that respect to reflections. The first argument would require examination of Plato's comments on the nature of mirror reflections, especially at *Timaeus* 46a-b and *Sophist* 266c. Allen offers an argument which shows why *he* thinks mirror images do not resemble their models (50, n.1) but does not undertake to examine Plato's views. For reasons which will become apparent soon, it is necessary to consider only the second point here. With regard to that second point Allen writes (51):

> It will be objected that Plato compares particulars with reflections and pictures indiscriminately; that pictures are not merely resemblances of, but stand in the relation of resemblance to, their originals; and that, therefore, the above interpretation cannot be attributed to Plato. But this objection overlooks the nature of his theory of art. The analogy is drawn, not to the picture *as* a picture, but to the art object – a 'man-made dream for waking eyes'. The picture does not differ in type or degree of reality from its original; it is an artifact, an object of πίστις; to apprehend it so is to apprehend it *as* a picture; and to be able to compare it, we cannot confuse it with that original. But the artist holds a mirror up to nature; it is essential to apprehending a picture as an art object that we may take it to be, not a resemblance, but the very thing it resembles, as we may mistake a reflection in a mirror for the thing reflected. Viewed as an art object, the picture no longer retains its independent character; it is assimilated to that of a reflection, which is to say that its full meaning is relational, dependent upon the nature of its original.

Now Allen is clearly right in saying that the image F (the painting of a red scarf) does not resemble its model in being F (the painting is not a real scarf at all). But his argument is supposed to show that, *qua* art object, the painting does not resemble the real thing with respect to being red, either. And while he is again right in concluding that resemblance to the Form of F in respects other than F is no part of participation in F, his argument for these conclusions has, it seems to me, skipped the rails.

A statue of Cratylus may be thought of as a kind of Cratylus (as when it is labeled "Cratylus" in a museum) or as a tall, painted piece of marble of such-and-such dimensions. Considered as a Cratylus it does not in that respect resemble its model since it is not in fact "another Cratylus" (recall *Cratylus* 432c), not "another real thing of the same sort" as its model (*Sophist* 240a-b). In other respects, however, it may well resemble its model by duplicating Cratylus' color, size, or shape. This is perhaps what lies behind Allen's distinction between the image "*qua* art object" and the image "*qua* picture" or statue. Assuming the classification scheme of *Republic* X, one could also put the point this way: The painter's horse does not participate in the Form of Horse, as does the trainer's horse; the painter's horse is an image not of the Form but of the living horse. It will, however, participate in such Forms as Brown (if there is such a Form) and in the appropriate geometrical Forms, along with the trainer's horse. In those respects it does plainly resemble its model. Allen would say, however, that those points of resemblance obtain only if the image is considered "as a picture" rather than "as an art object."

What is most worrisome about Allen's way of putting the matter is that the distinction crucial to his argument does not seem to be found in Plato. Allen alludes to Plato's theory of art and to Plato's talk of a "man-made dream for waking eyes." But insofar as Plato himself comments explicitly on the relation of painting to model, he asserts, first, that the very same paintings which are only image or imitation *F*s can and do resemble their models in other respects. We have seen this emphasized in the *Cratylus* and *Sophist*, and it is clearly assumed in *Republic* X where the painter duplicates the phenomenal properties of his models in order to produce mere phantasms. That is, Plato maintains in the first place that the products of the fine arts can and typically do resemble their models in some respects other than *F*.

Moreover, Plato seems to think we may very well regard a painting, say of a red scarf, *both* as an art object and at the same time as something resembling its model with respect to its color. Indeed we very often do this when we assess the accuracy, faithfulness, or correctness of an art object by comparing it with its original (*Cratylus* 430d-431c, *et al.*). In Allen's terminology, the painting "*qua* art object" would be, on Plato's view, *both* a mere imitation scarf and a "really" red object.

So, while Allen is right about lack of resemblance in respect *F* between image *F* and real *F*, and also right about lack of resemblance in other respects between sensible *F* and Form *F*, his argument for the latter is not viable.

E.N. Lee's approach has much in common with Allen's ["On the Meta-physics of the Image in Plato's *Timaeus*," *Monist* 50 (1966): 341-368.] He too thinks of participants as things whose being is "relational, adjectival, dependent." Like Allen, he focuses on reflections as a good illustration of this particular point—if not of certain other points of Plato's theory (366)—agreeing that "the very being of a reflection is relational, wholly dependent upon what is other than itself; the original, and the reflecting medium" (364). But he is concerned to base his case on careful textual analysis, and instead of trying to assimilate pictures and statues to reflections, he argues that Plato himself, in a key passage of the *Timaeus*, moves decisively to an ontology properly illustrated by such images as mirror reflections rather than paintings and statues.

Lee's reading of *Timaeus* 48e-52c brings out well the internal coherence of the passage and the fact that it *is* an important text in which Plato at-tempted something special and quite difficult. Lee correctly stresses also that the text does not just "add on" a theory of the receptacle, but tries to integrate it with Plato's larger theory of Form (model) and sensible (im-age), and that the text stresses a double dependence of the "intermediate" image—dependence at once on the model *of* which it is an image and on the medium *in* which it must come to be if it is to be anything at all. I must disagree, however, with the radical interpretation Lee gives of the nature of sensibles and of their dependence on Forms. He argues that in this pas-sage of the *Timaeus* Plato gives us an exposition of the metaphysics of the image which implies something more extreme than we had seen (or at least, clearly seen) in the *Phaedo, Republic*, or even the balance of the *Timaeus*, namely, an ontology of the "insubstantial image." Such images include mirror reflections, for example, which depend "for their existence on a continuing relation to their original, and if that original is removed or destroyed, the image must also disappear . . . they have no reality on 'their own,' but wholly derive their being from their original and from the medium in which they appear." Such images are not "substantial images" like paintings, statues, or "items with some independent physical identity of their own, a kind of image that can survive the destruction of the origi-nal it represents" (353).

Lee writes:

What Plato does at 48e-52d is to disclose the presence of the mirror. By introducing his "third kind" as the medium "in which" phenomena as images appear, he exposes the "magic trick" by which images so much as seem to have reality on their own . . . he moves decisively from an ontology of the "substantial image" (one at least tolerated, if not encouraged in the previous part of the *Timaeus*) to one specifically restricted to the "insubstantial image"; from a straightforward two-level structure where one item is an image of the other, to a three-term system where the third term (the image) is resultant from the inter-action of the other two.

The introduction of the receptacle is one key element in Lee's reading. He points to the witholding even of deictic terms from phenomena (*Timaeus* 49b7-50a4); to the gold example of 50a5-b5 (in which the only thing with an enduring nature is the medium rather than the ever-changing shapes molded in that medium [see Lee's article, "On the Gold-Example in Plato's *Timaeus* (50A5-B5)" in *Essays in Ancient Greek Philosophy*, ed. John Anton and George Kustas (Albany, 1971), 219-235] and the fact that "such definiteness of character as an image exhibits belongs, not to the image itself, but to that which it signifies" (357-360). These considerations all point to what Lee calls a "radical insubstantiality" of sensibles—they are entirely dependent on an interaction between model (Form) and medium (receptacle). If one grants phenomena any substantiality of their own, Lee argues, then, as with a substantial image, "the relatedness of the image to its original is, so to say, extrinsic to its simply *being*" (360); one misses the "key idea," which is "the internal, continuing, essential relatedness to an original" (354, n. 27).

My general response is as follows. First, one can do justice to the impor-tance of the *Timaeus* text, and capture the key idea about relatedness to an original, without such radical measures as Lee proposes.

Second, Lee's position makes the nature of sensibles and of their par-ticipation in Forms quite obscure. Third, his reading is open to what seem to me fatal objections on both textual and philosophical grounds. I hope my estimate of the importance of the receptacle and its integration with other Platonic ideas was clear in chapter 5. Even if the doctrine of the receptacle reflects earlier (*Phaedo, Symposium*) ways of looking at sen-sibles, the very attempt to formulate those intuitions explicitly is impor-tant. And the formulation arrived at, obscure as it may be on some points, is an important achievement. I also argued that the receptacle underlies virtually all the standard marks of inferiority of sensibles and serves to consolidate Plato's picture of the way in which sensibles are F, and earn the *onoma* "F." I believe also that the key idea mentioned by Lee is captured on my interpretation, for the of-ness of an image *is* a "continuing, essential" relation to its model. Again, we saw in chapter 3 that this holds for *all* sorts of images, even substantial ones that do survive their originals. Lee does recognize the essential of-ness of images (253). But he underestimates its potential for illustrating the way in which the being F of sensibles is dependent on participation in the Form of F.

Beyond this, Lee's reading unjustifiably leaves the nature of phenomena and of participation a mystery. Sensibles are "radically insubstantial" and, Lee says (in correspondence) not the logical subjects of predication. Yet he also maintains that a sensible's "essence (so far as it has any) just *is* its striving to be like the Form. 'It' is a locus of striving. It *is* any definite 'something' only insofar as it strives *for* some definite Form" (362, n. 46). On the other hand, sensibles *are* allowed to be objects of sense perception (366). Moreover, one would imagine any particular locus of striving (located at some particular part of the receptacle) would be a striving of a particular sort, the sort being the Form after which it strives. Also, any particular locus of striving will presumably have *these* rather than *those* phenomenal properties—otherwise they could not be the objects of sense perception. So phenomena are locatable, perceptible, and describable even if their correct apprehension and description depends on the Forms in which they participate. This will hold despite the fact that phenomena are nothing apart from the receptacle, or if in some sense the receptacle is the only proper (worldly) object of predication. But all these claims can be given good sense on the interpretation defended in this study; they do not require any more "radical" account.

In addition, on Lee's reading there is obscurity about *how* sensibles come into being. Lee says this arises through "interaction of Form and receptacle." But in this same passage of the *Timaeus* Forms are said never to go out to anything, be in anything, or admit anything into themselves. How, then, is the interaction to be accomplished? Lee says he does not consider Forms efficient causes of sensibles, but he does not explain what this interaction could amount to. Moreover, one would not like to see "the works of reason" eliminated. Plato's usual view, in the *Timaeus* and elsewhere, is that *craftsmen* create artifacts, human beings perform actions, with an eye to the appropriate Forms. What becomes of their contributions if interaction of Form and receptacle is responsible for sensibles? (Here one wants to protest also that Lee's treatment of the *mirror image* leaves out a corresponding factor crucial to Plato's own analysis, namely, light. It is not, after all, interaction of model and medium alone that gives rise to the image, even in the case of mirror reflections.)

Furthermore, even if insubstantial images were "radically insubstantial" (a view which, in Allen also, has not been founded on *Plato's* analysis of mirror images), this text of the *Timaeus* would tell against rather than for such an ontology, since it repeatedly appeals to *substantial* rather than insubstantial images. It most frequently uses the language of a wax impression, which would be a substantial image, able to survive destruction of its original (such as a seal or signet ring), just as a properly sculpted stone is a substantial image of Cratylus. Lee candidly acknowledges this possible objection but cites the application of "impress" language (*Timaeus* 71b, *Theatetus* 206d) to mirrors and infers that the occurrence of such language at *Timaeus* 50 "does not disqualify our mirror analogy" (357, n. 32). But even if in other passages Plato does apply impress language to mirrors, it is at least odd that at 48e-52d Plato makes no mention of mirrors whatever. The real difficulty is that the "impress" language is not used neutrally in our passage, but is unequivocally linked to impressions such as those in wax, and so cannot be neutralized by citing the use of that language elsewhere to describe mirror images:

> So, too, just as the receptacle does not present any characteristics of its own, those who try taking impressions of shapes in soft substances do not allow any shape whatever to appear there, smoothing them down beforehand and making them as smooth as possible. (*Timaeus*, 50e8-10)

Nor, finally, does the disclosure of the medium of sensible participants tell in favor of Lee's interpretation. Substantial images are just as dependent on a medium as insubstantial ones; one image will appear in a medium of wax or some "soft substance," another in stone, another in pigment, still others in water or in a mirror. Plato's point about dependence on a medium will hold for all sorts of images; there is no need to understand it in terms of insubstantial images.

In a related article, Lee develops an interesting response to the *Parmenides* regress of similarities using the concept of a dynamic, as opposed to static, image. (See "The Second 'Third Man': An Interpretation," in *Patterns in Plato's Thought*, ed. J.M.E. Moravcsik.) This dynamism, or "striving," whether or not it involves motion or conscious striving on the part of the image, establishes a non-accidental connection between the image and its model. (They are not associated, like some objects, because they *just happen* to be similar.) Now, in some cases of imaging, Lee continues, the image will be close enough to the model to be considered similar to it. There one finds the asymmetrical relation of imaging *and* the symmetrical relation of similarity (Lee's "group b"). If Plato's participants were analogues of those images, Plato would be open to the regress argument. But there is a kind of image which manifests that essential "striving-to-be-like" its model, but which is so radically deficient it cannot be said to be similar to its model ("group c"). One example, with which academics generally may sympathize, is Lee's bank account, which he is striving to raise to the level of Rockefeller's. Since Lee's account contains only $256.25, it is not similar to Rockefeller's fortune. Another example is a map that hardly resembles the terrain it maps, yet is a very useful image of that terrain for those who know the relevant projection rules.

The crucial consideration is that "group c includes directed processes of imitations that are marked (no matter how good they may actually be as imitations) by an essential feature of deficiency. Because of that essential feature of deficiency (their being radically short of their goal), assertions of any achieved degree of symmetrical resemblance to the standard are precluded" (page 110).

Although, again, I agree with Lee's main conclusion, I have doubts about his particular arguments for it. The main problem—and here I must omit many stimulating details of Lee's discussion—is that the critical distinction between images that are fairly close to their models and those whose deficiency is so extreme as to preclude judgments of resemblance, is simply not drawn by Plato in any of the familiar passages in which he constructively appeals to the image analogy.

Second, such a distinction is not necessary to meet the regress. All images, be they paintings or statues, dreams or mirror reflections, dynamic or static, manifest both an essential relatedness to a model *and* a deficiency, a lack of resemblance, of precisely the sort needed to block the regress.

Abbreviations

AJP   *American Journal of Philology*

ACPA   Cherniss, Harold. *Aristotle's Criticism of Plato and the Acad-
             emy.* Baltimore: The Johns Hopkins University Press,
             1944; reprint, New York: Russell & Russell Inc., 1962

APQ   *American Philosophical Quarterly*

Archiv   *Archiv für Geschichte der Philosophie*

CQ   *Classical Quarterly*

CR   *Classical Review*

JHS   *Journal of Hellenic Studies*

PAS   *Proceedings of the Aristotelian Society*

PQ   *Philosophical Quarterly*

PR   *Philosophical Review*

PS   Vlastos, Gregory. *Platonic Studies.* Princeton: Princeton
             University Press, 1973.

Plato I,   Vlastos, Gregory, ed. *Plato: A Collection of Critical Essays.*
   II   Vol. I, *Metaphysics and Epistemology.* Vol. II, *Ethics,
             Politics, and the Philosophy of Art and Religion.* Garden
             City, N.Y.: Doubleday & Company, 1971

RM   *Review of Metaphysics*

SPM   Allen, R.E., ed. *Studies in Plato's Metaphysics.* London:
             Routledge and Kegan Paul Ltd., 1965

Notes

1   Introduction

1.   I detect already a slightly incredulous query: "What about the Pythagoreans?" Well, it may be, as Aristotle says, that some early Pythagoreans believed things "imitated numbers." But even taking this testimony at face value, there is nothing in Aristotle's actual description of the Pythagoreans or in any extant Pythagorean fragments to suggest that they held the Platonistic theory (or some limited version of it) that I shall attribute to Plato.

2.   G.M.A. Grube, *Plato's Thought* (Indianapolis, 1980), 35.

3.   Paul Shorey, *The Unity of Plato's Thought*, (Chicago, 1903; repr. New York, 1968), 37. Aristotle less patiently dismisses the figure as empty metaphor (*Metaph.* 991a20-22).

4.   The most influential contemporary proponents of what I broadly call paradigm case interpretations are Gregory Vlastos and G.E.L. Owen. Owen especially

would, I think, claim Aristotelian ancestry for his interpretation of paradigmatic
Forms as "unqualified exemplars." See, for example, "A Proof in the *Peri Ideōn*,"
JHS 77 (1957, Part I): 103-111; repr. in *SPM*, 293-312. The view is explained further in chapter 2 below. For a similar reading see Gunther Patzig, "Platons Ideenlehre, kritisch betrachtet," *Antike und Abendlände* 16 (1970): 113-126. Aristotle's
own views on Plato's theory of Forms are often problematic, but do belong to the
general category of paradigm case interpretations.

Vlastos' "The Third Man Argument in the *Parmenides*," *PR* 63 (1954): 319-349
(*SPM*, 231-263), unleashed a still raging torrent of analysis and commentary on
the regress arguments of the *Parmenides*. The article provided a broad-based de-
fense of an "approximation" reading of participation (the view that each Form *F*
is itself perfectly *F* whereas worldly participants are only more or less imperfectly
F). Vlastos himself has since moved away from a *general* self-predicational interpretation, arguing that Forms will be instances of themselves only where that is
required in particular cases (Difference is different from other Forms; Beauty is
beautiful, and so on). But his earlier views are still widespread and in any case
comprise a clear and forceful presentation of an important type of reading.

5.   Martin Suhr, *Platons Kritik an den Eleaten* (Hamburg, 1969), 108. Cf. Harold
Cherniss' remarks on Aristotle's use of "*paradeigma*" at *Metaph.* 1013a 26-27 =
Ph. 194b 26, in *ACPA*, 464, n. 411.

6.   Hans Vater, *Die Dialektik von Idee und Teilhabe in Platons "Parmenides"*
(Hamburg, 1972), 106. Cf. J. Moreau, "Sur la signification du *Parmenide*," *Revue
Philosophique* 139 (1949): 97-131.

7.   The best known statement of this point is probably R.E. Allen's, in "Participation and Predication in Plato's Middle Dialogues," *PR* 69 (1960): 147-164 (*SPM*,
167-183).

8.   I will be using the variable "*F*" somewhat more promiscuously than might be
approved in our straight-laced times, to range over Forms, sensible participants,
universals, *et al.* To some extent, this generalizes the oft-noted ambiguity of the
Greek. For example, "*to kalon*" may in different contexts denote the Form of
Beauty and any and all things possessing beauty, in our world or the next. I have
tried to be sure my usage does not confuse or mislead.

9.   The views of R.E. Allen and E.N. Lee on how the analogy is to be applied
and on how this affects one's understanding of Plato's metaphysics are discussed
also in appendix 2.

10.   Thus Aristotle apparently considered it impossible that Forms which were in
no way immanent in worldly objects could be the *ousiai* of those objects. See

Metaph. 992a26-29, 991a 12-14. Cf. G. Vlastos: "If the Forms *were* attributes of particulars, 'Separation' would make no sense. . . . " ("The Third Man Argument in the *Parmenides," SPM*, 254 n.).

11. See E.N. Lee, "On the Metaphysics of the Image in Plato's *Timaeus," Monist* 50 (1966): 341-368. This is the implication also of Paul Shorey's remarks about "the inexpressible," and is the practical effect of interpretations that take "participation" not only as a primitive term, but as one about which nothing interesting can be said.

2   Varieties of *Paradeigmata*

1. The use of bad men as *paradeigmata* is recommended also at *Laws* 854e and 862e.

2. Of course a single example will sometimes suffice. Socrates explains the Delphic oracle concerning his wisdom by the god's intent to make of him a *paradeigma*, as if to say "that man is wise who, like Socrates, realizes that in wisdom he is really of no account" (*Ap.* 23b). Socrates is an example of a man who knows that he does not know, and so is used by the god to illustrate an important truth about human wisdom. (See *Soph.* 251a7, *Phdr.* 262c, *Politicus* 277d, *Laws* 663e, 801b, 961e).

3. See also *Phlb.* 12e-13c, where colors and shapes are *paradeigmata* illustrating the fact that things different from one another, or even opposite, may yet belong to a single *genos*. Protarchus is supposed to see that this is true also of pleasures.

In *Prt.* 330a-b, Socrates' question whether the parts of virtue are alike or unlike is framed in terms of the *paradeigma* of the parts of the face; the parts will be unlike one another "if they are like the *paradeigma*." The parts of the face provide a clear example of dissimilarity and independence of function among the parts of a thing: Are we to view the virtues as another instance of the same sort? Victor Goldschmidt's *Le Paradigme dans la Dialectique Platonicienne* (Paris, 1947) contains useful observations on individual texts of this sort, but tries to fit almost all the dialogues into a rather tenuous four-fold scheme of Platonic dialectic.

4. It may be disputed whether the angler himself is the *paradeigma*, or the definition of the angler, or the particular process of defining the angler, but it does not matter for present purposes.

5. The *paradeigmata* need not be particulars. They may often in fact be specific *kinds* of something still more general. The *paradeigmata* of *Phlb.* 12-13, for instance, could be understood as types of color and shape rather than particular ob-

jects having some color or shape, or concrete instances of color. The stranger's examples of "discrimination" (*Soph.* 226b-c) could also be various *kinds* of activities rather than particular performances of those activities. As Alexander Nehamas has pointed out, "In this context [in which some respondent is trying to answer Socrates' question "What is . . . ?"] the word 'example' is peculiarly ambiguous." See his "Confusing Universals and Particulars in Plato's Early Dialogues," *RM* 29 (1975): 295.

6.   See especially Richard Robinson's helpful discussion in *Plato's Earlier Dialectic* (Oxford, 1953), 204-217.

7.   Homeric *paradeigmata* (the term is common in Homeric criticism but not found in Homer) are usually examples of what was said and done in a certain situation by some hero of the past, indicating what ought to be done now, in a similar situation. These, and any other *paradeigmata* taken as examples to be followed (or avoided), have normative connotations and so begin to shade over into type B: *paradeigmata* as standards. Most precedents or examples to be followed could find a place either among illustrative examples or among standards, depending on the emphasis of a given occurrence.

8.   Herodotus *may* refer to such a *paradeigma* at v. 62, if he has in mind something like a sample block of a certain type, composition, and workmanship. J.J. Pollitt lists thirteen such architectural *paradeigmata* attested epigraphically, including "a splendid Corinthian capital in stone, apparently the model for the capitals in the interior of the Tholos found at Epidaurus." See his *The Ancient View of Greek Art* (New Haven, 1974), 204-211, 212 n. 6.

9.   *Jahrbuch des Deutschen Archäologischen Instituts* 88 (1973). This example was pointed out to me by Charles Kahn, on information from Walter Burkert.

10.   The *Euthryphro* contains a notorious occurrence of *paradeigma* in the sense of "standard":

> Then tell me what this character [*idea*] itself is, so that by looking to and using it as a standard [*paradeigma*], I may declare whatever you or anyone else may do that is of that sort [*toiouton*] to be holy, and declare whatever is not of that sort to be unholy. (6e)

The passage is at least a harbinger of the theory of Forms, and is often thought to treat its *idea* as a paradigm case or standard instance of holiness. But I do not set it down here as an example of *paradeigmata* type B, because it seems quite impossible to say what sort of standard Socrates intends. The fact is that *any* of our *paradeigmata* (except those of type A) may be *standards* to which one may look in judging whether particulars are or are not "of a certain sort"; this feature of the passage cannot determine any one reading in particular. Socrates' use of *toiouton* does not help because it is just as much at home in talk about images and models (section D) where the image *F* is said not to be another real *F*, as it is in the case of paradigm and non-paradigm *F*s. The term could even be used with a "pattern" interpretation of the *eidos* in mind (section C).

Nor does Socrates' request hinge in any way on narrowing the sense of *paradeigma*, rather than taking it in a broad sense that would encompass various sorts of standard. On the contrary, the course of the ensuing search for the *eidos* of holiness, during which it appears in turn as "being loved by the gods," "being loved by all the gods," "service to the gods," and "the art of prayer and sacrifice," calls rather for a loose sense of standard: for a broad conception of the Holy itself as simply that to which we look in deciding whether given acts are holy or unholy. Nothing is implied or presupposed about the particular manner in which the comparison or reference is to be made.

11. See P.T. Geach, "The Third Man Again," *SPM*, 276; R.S. Bluck, "Forms as Standards," *Phronesis* 2 (1957): 115ff.; Wittgenstein, *Philosophical Investigations*, sec. 50. A doctrine of analogous predication could of course be developed so as to cover cases in which the analogues are not similar in the manner of paradigm and non-paradigm *F*. This sometimes occurs in theological discussions of how a given term can apply both to God and to worldly creatures.

12. See Colin Strang's citation from Norman Feather in "Plato and the Third Man," *Plato I*, 190.

13. A further variant on this approach to Forms as paradigm cases, consistent with all three versions described above, and perhaps actually part of what their advocates intend, would make the Form an exemplar which has *only* the property of being *F* (something like an "idealized, frictionless plane"). This would also reflect one possible reading of the Form's being "single-natured" (*monoeides*). Such a reading would bring along all those problems common to every self-exemplificational interpretation, plus one of its own: the impossibility of being just *F* and nothing more.

14. The idea finds expression in Charles Bigger's *Participation: A Platonic Inquiry* (Baton Rouge, 1968). Forms receive a "dynamical interpretation": They must be not merely principles of determinateness, but immanent in their participants, "real constituents in effectively channeling the flux" (128). See esp. the whole of Bigger's chapter 4. For a different immanent Form approach, on which Plato attempts to "deconstruct particulars" into Forms or portions of Forms without

remainder, see John Moline, *Plato's Theory of Understanding* (Madison, 1981), 116. Moline's discussion of the *dynameis*, or power elements, present in particulars and the possible connection of early medical uses of *"eidos"* and *"dynamis"* to Plato's thought is extremely interesting and should be read in connection with the question of the nature of worldly particulars regardless of how one asesses its bearing on the nature of separate Forms.

15. Paul Natorp, *Platos Ideenlehre* (Leipzig, 1903). For references to other proponents of this approach (J.A. Stewart, Constantine Ritter *et al.*) and to some of their principal critics, see Harold Cherniss, *ACPA*, 207, n. 124.

16. Carl Friedrich von Weizäcker, "Platonic Natural Science in the Course of History," *Main Currents in Modern Thought* 29 (1972): 8.

17. Gilbert Ryle believed that Plato's "Italian principle of the limit/limitable (prominent in the *Philebus*) led away from a two-worlds view towards a two-factors view. . . ." Ryle stops short of asserting that Plato himself realized where his principle led: Platonism was for Plato still a "deference," but "no longer a passion." Ryle, *Plato's Progress* (Cambridge, 1966), 252.

18. Shape need not be regarded as primary among structural properties. What is at issue is the specificity with which any of the structural properties of a thing (size, shape, spatial arrangement of parts) are determined. One might specify all of them quite narrowly, or specify some or all of them only within some wider range, or specify some while leaving others totally open.

19. J.L. Austin, *Sense and Sensibilia* (Oxford, 1962), lecture 7. Cf. Gregory Vlastos' use, in "A Metaphysical Paradox," *Platonic Studies* (Princeton, 1973), 46, of this sense of "real" to correct R.C. Cross's and A.D. Woozley's error of regarding "is real" and "exists" as synonymous in their *Plato's Republic: A Philosophical Commentary* (London, 1964). In a similar spirit, John Brentlinger has called this the "authenticating," as opposed to the "comparative" or "evaluative" use of "real." On the former use, "real" has the force of "genuine" or "authentic" as opposed to "imitation" in "imitation leather is not real leather." On the latter use one means, in saying something is a real *F*, that it is a good *F* or a very good *F*, as in "Abe is a real friend." (The example *could* be taken in the sense of "authentic," depending on context.) See "Particulars in Plato's Middle Dialogues," *Archiv* (1972): 150ff. Brentlinger sees clearly that a painting of a bed, say, is not another bed, not even an imperfect one, and also that the painting can be labeled "bed" although it is not literally a bed at all. He may also be right that Vlastos' interpretation of the Forms' being "really real" as compared with sensibles, goes wrong in that it fails to make full use of the "authenticating" sense of "real." Cf. Vlastos, "Degrees

of Reality in Plato," in *New Essays on Plato and Aristotle*, ed. R. Bambrough (New York, 1965), 1-20.

20. Austin, *Sense and Sensibilia*, 271.

21. I refer to "apparent" exceptions because, strictly speaking, the basic principles have not been violated; it is rather that one must recognize, though it may not be obvious, that the painting or reflection of a real *F* is not necessarily an image or imitation *F*.

22. From this point of view, a "scale model" or "modello" (which may have been employed by Greek architects and artists along with architectural *paradeigma*) would be an *eidōlon* or *mimēma* relative to the intended "real" artifact.

3   Image and Reality

1. "Metaphor," in *Models and Metaphors* (Ithaca, 1962), 25.

2. Note the substitution of "*eikōn*" for "*mimēma*" in this context. A third frequent variant is "*eidōlon*," image or likeness. In both the *Republic* and *Sophist*, Plato characterizes *mimēsis* as the production of *eidola* (*Rep.* 599d, *Soph.* 265a-b). This is not to say that all three terms may substitute for one another in all contexts.

3. I take it the non-sensibles studied in geometry are mathematical Forms, rather than "intermediate mathematicals." These objects of study are said to be *noēta* when connected with an unhypothetical first principle (511d2), and it is the *Form* that is the object of *noēsis*, and that gets connected in this passage to the ultimate first principle.

4. On this point see especially *Rep.* 501b. See also 484c-d and other references to molding a city (374a, 466a-b), sketching a constitution (414a), and shaping (*plattein*) moral character (377b-c, 500d).

5. As Harold Cherniss observes in "The Relation of the *Timaeus* to Plato's Later Dialogues," *SPM*, 361, the language of *Phdr.* 250a-d is recalled in the *Politicus*:

> Most people have failed to notice that, while some of the real entities naturally have certain sensible likenesses (αἰσθηταὶ τινες ὁμοιότητες) . . . , of the greatest and most precious entities no image (εἴδωλον) has been made clearly perceptible to men.

Whether the *thought* of the *Phaedrus* is recalled, or whether the *Statesman* has in mind only man-made images of earthly originals, is more controversial. (See G.E.L. Owen, "Plato on the Undepictable," in *Exegesis and Argument: Studies in Greek Philosophy Presented to Gregory Vlastos*, ed. E. N. Lee *et al.* (Assen,

1973), 349-361. Notice that the passage will in either case illustrate the opposition of mere image to real thing; whatever larger point Plato has in mind, he makes the point in part by appeal to the opposition of image *F* to real *F* (here, something like a lion and a picture of a lion).

6. F.C. White may well be right that Plato "only gradually worked out the refinements of such a doctrine" ("Plato's Middle Dialogues and the Independence of Particulars," *PQ* 27 (1977): 202). But his claim that Plato "came to such a view after the *Phaedo*," or "that there is in the *Phaedo* no mention at all of particulars as images (*eikones*), likeness (*homoiōmata*), imitations (*mimēmata*) or anything of the kind," misses the importance of the passages just cited.

7. It will be clear in many contexts, including the present one, that I talk of a difference in sort, kind, or type between *F*s in a sense strong enough to rule out property sharing between image *F* and model *F* with respect to being *F*. We saw that in a weaker sense the copy-standard relation can also preserve a distinction in kind between paradigm and non-paradigm cases, even while the two are similar in respect *F* (chapter 2, B).

8. For an excellent survey and discussion of *fifth* century occurrences of "*mimesis*" and relevant cognates see Gerald F. Else, "Imitation in the Fifth Century", *CP* (1958): 73-90.

9. At the same time these examples set off Plato's notion of image *F* as contrasted with real *F* from most contemporary theories of representation and thing represented. The two views are similar in rejecting certain assumptions about the role of similarity in imaging (or representation). Nonetheless these are importantly different sorts of theory. On the latter, but not the former, one real *F* can represent, symbolize, or even depict another real *F*—or *itself*, for that matter. Thus a representation of an *F* would not necessarily be an image *F* or imitation *F* in Plato's sense. In fact either a (Platonic) image *F* or a real *F* could perfectly well represent a real *F*.

10. I am indebted here to Eva Keul's remarks on the passage in *Plato and Greek Painting*, Columbia Studies in the Classical Tradition, 5 (1978): 83. On the controversy about the exact nature of *skiagraphia* see Keul's chapter 4. Cf. J.J. Pollitt, *The Ancient View of Greek Art: Criticism, History and Terminology* (New Haven, 1974), 247-254, and Elizabeth G. Pemberton, "A Note on *Skiagraphia*," *American Journal of Archaeology*, 80 (1976): 82-92.

11. Cf. Alexander Nehamas: "As the products of *mimesis* are images of real things, so the practice of *mimesis* is the image of a real practice." See his "Plato on Imitation and Poetry in *Republic* 10," in *Plato on Beauty, Wisdom, and the Arts*,

ed. J.M.E. Moravcsik and P. Temko (1982), 63. Plato can still distinguish his own production of a soul or city in *logos* from that of Homer or Zeuxis by the fact that *they* are guided by appearance while his production is based on knowledge of the Good and the Just. The point is well put by David Gallop, in "Image and Reality in Plato's *Republic*," *Archiv* 47 (1965): 130.

12.   D.R. Grey, "Art in the *Republic*," *Philosophy* 27 (1952): 296.

13.   Thus it seems to me G.E.L. Owen misses this crucial implication of the image analogy:

> . . . certainly Plato later concluded that the *eidos* should be regarded as "*being* that which the particular *has* as an attribute" . . . – the necessary type distinctions are forced by Parmenides' first regress (132a1-b2) and sketched in *Tht.*, 156e, 182a-b; but to expound μέθεξις in the idioms of resemblance and copying is just to show that one has not yet grasped these type-distinctions.

("The Place of the *Timaeus* in Plato's Dialogues," *SPM*, 320, n. 4.)

14.   Actually Cratylus' position is even more extreme. He wants imaging (like naming) to be an all-or-nothing affair, so that strictly speaking only an exact duplicate will be an image of a given model. But because an exact duplicate would be another real Cratylus, it turns out that *none* of the images acknowledged by Cratylus will be images. Nor do I find any suggestion that in Socrates' general view an image of *F* is an incomplete (genuine) *F*. One might be tempted to view the particular example in this way, as it gradually approaches, then reaches the point of no longer being an image, but another Cratylus. But the argument does not depend on such a view of images; even here the logically operative dichotomy is "image of Cratylus/second (genuine) Cratylus." Recall Plato's description of imitation virtue; those *idola* and imitations were most definitely not cases of incomplete genuine virtue, but cases of non-virtue (or even the opposite of virtue).

15.   See Richard Robinson, *Plato's Earlier Dialectic* (Oxford, 1953), 218, 220; Cherniss, *SPM*, 375; J. Gosling, "Similarity in *Phaedo* 73b seq.," *Phronesis* 10 (1965): 155, 158; Alexander Nehamas, "Plato on the Imperfection of the Sensible World," *APQ* 12 (1975): 113; Sixten Ringbom, "Plato on Images," *Theoria* 31 (1965): 89, 96.

16.   The *Sophist's* distinction between *eikōn* and *phantasma* (235-6) is not that between duplicate or copy and image, but between two kinds of image – one whose form and color do reproduce those of its model, and one whose properties do not, although they appear to do so. Plato's examples are two statues, one true to life, one departing from the proportions of its original so that it will look right when

placed high above an observer. Richard Robinson (*Plato's Earlier Dialectic*, 220) corrects Cornford on this point (*Plato's Theory of Knowledge*, 198). Of course neither the accurate nor the deliberately disproportioned statue will be an Olympian god at all.

17.   With regard to *Phd.* 73b seq., Gosling observes "the point of similarity between *tauta ta isa* and *auto to ison* is *isotēs*, between *tauta ta kala* and *auto to kalon, kallos*, and so on." (See "Similarity in *Phaedo* 73b seq.," *Phronesis* 10 (1965): 152.

18.   See Aristotle, *Part. An.* 640b35-641a4 on the physician in a painting and the sculpted flute. See *De An.* 412b22 on the painted or sculpted eye (and cf. *Metaph.* 991a6-8). These images are not hands, eyes, or flutes "except in name" (*ouk et' ophthalmos, plēn homōnumōs*, according to *De An.*412b21). They are not classed as *pros hen legomena*—things called by a common name not equivocally but because they bear an appropriate relation to an item correctly and strictly called by that *onoma*.

19.   *On the Interpretation of Plato's Timaeus* (London, 1899), 109 ff.

20.   Cherniss, *SPM*, 376-377.

21.   Of course a statue or painting may be depicted in a painting, too. Also, one could produce an unending series of "levels" of *F*s since there could be images of images of images of *F* itself. But Plato wants, in most contexts, to place all and only "real" *F*s (*living* horses, *useful* shuttles, participants in the relevant Forms) on the second level. To collapse all the images of lower levels into a single category, one could simply place on the third level all *F*s called "*F*" because they are related to some second-level *F* by the ancestral of the relation *being an image of*. In other contexts, however, one might regard an image (say a statue) as "real" relative to its own shadow or reflection. This Plato does in the simile of the cave.

22.   My thanks for this point to Hide Ishiguro.

23.   Arthur Danto, "Representational Properties and Mind-Body Identity", *RM* 26 (1973): 405.

24.   In his arguments prior to the second regress (131a-132c), Parmenides uses the terms "*metechein*" and "*metalambanein*" (that is, "have a share of or in"). As terms of Plato's metaphysics these provide a less colorful and less suggestive metaphor than "imaging" or "imitation." It is worth noting that, on philological grounds, neither term need carry the meaning Parmenides gives them ("having a piece of") in his argument at 131a8-c5. The phrase "*metechein tēs poleōs*" ("have a share in, or participate in, the city"), for example, found in Pericles' citizenship law of 451-450, does not mean that each citizen shares in the *polis* only when, and

so far as, he possesses one bit of the city rather than another. (See Cynthia Patterson, *Pericles' Citizenship Law of 451-450* [New York, 1981] for a full discussion of these and other occurrences.) It would be better to say that although different citizens may participate in different ways, each has a share in civic life considered as a whole. This is more in line with Socrates' image (131b) of the day, which is everywhere at once without being split up into parts or separated from itself. Parmenides quickly diverts attention away from this line of thought, however, by appealing to his own figure of the sail spread over many sailors, where one can say that this piece, rather than that, is over each particular sailor.

With regard to the image analogy, one could say that various portraits, statues, etc., image Napolean from different viewpoints and by different means, but are all images of one and the same human being and can all be labeled "Napolean" rather than "Napolean's left side" or "Napolean's front," even if in another sense they image only parts, or views, of him.

The "political" use of "*metechein/metalambanein*" is also more in line with the idea that each Form "is present as a whole" to each participant. In Plato's Platonism, the Form is not spatially present to each participant, thus "separated from itself." Rather, each participant participates in the Form of the whole: Each ox participates in the Form of Ox—rather than in one piece of the Form. This holds even if sensibles participate in some generic Form (e.g., Animal) *by* participating in one of its parts (human) rather than another.

Perhaps one advantage "*metechein*" has over "*mimeisthai*" is that it carries the suggestion of communality, of common sharing among participants. The point can be conveyed by the image analogy, however.

25.   Review of Paul Wilpert, *Zwei Aristotelische Früschriften über die Ideenlehre* (Regensburg, 1949), *Mind* 61 (1952): 108ff. Ackrill also observes "The relation between Man and men is for Plato analogous to that between men and imaginary men. Imaginary men do not constitute an extra sort of man alongside Frenchmen, Italians, etc. . . . "

26.   Cherniss, *SPM*, 366 ff.

27.   This is similar to a point made by Vlastos in his discussion of the first regress ("The Third Man Argument in the *Parmenides*," *SPM*, 233.)

28.   The only serious attempt I know of to work through recent research on relevance logic and to evaluate its importance for the study of Plato is contained in William Rumsey's *A Commentary on Plato's Sophist* (Ph.D. dissertation, Columbia University, 1980).

29.   "The Logic of the Third Man," *PR* 80 (1971): 448-475.

30. Advocates of this approach include Proclus, *In Parmenidem* (V. 125, Cousin); Taylor, *The Parmenides of Plato* (Oxford, 1934), 26; Cornford, *Plato and Parmenides*, 94; V. Goldschmidt, *Le Paradigme Dans la Dialectique Platonicienne*, (Paris, 1947), 44; *et al.* For helpful discussion of Proclus' particular version, see R.F. Hathaway, "The Second Third Man," in *Patterns in Plato's Thought*, ed. J.M.E. Moravcsik (Dordrecht, 1973), 89 ff.

31. Cf. G.E.L. Owen, "The Place of the *Timaeus* in Plato's Dialogues", *SPM*, 319 n. 3.

32. Or, if Platonism entered at all, it would be only *via* a realist account of similarity itself.

33. See the references to Wittgenstein, Geach, and Bluck in chapter 2, n. 10. The approach is developed in greater detail by William Prior, "Parmenides 132c-133a and the Development of Plato's Thought," *Phronesis* 24 (1979): 230-240. Prior has since reconsidered his endorsement of this position.

34. So also Cherniss, "The Relation of the *Timaeus* to Plato's Later Dialogues," *SPM*, 364. It would hardly be possible or fruitful to review here all extent replies to the regress. Ed Lee's detailed proposal in "The Second 'Third Man': An Interpretation," in *Patterns in Plato's Thought*, ed. J.M.E. Moravcsik (Reidel, 1973), is discussed in appendix 2.

35. This sort of argument could be derived from remarks of John Brentlinger, "Particulars in Plato's Middle Dialogues," *Archiv für Geschichte der Philosophie*, 64 (1972): 152 (although he does not himself have such an argument in mind). The basic form of the argument used here was suggested to me by Ed Lee, and can be related naturally to his discussion of resemblance and imitation in "The Second 'Third Man': An Interpretation."

36. The only clear statement I have found of this argument is in F.C. White, "Plato's Middle Dialogues and the Independence of Particulars," *PQ* 27 (1977): 208. R.E. Allen anticipates it and proposes an answer in "Participation and Predication in Plato's Middle Dialogues," *SPM*, 50-51. White does not mention Allen's argument; my objections to Allen are aired in Appendix 2.

4   Predicates, Perfection, and *Paradeigmata*

1. See G. E. L. Owen, "A Proof in the *Peri Ideōn*," *SPM*, 301. Plato's use of the term "homonymous" leaves open the question of *why* homonymous things have the same *onoma*. Plato's usage differs from Aristotle's "(bare) homonymy" where

the homonymous things have, one might say, nothing in common but the *onoma*. On Plato's theory it will be participation, however that is to be explicated, which grounds the application of the same *onoma* to participant as to Form.

2.   Thomas Bestor might insist that strictly speaking only certain compounds with "*F*" ("the *F* itself" or "what-is-*F*"), rather than "*F*" *simpliciter*, apply to Forms. See his "Plato's Semantics and Plato's *Parmenides*," *Phronesis* 25 (1980): 38-75. Bestor's evidence for this claim seems to me slight and far from conclusive. In any case, I will try to show that (a) the supposedly calamitous results of letting *F* itself have the preeminent claim to the onoma "*F*" do not in fact come about, and (b) Plato had definite reasons for insisting on the Forms' prior and strict right to be called "*F*." On my view, the fact that Forms are routinely referred to by such compounds as "what-is-*F*" or "the *F* itself" reflects not a desire to avoid calling them "*F*," but an emphatic affirmation of their special claim to the *onoma*.

A final terminological aside: *Eponomadzein* does not by itself mean naming one thing *after* another, but only naming, dubbing, or calling something by a name. However, the occurrences in which we will be interested do involve the calling of sensibles after Forms in which they participate.

3.   See Allen, "Participation and Predication . . . ," *SPM*, 46; Cherniss, "The Relation of the *Timaeus* . . . ," *SPM*, 370 ff.; and Bestor, "Plato's Semantics and Plato's *Parmenides*," *Phronesis* 25 (1980): 58.

4.   Richard Patterson, "The Unique Worlds of the *Timaeus*," *Phoenix* 35 (1981): 105-119.

5.   At one time Gregory Vlastos saw *Prt.* 330c as a "star instance of [regress-prone] self-predication" ("The Third Man Argument in Plato's *Parmenides*," *SPM*, 249) asserting that the Form is itself virtuous—as if it were a moral agent rather than the intelligible Nature of justice. He now regards it instead as a case of Pauline predication (after St. Paul's "Charity suffereth long and is kind") asserting that everyone who is just is just, everyone just is holy, and so on, or that the Forms' instances are related in the way indicated (*PS*, 252, and "A Note on 'Pauline Predications' in Plato," *Phronesis* 19 (1974): 95-101). Whatever reservations one may have about this interpretation of the passage and about those two formulations of Pauline predication, Vlastos has shown that certain statements which could be used to predicate justice or piety absurdly of an abstract Form would normally be understood, in a conversational context, as perfectly reasonable, even obviously true statements about moral agents. In this constructive spirit I would add that in their own context the statements of *Prt.* 330 need not be thought of as speaking metaphorically or indirectly about *people* (though they imply statements about people),

but could be literally or directly about justice as a "dispositional quality manifesting itself in action" (*PS*, 229 n. 20), a "permanent organizational state of the soul" (C.C.W. Taylor, *Protagoras*, 110), "motive forces" (Terry Penner, "Thought and Desire in Plato," *Plato II*, 96-118), something like a person's "moral sense" (Hutcheson, cited by Grote, *Plato and the Other Companions of Socrates*, II, 304 n. 2), or an "innate characteristic" (J.W. Forrester, "Some Perils of Paulinity," *Phronesis* 20 [1975]: 11-21). That is, the interlocutors could have in mind some version of what Socrates in the *Phd*. calls the "*F*-in-us*." To say it is absurd to call such things just or unjust, on grounds that people rather than dispositions or states are just or unjust, would be willfully parochial. In any case such statements do arise in conversational contexts: A rancorous disposition is one that makes its possessor rancorous. Honorable intentions make the intender honorable; deviant tendencies make their possessor deviant. Here one has a way different from Vlastos' of reading the *Prt*. statements as normal, everyday discourse rather than absurd statements about Platonic Forms. (Against the interpretation of *Prt*. 330c as obliquely about people rather than directly about the "things" [*pragmata*] justice and piety as characteristics of people, see esp. Forrester, 20 ff.)

Considered as an interpretation of Socrates' language in its own context, this sort of reading of justice and piety also has the advantage (over readings of the just itself as a Platonic Form) of making sense of Protagoras' immediate agreement that there is such a thing as justice, that it is just, and so on. Surely Protagoras would not begin a discussion of the unity of virtue by freely admitting there are Platonic Forms.

One reason readers do see Forms at 330c is Socrates' use of the terminology of the theory of Forms: "*auto to dikaion*" and "*auto to hosion*." But this language is also used by Plato in the *Phd*. of the *F*-in-us, which is what justice turned out to be on any of those readings surveyed above. Again, in *Cra*. 413b-c, justice is first said, on inspired etymological grounds, to be the sun, then to be "fire itself" (*auto to pur*), then "the heat itself in the fire" (*auto to thermon to en tōi puri enon*). Socrates has not changed the subject from the sun to a Form of Fire, then to a Form of Heat. Moreover, I know of no one who takes Socrates to be speaking of Forms at *Prt*. 351e when he refers to "pleasure itself" as *tēn hedonēn autēn*.

In sum, the passage provides no firm evidence for any inference about the nature of separate Platonic Forms. If one *must* find a way of construing *Prt*. 330c as about Forms, the balance of this chapter will suggest how that might be done. But even that would be a treacherous business because the passage poses the especially difficult problem of distinguishing what Socrates can reasonably be said to believe from what Socrates, for whatever purposes are guiding the discussion at that point, gets Protagoras to agree to.

6. Whether or not the emendation of Boeckh (followed by Burnet) at c1-2 is accepted makes no difference here. The translation given follows the text of the manuscripts.

7. I would stress the "we" because I do not wish to presuppose (or deny) on Plato's part a theory of the use(s) of "is" dividing them into copulative or predicative, existential, and identifying. The points I wish to make here are neutral concerning that issue. Also, I have not claimed that *"einai ti"* has, of itself, the force of an existence claim. One might say that more often the *"ti"* will, in both Plato and Aristotle, stand for a predicable, so that saying a thing is something or other will presuppose, but not directly assert, the thing's existence. The present point is that in *this* context Plato has used the phrase, in part, to assert existence in a more direct way.

8. Strictly speaking only Beauty itself is securely *kalon*; other things must participate in Beauty if they are to be *kalon*. See Nehamas, "Self-Predication and Plato's Theory of Forms," *APQ* 16 (1979): 93 ff.

9. For this reason Helmut Meinhardt's study, *Teilhabe bei Platon*, concentrating as it does on relations among Forms and treating the sensible/Form relation quite perfunctorily, is somewhat incomplete, considered as the general study of participation promised in the title.

10. Colin Strang, "Plato and the Third Man," *Plato I*, ed. Vlastos, 193.

11. Nicholas White also speaks with evident disapproval of Plato's being "willing to think of the term 'Simmias' as correctly applicable both to the man Simmias and to a portrait of him (the latter application being somehow less proper and privileged than the former)," *Plato On Knowledge and Reality* (Indianapolis, 1976), 68. Also see 86, n. 54, on Plato's "slide" from denoting to describing the Form as *"F."* White expresses a doubt probably shared by many readers of Plato. But the willingness of which he speaks is ours as well as Plato's, as one can verify through most any newspaper, magazine, illustrated encyclopedia or dictionary, textbook of anatomy, child's picture book, or museum. The practice of calling, captioning, or labeling an image after its model is so habitual it seems easily to escape notice, so that when encountered explicitly in Plato it can strike one as something strange.

12. The point does *not* presuppose a Form of Horse at any particular stage in Plato's writings. The relation of picture or reflection to real horse will illustrate the relation of sensible to Form (say, visible equals to Equal) whether or not there happens to be a Form of Horse.

13.   The last phrase is not commonly used by Plato himself, though its use is clearly justified by what he does say. *"Auto to F"* occasionally applies to things other than Forms. It is used of the *F*-in-us at *Phd.* 103b (and perhaps also at *Prt.* 330c-e) and of sensible particulars at *Rep.* 532a3-5. Where Forms are also involved in such passages, other devices may distinguish the Form itself (e.g., the sensible/intelligible contrast).

14.   For other passages from the *Republic* concerned with the question of whether something deserves a certain name, or is rightly called by the same name (or a different name) from something else, see esp. 422e, 429a, 431b,d, 458c, 470d-e, 476b (with 480a6-7,11-12), 576a, and the interestingly Thucydidean passage on how, under extreme cirsumstances, good qualities of the soul come to be called by names of their opposites, and *vice versa* (560d).

15.   In certain contexts Plato makes further refinements. At *Soph.* 261e-262e he marks out, within the broad range of *onomata*, two categories crucial to the concept of a *prōtos logos*, namely, *onomata* and *rhēmata*. This is not a distinction between names and descriptions or predicates and does not affect the point made above. He also sometimes is stingy with *onomata*, maintaining only natural sorts of things, as opposed to arbitrary ones, deserve an *onoma* (see *Soph.* 225c). For discussion of the point see Norman Kretzmann, "Plato on the Correctness of Names" *APQ* 8 (1971): 126-139; Gail Fine in *Philosophical Quarterly* 27 (1977): 296 ff.; chapter 6, below.

16.   Thomas Bestor argues the point well in "Common Properties and Eponymy in Plato," *Philosophical Quarterly* 28 (1978): 189-208.

17.   See J.M.E. Moravcsik, "The 'Third Man' Argument and Plato's Theory of Forms," *Phronesis* 8 (1963): 52, and Vlastos, "Self-Predication and Self-Participation in Plato's Later Period," *PS*, 337 n. 8.

18.   R. Martin "Selbstprädikation bei Platon," *Kantstudien* 58 (1967): 209-228.

19.   Not to be too glib about an important matter: There is some danger, especially on a paradigm-case reading of Forms, of trivializing this ultimate revelation, as if the initiate encounters things pretty, prettier, and prettiest (Miss Universal?). To understand why Beauty is surpassingly beautiful even among Forms one must not only acknowledge the potential beauty of abstract objects, but also, I think, appreciate the key position of Beauty among the Forms and its role as *aitia* of all beauty in the created world. If Beauty is the same Form as the Good, chapter 6 will have something more to say about this question.

20.   For discussion of this generalizing step see especially Nehamas, "Participation and Predication in Plato's Late Dialogues", *RM* 63 (1982): 343-374.

21. Hence, in G.E.L Owen's apt phrase, they are "non-relative relatives."

22. See Moravcsik, "Recollecting the Theory of Forms," in *Facets of Plato's Philosophy*, ed. W.H. Werkmeister (Assen/Amsterdam, 1976), 11.

5   The Imperfection of the Sensible World

1. See *Phd.* 102d9, 104c1, d1, d6, e10, 105d3, d10, 106a4, and Burnet's notes on these passages in *Plato's Phaedo* (Oxford, 1911). Cf. D. O'Brien, "A Metaphor in Plato: 'Running Away' and 'Staying Behind' in the *Phaedo* and the *Timaeus*," *CQ* 27 (1977): 297-299.

2. See Robert Turnbull, "Aristotle's Debt to the Natural Philosophy of the *Phaedo*," *PQ* 8 (1958): 133. Diotima's notion is in one way broader than Timaeus', for her images of excellence, including various kinds of learning, would be in souls as well as in corporeal things. Timaeus' medium for psychic images of Forms would be not the receptacle but the intermediate material of which souls are composed.

3. Compare Aristotle's use in *Cat.* of *being in something* as a mark of dependence on that subject in which a thing is found. Diotima and Timaeus would agree that Forms show no such dependence on particulars or on place in general.

4. A related issue may be troubling some readers: It is generally, if not quite universally, assumed the images of Forms are worldly individuals rather than particular property instances or characters of things. (Thus Socrates for example, rather than the F-in-Socrates, is an image of the Form of F.) The general assumption seems to me to be correct. The *Phd.* tells us worldly participants are named after (*eponomian echein*) the Forms in which they participate (102b). Simmias is then said to be called (*eponomian echei*) both small and great (102c, cf. 102b, e). The point is reflected precisely in the statement of the young "Socrates" in *Prm.*, according to which the things in our world get their names from the Forms in which they participate. Thus various humans (not the properties of humans) are called "slave" or "master" (133c-e). Similarly, possession of opposite properties by worldly participants is accounted for by their participating in Forms of opposites. In this way, *I* am one and many (129c-d), *sticks and stones* are one and many (129d). Notice both here and in the *Phd.* if part of the inferiority of images of F is that they admit of being un$F$ as well as F, the images cannot be identified with the F-in-us, because the latter never admits of being un$F$ (*Phd.* 103b).

The *Ti.* as a whole centers on creation of a vast sensible animal as an image of the divine intelligible animal (29a). In the difficult passage introducing the receptacle (48e-52c),Timaeus' basic distinction between Form and worldly image is retained, yet complicated by an account of one dark, hardly-to-be-expressed general condition of the generation of sensibles. Timaeus emphasizes that this gives a three-fold account of reality; he does not allow that a fourth has been introduced along with it (the recurrent characters of things, some have thought) — much less that some fourth sort now comprises the images of Forms.

Rep. X implicitly recognizes the carpenter's couch as an image of the Couch-in-Nature. In the middle books, just cities and human souls (rather than the justice in them, taken by itself) seem to be treated as images of the Just in Nature (500e).

I know of no passage in which a character or property instance is clearly treated as an image of a Form.

5. Plato usually speaks of an individual (rather than some plurality of individuals) as being equal, or as participating in Equal, Greater, or Less. One person participates in Equal because his size, in some respect, is the same as the size of something else. See, e.g., *Phd.* 102b-d on the relative heights of Socrates, Simmias, and Cebes.

6. Terence Irwin notes that an equal stick must have some definite length; that being, say, three feet long is not the same as being equal, and that being three feet long (a fact which we may *perceive*) is not a good guide to the nature of equality (*Plato's Moral Theory*, 150). This is true, but I have tried to bring out two underlying points. First, in being any particular number of feet long a sensible will be "scattered," composite, subject to dissolution, and cognitively accessible only through multifarious perturbations of our sense organs. Second, I believe the facts to which Irwin refers can be seen as symptomatic of the *incompleteness* of sensible equals. Each must have not only some definite length, but some length equal to the length *of some* (*other*) *thing*. As Irwin says, three feet long is not the same as being equal, and perceiving that a stick is three feet long does not tell us what equality is; it does not matter what the length is, so long as some other stick also has that length.

7. In one sense there are exceptions (see chapter 4, sec. D) in that some Forms are characterized by themselves and their opposites. (There, of course, Forms *are* *F* in relation to one relatum, un*F* in relation to another.) In these cases the ground-level exclusion of opposites still obtains, since the Form will not equally be the nature of *F* and the nature of un*F*.

8. With human justice one must generalize from sensibles, since souls are not sensible. The point is easily generalized, however, so long as souls can be regarded

as having relevant parts. See *Rep.* 435 ff. for one account of the relevant parts of the soul. A different description of the right ordering of the parts – and motions – of the soul is given in the *Ti.* (See 37a-c, 44b-c.)

9.   I agree with Irwin (*Plato's Moral Theory*, 319, n.34) that particular *kinds* of acts are just and unjust in the sense that some particular acts of each kind (returning what has been loaned to one, telling the truth) will be just, others unjust. Thus returning what has been loaned is, of itself, no more just than unjust, and cannot itself be the *aitia* of any act's being just. Individual *acts* need not be just and unjust, though their being one or the other still depends on their occurring in this or that specific context so that they are still incomplete.

10.   *If* coming-to-be and perishing entail being *F* and un*F*, then most members of kinds of living things and most artifacts will manifest this kind of being *F* and un*F*. (The question is complicated by the fact that, in the case of total destruction, it is not clear in what sense there is still a subject to *be* un*F*.) Even so, however, everlasting sensible animals like the cosmos and the created gods of the *Timaeus* will not be *F* and un*F* in that way, unless on a literal reading of the creation story.

11.   There is less *direct* evidence concerning numbers, but Plato's "unaddable" (*asymblētoi*) numbers seem, like the abstract numbers of some more recent Platonists, *not* to consist of pluralities of units. They do not earn *onomata* such as "three" or "even" by containing three or an even number of units, any more than Circle itself earns the *onoma* "circle" by having that shape. They seem to be distinguished from one another through relations of priority and posteriority, rather than through size. They are imaged by sensible pairs or trios or whatever, but are not themselves pairs or trios of intelligible monads. For helpful discussion of this question see John Cook Wilson, "On the Platonist Doctrine of the ἀσύμβλητοι ἀριθμοι," *Classical Review* 18 (1904). Cf. Sir David Ross, *Plato's Theory of Ideas* (Oxford, 1951), 180 ff.

12.   The epistemological parallel is that any sensible *F*, hence any sensible unity, can be perceived only *via* its direct and indirect effect on our corporeal organs of sense. The appearances of a given object are multifarious, as indefinitely numerous as the points of view from which it may be observed, and changing over time. We *see* it *as* one sensible by viewing these various and sundry appearances as *phainomena of* some one thing – e.g., one participant in some particular Form. So also one *sees* the diverse areas of color on a canvas, or light playing on a smooth surface, or darkness on a cave wall *as* a unity when one sees each as the image of some original. More graphically, one may think again of the components of

skiagraphia, which from close up appear multifarious (*polla kai hetera kai anomoia*), but from a distance appears coherent (*hen kai tauton kai homoion*). See *Prm.* 165c-d.

13.   I have discussed Timaeus' various descriptions of time and eternity in "The Eternality of Platonic Forms," forthcoming in the *Archiv für Geschichte der Philosophie.*

14.   If there are Forms of Uniqueness and Completeness we will have, as in the cases of Sameness, Difference, *et al.*, Forms that are abstract, intelligible exemplars of themselves. On why this does not jeopardize Plato's "Two World" ontology, see chapter 4, sec. D. For further treatment of the passage, see my "The Unique Worlds of the *Timaeus*," *Phoenix* 35 (1981). In that article, I also argued that the demiurge, perhaps unwittingly, conflates two matters: making the cosmos *better* in a way that brings it into closer resemblance with its model, and making the sensible cosmos a better *image* (a more faithful, accurate *eikōn*) of its model. Making the cosmos unique, e.g., may achieve the former, but it has no bearing on the latter. This conflation neither undermines the main features of Plato's general picture of craftsmanship, nor imports significant problems into Plato's his metaphysics.

15.   Ryle, "Plato's *Parmenides*," *SPM*, 105.

16.   This last way of putting the matter, in terms of having vs. being a Form, is potentially controversial, as it is usually thought to reflect a Platonistic interpretation of Forms as opposed to one or another paradigm-case interpretation. (For Plato's use of these terms, see *Cra.* 389b9-10, *Phd.* 103b3-c1, *Rep.* 597c7-9; cf. *Meno* 72c6 and the early *Lysis* 217d7-e1.) But in fact Plato's usage here seems to be as broad as his use of "participation." Both phrases can cover relationships between one *kind* of thing and another as well as between a kind (or a Form) and sensible members of that kind. Just as it is possible for Forms to participate in other Forms, so some intelligible natures can be said to possess or have others. So one cannot settle the central issues about the nature of Forms by supposing only worldly things (as opposed to intelligible natures) can *have* Forms. The fact which shows there is a strong type distinction between sensible and intelligible F is not, in itself, Plato's talk of "having" and "being" a Form, but his characterization of that type distinction through appropriate categorical distinctions between Form and sensible and, of course, through the image analogy.

17.   I say "tend" to share because this is not essential to the exclusive F-and-un$F$ reading of worldly inferiority. If being F at one time and un$F$ at another counts as a kind of being-F-and-un$F$, this approach can *perhaps* be extended to allow for

Forms corresponding to sortal notions (man, ox, shuttle). Besides the problem mentioned in n. 10, above, this would involve loosening the notion of an opposite, since *being man, ox, shuttle*, etc., have no natural opposites.

18.   The passages distinguishing disputed predicates are *Alc*. I, 111b, e; *Phdr*. 263a6-7; *Euthphr*. 7b-d. Irwin emphasizes the three-fold distinction established in these passages: disputed cases with no established "decision procedure" (as with *just*, beautiful); disputed cases in which there is a decision procedure (as with quantitative properties one can determine by counting, weighing, or the like); non-disputed cases, such as gold, iron. (C. Strang and G.E.L. Owen speak only of a two-fold distinction, but as Irwin points out, conflation of the first two categories can lead to error.)

19.   See Owen, *SPM*, 307. Cf. Patzig, "Platons Ideenlehre kritisch betrachtet," *Antike und Abendlände* 16 (1970): 116.

20.   Nehamas brings out clearly how a limited population of Forms, an exclusive *F*-and-un*F* reading of inferiority, and a specific motivation for postulating Forms (as *definienda*) may go together. "Plato on the Inferiority of the Sensible World," *APQ* 12 (1975); see page 108 on Forms in the *Phd.* and middle *Rep.* only for incomplete predicates; 109 on imperfection as incompleteness (or accidental possession of properties); 116 ff. for Plato's motivation. (See below, however, on an important difference between predicates for *opposites* and *incomplete* predicates.)

21.   Explicit recognition of this point is rare, but see J. Annas, *An Introduction to Plato's Republic* (Oxford, 1981), 234.

22.   G. Fine, "The One over Many." *PR* 89 (1980): 231, 234.

23.   See F.C. White, "The *Phaedo* and *Republic* V on Essences," *JHS* 98 (1978): 144 ff. Cf. Nehamas, "Plato on the Inferiority of the Sensible World," *APQ* 12 (1975): 108 ff., who seems to use "being completely *F* " and "being essentially *F* " interchangeably. White takes considerable pains to formulate and assess different possible versions of a Platonic essentialism.

24.   As F.C. White points out, *art. cit.*, 148, n. 22.

25.   As F.C. White does, *ibid.*

26.   To say Plato believed *logoi* said something about something is not to imply he always had worked out a theory of *logos*, like that of the *Soph.* distinguishing different categories of linguistic expressions found in a "primary sentence," one of which (the *onoma*) indicates the subject about which something else is said by means of the other (the *rhēma*). It does not require mastery of even that much explicit theory to regard opinions and *logoi* as saying something about something.

27.   Again, within the realm of corporeal imitations the image will try to duplicate

its model in certain respects. "Like" here refers to the "literal" similarity Socrates has been emphasizing, prior to his rejection of such similarity as the criterion of correctness at 432a-d. I take truthfulness, or faithfulness, as a general counterpart to the truth of *logoi*, to be the crucial and *universalizable* feature of images here; it would generalize to images whose faithfulness or correctness did not involve duplication of the model in respects other than F (again, dreams, and probably *logoi*, would serve as examples).

28. See, for example, Nelson Goodman's "Seven Strictures on Similarity," in *Problems and Projects* (Indianapolis, 1972), 437-447.

6   Models, the Good, and Participation

1. Socrates says sensible beauties are beautiful by participation in Beauty itself and that the same holds for all cases. He does not specify the range of "all cases"; this will become an important issue later on.

2. Abner Shimony, "The Nature and Status of Essences," *RM* 1 (1948): 48. Cf. Aristotle, *Metaph.* 992a 26-29, 99la 12-14, 1079b 15-18.

3. *Plato's Theory of Ideas* (Oxford, 1951), 226.

4. See Cherniss, *ACPA*, 298; Owen, *SPM*, 320 n. 4; Vlastos, *SPM*, 253 n. 1.

5. Discussions of Forms as *aitiai*, often concerned in large part with the notion of Forms as efficient causes, could use reorientation. Vlastos' treatment of Socrates' "simple" causes, in "Reasons and Causes in the *Phaedo*," *PR* 78 (1969): 291-325 (repr. *Plato I*, 132-166), ought to have advanced matters considerably in the right direction. Cherniss is especially helpful on the matter of souls, rather than Forms, as Platonic sources of motion (*ACPA*, esp. 413 ff.), although his conclusion that certain initial static images must be caused *directly* by Forms is disturbing. Explaining such images may be a problem, but I do not see how direct causality by separate Forms can be a solution.

Plato's analogy at *Ti.* 50d on which the Forms are father and the receptacle mother of participants as offspring might, if taken in isolation, suggest Forms not only constitute a source of determinateness for sensibles, but also serve as their efficient cause. Since, however, Timaeus goes on to say Forms "never receive anything from without or go out to anything else" (52a) it is hard to believe he means to portray them as efficient causes. Moreover, he supplies such a cause for the principal offspring in question in the passage (earth, air, fire, water) — namely, the Demiurge (53b). Plato's employment of this creator god tells against reading Forms as moving causes, whether the creator is intended literally or only as a symbol for rationality in the functioning of the cosmos. In fact the analogy at 50d illustrates *receptacle*—intrinsically indeterminate but entirely determinable—apparently by drawing upon a reproductive theory according to which the mother contributes, aside from nourishment, only unformed matter capable of taking on suitable form (51a-b). This is a feature of Aristotle's theory in *Gen. An.*

6. Obviously, many of those willing to consider governmental types as abstract objects would balk at giving them independent ontological status. That in itself is beside the present point, which is only to produce a coherent, even if counterfactual, analogue of what one takes Plato to be talking about.

7. Here I am indebted to a formulation of Ed Lee's, "The Second Third Man: An Interpretation," in *Patterns in Plato's Thought*, ed. J.M.E. Moravcsik, 102.

8. On another interpretation of the passage, even the argument just given becomes irrelevant (and unnecessary). It may be the passage should be translated not in the usual way, along the lines given above, but as saying only that, if there is an Idea, that Idea is indiscerptibly one, and must not be divided or multiplied. On this see J.A. Smith, "General Relative Clauses in Greek," *CR* 31 (1917): 69-71. This reading is attractive, especially with emphasis on the "one" (*"hen,"* a6) in reading and a comma after "plurality" (*"polla,"* a7). Smith argues that a reading on which a Form is posited for *every* plurality to which a common *onoma* is applied would require a relative clause employing either αν with the subjunctive or some form of the relative other than οἵς, such as οἵστισι or ὅσοις. This will not establish his own reading. See the reply to Smith by E.A. Sonnenschein, "The Indicative in Relative Clauses,"*CR* 32 (1918): 68-69. (Thanks, for this reference, to Nicholas White.) This is not, of course, to question the plausibility of the reading, but only to say a certain argument does not establish it. For yet another possible approach to the passage, see note 10, below.

9. The Stranger's wording may seem surprising, given his comments on (natural) *eidē* as opposed to (mere) *merē* in the *Statesman* (quoted above). The *eidē* of the *Statesman* presumably deserve an *onoma*—the dialectician's official place-marker for natural divisions—whereas mere *merē* do not. In the *Soph.* it is *eidē* that do not automatically deserve an *onoma*. The context of the later passage indicates, however, that the same point is being made: *"Eidos"* is now used in its generic sense to cover all sorts of divisions the mind of man (*logos*) may devise or imagine; natural *eidē* are those discovered by *nous* (227b1), which here serves to introduce the desired normative implication. (All this can be true, of course, even if in a later passage of the *Soph.* *"eidē"* does clearly refer, again, in context, to genuine Forms —as at 258c3.)

10. Gail Fine suggests, in "The One Over Many," *PR* 89 (1980): 214, that Socrates may have this use of "*onoma*" in mind at *Rep.* 596a, so that he there acknowledges a Form only for every natural grouping of many things, not for every term applied in common to many things.

11. See esp. *Cra.* 390c-d; *Statesman* 275d.; *Soph.* 225c, 227a-b; cf.*Rep.* 405d, 470b. Here I endorse a view argued more fully by Norman Kretzmann, "Plato On the Correctness of Names," *APQ* 8 (1971): 126-138.

12. See, e.g., David Wiggins, "Sentence Meaning, Negation, and Plato's Problem of Non-Being," in *Plato I*, 300; Gail Fine, *art. cit.*, 224ff.

13. Michael Frede, in *Prädikation und Existenzaussage* (Göttingen, 1967), 92 ff., put his finger on the single most puzzling case: The *Statesman* rejects a Form for *number different from 10,000*, although the *Soph.* discussion of Difference would imply (given a Form for the number 10,000) a Form for *different than 10,000*. I believe, however, the two dialogues are in agreement. *Different from 10,000* is a Form, because it is a natural part of Difference; *number different from 10,000* is not a Form because it neither fits the stated requirement for being a part of the Different, nor (unlike Odd or Even) constitutes a natural part of Number as such. It is just an arbitrary part of Number.

14. For further discussion of Aristotle's testimony concerning the naturalness of Forms, see above all Cherniss, *ACPA*, 239-260. Fine's examination of Aristotle's comments on an allegedly Platonic one-over-many argument (*art. cit.*) shows Aristotle did not take Plato to postulate a Form for every Greek predicate. Fine also correctly points out that (a) Plato himself nowhere argues for separate Forms simply by a one/many argument; (b) Plato wants separate Forms only for "genuine properties" of things, not for any and every aspect of things; (c) certain passages sometimes adduced as evidence for a more liberal population of separate Forms are in fact indifferent concerning that issue (e.g., *Meno* 75d5-e1, *Phd.* 102b2, c10-11, 103b7-8; *Chrm.* 175b2-4).

15. I.M. Crombie sees clearly the connection between the separateness of forms and the role of the Good as guarantor of their being and intelligibility. See *An Examination of Plato's Doctrines*, vol. 2 (London, 1963), 155 ff.

16. For fuller discussion and references, see Michael Rohr, "Empty Forms in Plato," *Archiv* 60 (1980): 268-283. Rohr actually argues for a stronger version of Platonic plenitude, but that need not be pursued here.

17. See Aristotle, *Metaph.* 1040b 27-34; 1086b 5-13. Cf. Vlastos, *SPM*, 253 n. 1. In between, the objection was expressed for several centuries in terms of the reification of universals.

One sometimes encounters a decided reluctance to believe Aristotle could have so misunderstood the theory of Forms. After all, he spent eighteen years in the Academy, was intensely interested in such issues as we have been discussing, and was himself a great metaphysician. True, but one must not forget, what is sometimes forgotten, that Plato's associates in that period included other competent philosophers (e.g., Speusippus, Xenocrates), and prominent early members of the Academy were divided from the start over Plato's meaning on key questions. It is puzzling such disagreement arose, but I do not see how one can assume Aristotle in particular must have had things right, on grounds that he was a philosopher, and that he was there. Still, I would be willing to hazard a more positive suggestion as to how Aristotle might have gone wrong in the way he did. First, the dialogues include passages that can reasonably and without perversity be read as Aristotle, and as many able commentators since, have read them. I have tried to show the Aristotelian reading in many cases does not hold up under close scrutiny, but that is hardly to say it is in any way bizarre or arbitrary. Aristotle had very strong views of his own about *eidē* as formal causes of sensibles. His position may have developed over time, and some aspects of it may have remained problematic. But he seems to have been deeply and unshakably convinced the form of a sense object could not exist apart from that object.

18. See Augustine, *De Diversis Quaestionibus* 83, q. 23; Aquinas, *ST*, I, 15, 2; Ralph Cudworth, *The True Intellectual System of the Universe*, vol. 3 (London, 1820), 66 ff.

19. Socrates affirms at the end of *Rep.* IX that even if no city such as he has described should ever exist on earth there is a *paradeigma* of it "laid up in heaven" (592a-b). The *paradeigma* determines the specific kinds of inhabitants, kinds of activities, and kinds of responsibilities (guardians, auxiliaries, carpenters, etc., and their functions) necessary for a just city.

20. To say the Good determines the population of Forms is not to deny the existence of "bad" Forms (Injustice, Ugliness, or Disease). If there are such Forms one may say the intelligible order includes Forms not only for the natural excellence of animals, plants, and artifacts, but also for the natural opposites of those excellences. That is, the "moral" Forms will, like *all* opposites, come paired with their own opposites and with the natural subspecies of those opposites. Epistemologically, the "bad" opposites are as objective as their correlatives, and known by the same knowledge. (This is *not* to say it is, in itself, good that the bad ones be exemplified in the cosmos!)

21. The interpretation of participation and of the nature of Forms as abstract ob-

jects given here is consistent with different views on the population of Forms in this or that period of Plato's career. The interpretation does not depend on assuming Forms of artifacts or living things as early as the *Phd.* A survey of various sorts of Forms will show how they are accomodated under one principle, whether or not Plato felt a need to expand or contract application of that principle over time.

22. Cf. Cherniss, *ACPA*, 254.

23. Jerry Fodor, *The Language of Thought*, (New York, 1975), 14.

24. This important similarity has not gone entirely unnoticed; some recent commentators portray Forms as very like natural kinds in a modern sense, or like properties in a sense used, for example, by Hilary Putnam or D.M. Armstrong. See Putnam, "On Properties," in *Essays in Honor of Carl G. Hempel*, ed. Nicholas Rescher (New York, 1970), 235-254, and Armstrong, "Towards a Theory of Properties," *Philosophy* 50 (1975): 145-155. For the comparison to Putnam and Armstrong, see Rohr, *art. cit.*, 274 n. 25. For a lengthier discussion of Plato in a similar vein see Crombie, *op. cit.*, vol. 2, 153-246. Cf. Fine, *art. cit.*

25. It is an important issue, but slightly to the side of present concerns, whether there is in Plato any independent epistemological argument for separate Forms. It is often taken as fairly obvious that *Rep.* 475 ff. or *Ti.* 51d-e contain such an argument. But if *epistēmē* of what is "really real" (in the former passage) or true *nous* (in the latter) must involve comprehension of the Forms' connection to the Good, then there will be no value-free (or, in a Platonic sense, "denatured") argument from certainty, or *aprioricity*, or the like. The point is especially obvious if one thinks of grasping Forms as a matter of gaining true understanding (and perhaps certainty) rather than attaining certainty, or *a priori* knowledge, alone.

26. On Plato's assimilation of *nature* (in the popular sense) to art, see especially Cherniss, *ACPA*, 240-259. Perhaps I should add that not every use of a natural artifact, not every performance of a "natural act," or every creation of a new member of some natural species will be good. These things must be done, as Plato emphasizes, at the right time, in the right way, in the appropriate context. The abstract natures of artifacts and living things do not themselves give us that sort of guidance. For that, one needs knowledge of such Forms as the Just or the Good.

27. Robert Turnbull's approach to the *Phaedo's* "theory of nature" in terms of Forms, the *F*-in-us, and things having *F* which "strive" to attain to the Form is thus much closer to Plato's own outlook than that of many ancient *physikoi*. See "Aristotle's Debt to the 'Natural Philosophy' of the *Phaedo*," *PQ* 8 (1958): 131-146. I would add that, in its ancient context, Plato's calling the Form (as opposed to the *F*-in-us or the things having *F*) the "*F-in-nature*" was surely quite pointed.

28. For these and other reasons, numbers, and certain types of distinctions and relations between them, find a place—in fact, a ground-floor position—in the order of natural essences. Recall also that harmonic ratios of numbers are essential for making the world (and human beings) rational, a vital step toward producing a good cosmos. For this purpose the Forms Being, Sameness, and Difference (whose function one might have supposed was more purely "logical") are also essential (*Ti.* 35a). Mathematics and various kinds of measure are also crucial for every natural art and science (see esp. *Rep.* 522c, *Statesman* 284d, *Philb.* 55d-57a).

29. The *Meno*'s examples of bees, strength, size, health, shape, color, and its main concern, virtue (71e ff.), are already suggestive of Plato's concern with the natural. So, too, is Socrates' tantalizing remark, in the course of his demonstration that learning is really recollection, that the soul can in principle recover all knowledge once it has gotten started "because all nature is akin" (81c9-d1).

30. G. Santas goes further, asserting that without regress-prone self-predication there is no way to understand the Good's being the source of the being and essence of any other Forms ("The Form of the Good . . . ," p.16).

31. If memory serves, I am indebted to Michael Rohr for this formulation.

32. We may note, if not resolve, a serious question for Plato: If, as *Rep.* 511c1-2 seems to suggest, there is (a) some principle of goodness entirely intrinsic to the intelligible realm which determines the realm of Forms, *why* should the principle yield (b) a system of Forms that is, as in the *Ti.*, the optimal model for a created cosmos? Perhaps the Good is, after all, the objective, eternal nature of goodness *for* a sensible cosmos. This would not jeopardize its ontological independence, since it would exist, perfectly well defined, awaiting apprehension and exemplification, even if no sensible cosmos ever came into being. Nor would its being defined in terms of Forms of worldly objects make it dependent upon any actual worldly things. I am not entirely comfortable with this answer; however, it is beside the main issues and is not connected with any particular interpretation of Forms. Presumably both (a) and (b) should be acknowledged in some guise by all interpretations.

33. E.N. Lee, "The Metaphysics of the Image in Plato's *Timaeus*," *Monist* 50 (1966): 341-368.

7   Conclusion

1. In view of chapter 6, one must not conclude that every predicate of Greek, or even every predicate true of many individuals, corresponds to a Form.

2. E.g. Cherniss, "The Philosophical Economy of the Theory of Ideas," *SPM*, 1-12; R.C. Cross and A.D. Woozley, *Plato's Republic: A Philosophical Commentary.* (London, 1966), esp. 178-179; J.M.E. Moravcsik, "Recollecting the Theory of Forms," in *Facets of Plato's Thought*, ed. W.H. Werkmeister (Assen, 1976), 1-20. These lists sometimes, but by no means always, distinguish between the two basic epistemological roles of Forms (as grounds of sense perception and objects of strict knowledge) and between their two *aitiological* roles (as formal *aitiai* and as models for making). Moravcsik surveys various lists in "Recollecting the Theory of Forms" and presses the questions whether any adequate list would be internally consistent, whether the functions assigned to Forms would fit Plato's general characterization of Forms, and whether all of these would harmonize with Plato's arguments for Forms.

3. See *Word and Object* (Cambridge, Mass., 1960), esp. chapter 7. This is obviously not a description of Quine's metaphysics, which would require discussion of *why* he countenances sets. Various alternative ontologies are discussed here only so far as is necessary for bringing out relevant contrasts with Platonic Forms.

4. I say "traditional" head because this familiar characterization, while adequate for present purposes, obscures some important subtleties and difficulties in Aristotle's views on universals.

5. For discussion of this sort of theory see the symposium "Are the Characteristics of Particular Things Universal or Particular?," G. Dawes-Hicks, G.E. Moore, and G.F. Stout, *PAS*, Suppl. Vol. 3 (1923): 95-128.

6. The realm of eternal possibilities *is* limited to some extent, since there will be no such possibility for round squares. But this falls far short of what Plato requires by way of population control.

7. See *Science and the Modern World* (New York, 1925), esp. "Abstraction." I do not say that Whitehead unambiguously intends this meaning of "ingression"; only that it looks to me like a reasonable (and controversial) reading. But it is more important for now that a certain theory type be described and contrasted with Platonic platonism than that a particular interpretation of Whitehead be established. Sir David Ross once attributed this sort of Plato to Aristotle on grounds that (a) Aristotle says Plato separated Forms and (b) Aristotle frequently mentions "participation" (*methexis*) of sensibles in Forms, which term implies (according to Ross) immanence of Forms (*Metaphysics* I, xlii). But (b) is without force, since Aristotle refuses to attach any such ontological import to this terminology. For a fuller reply to Ross see Cherniss, *ACPA*, 206, n. 123.

8. On God's ideas, models, or archetypes of kinds of things, and even of in-

dividual things (which introduces a further difference from Plato), see Aquinas, *ST*, I, 15, 1-2; cf. Augustine, *De Div. Quaest.* 83, q. 46; cf. qq. 23, 38.

9.   *ST* I, 15, 1, reply obj. 1.

10.   Frege sounds most like an extreme Platonist of the pure variety in "The Thought," when he postulates a realm of abstract propositional entities independent of the physical world and of minds. Applying these remarks to (Fregean) concepts corresponding to general terms produces strikingly Platonic claims.

11.   For discussion and illustration of "casual" and "structural" metaphors, see Abraham Edel's modest but rich article "Metaphors, Analogies, Models, and All That, in Ethical Theory," in *Philosophy, Science, and Method: Essays in Honor of Ernest Nagel*, ed. Sidney Morgenbesser *et al.* (New York, 1969), 364-381.

Appendix 1

1.   "Plato on Knowledge and Reality," review of I. M. Crombie, *An Examination of Plato's Doctrines, Vol. II*, in *PS*, 377.

2.   See, e.g., John Burnet, *Plato's Phaedo* (Oxford, 1911), 55; A. E. Taylor, *Plato, The Man and His Work* (Cleveland, 1956), 187; Ross, *Plato's Theory of Ideas*, 23; Paul Shorey, *What Plato Said* (Chicago, 1965), 124; Vlastos, *SPM*, 246; R. Hackforth, *Plato's Phaedo* (Cambridge, 1955), 69 n. 3, for a small sampling.

3.   The correct reading of the dative has been debated at very great length. But the argument of this appendix does not depend on any particular reading.

4.   On the "appears" reading the passage brings out, as Vlastos has observed, one aspect of the inferiority of sensible equals; they are, as he put it, "cognitively unreliable" ("Degrees of Reality in Plato," *PS*, 63.)

5.   The point is seen by Gosling in "Similarity in *Phaedo* 73b seq.," *Phronesis* 10 (1965): 152, and K. Dorter in "Equality, Recollection, and Purification," *Phronesis* 17 (1972): 204 ff. Cf. Alexander Nehamas, "Plato on the Imperfection of the Sensible World," *APQ* 12 (1975): 111.

6.   A lyre, a man; Simmias, Cebes; a pictured horse, a man; a pictured lyre, a man; pictured Simmias, Cebes; pictured Simmias, Simmias. The last four examples lead by steps to the "pictured Simmias, Simmias" example.

7.   Recollection of Cebes from perception of Simmias is not an example, since their association is based on not resemblance but constant (affectionate) conjunction.

8.   At *Phd.* 99d-100a, where Socrates maintains that by studying things through

words (*en logois*) he is not retreating into images (*eikona*) any more than they who study things "in deeds" (*en ergois*).

9.   I assume sticks can have *some* length, and given two of them, one will be longer than the other or they will have the same length. The discussion of the relative heights of Socrates, Simmias, and Cebes at 102b-d indicates the assumption is made by Plato also.

10.   A clever observer could always deny that two sticks are *eternal* equals, or point out with Plato that they may not *always* look equal even while they are equal (74b). But neither of these is the type of (ontological) deficiency alleged by the approximation reading.

11.   Cf. Bluck, "Forms as Standards," *Phronesis* 2 (1957): 117, and Allen, "Forms and Standards," *PQ* 8 (1959): 164-167.

12.   The plural "*auta ta isa*" of 74c1 (which I take to be a reference to the Form) does not tell one way or another regarding this issue. Kenneth Mills has provided a helpful critical summary of controversy over this phrase "Plato's *Phaedo*, 74b7-c6" Parts 1 and 2, *Phronesis* 2 (1957): 128-47, 3 (1958): 40-58. For a more recent treatment, and a bibliographical update, see Michael Wedin's "*Auta ta isa* and the Argument at *Phaedo* 74b-c5," *Phronesis* 22 (1977): 191-205.

13.   One desperate dodge may be mentioned. An approximationist could say the passage about the greater only means the Greater itself (or the Large itself) is larger than everything else (is the largest thing of all), and the Smaller is just the smallest thing of all (and the Equal is equal to everything?). It seems to me much less reasonable to take this way out (which in any case would face many other problems) than to construe the image analogy as described in chapter 3, and the inferiority of sensibles as described in chapter 5.

List of Works Cited

Ackrill, J. L. Review of *Zwei Aristotelische Frühschriften über die Ideen-lehre*, by Paul Wilpert. *Mind* n. s. 61 (1952): 108ff.

Allen, R. E., ed. *Studies in Plato's Metaphysics.* London: Routledge & Kegan Paul, Ltd., 1965.

_____. "Forms and Standards," *Philosophical Quarterly* 8 (1959): 164-67.

Annas, Julia. *An Introduction to Plato's Republic.* Oxford: Oxford University Press, 1981.

Anton, John, and George Kustas, eds. *Essays in Ancient Greek Philosophy.* Albany: State University of New York Press, 1971.

Armstrong, D. M. "Toward a Theory of Properties." *Philosophy* 50 (1975): 145-155.

Bestor, Thomas. "Plato's Semantics and Plato's *Parmenides*." *Phronesis* 25 (1980): 38-75.

————. "Common Properties and Eponymy in Plato." *Philosophical Quarterly* 28 (1978): 189-208.

Bigger, Charles. *Participation: A Platonic Inquiry*. Baton Rouge: Louisiana State University Press, 1968.

Black, Max. *Models and Metaphors*. Ithaca: Cornell University Press, 1962.

Bluck, R. S. "Forms as Standards." *Phronesis* 2 (1957): 115-127.

Brentlinger, John. "Particulars in Plato's Middle Dialogues." *Archiv für Geschichte der Philosophie* 64 (1972): 116-152.

Burnet, John, ed. *Plato's "Phaedo."* Oxford: Oxford University Press, 1911.

Cherniss, Harold. "*Timaeus* 52c2-5." in *Mélanges de Philosophie Greque Offert à Auguste Dies*, edited by J. Vrin, 49-60. Paris, 1956.

————. *Aristotle's Criticism of Plato and the Academy*. Baltimore: The Johns Hopkins Press, 1944. Reprint. New York: Russell & Russell Inc., 1962.

Cohen, S. Marc. "The Logic of the Third Man." *Philosophical Review* 80 (1971): 448-475.

Cornford, F. M. *Plato's Theory of Knowledge*. London: Routledge & Kegan Paul, 1935. Reprint. Indianapolis: Bobbs-Merrill, 1957.

————. *Plato and Parmenides*. London: Routledge & Kegan Paul, 1939.

Crombie, I. M. *An Examination of Plato's Doctrines*. 2 vols. London: Routledge & Kegan Paul, 1963.

Cross, R. C., and A. D. Woozley. *Plato's "Republic:" A Philosophical Commentary*. London: Macmillan, 1964.

Danto, Arthur. "Representational Properties and Mind-Body Identity." *Review of Metaphysics* 26 (1973): 401-411.

Dawes-Hicks, G., G. E. Moore, and G. F. Stout. "Are the Characteristics of Particular Things Universal or Particular?" *Proceedings of the Aristotelian Society*. Suppl. Vol. 3 (1923): 95-128.

De Laguna, Theodore. "Notes on the Theory of Ideas." *Philosophical Review* 43 (1934): 450-452.

Donagan, Alan. "Universals and Metaphysical Realism." In *The Problem of Universals*, edited by C. Landesman, 98-118. New York: Basic Books, 1971. First published in *Monist* 47 (1963).

Dorter, Kenneth. "Equality, Recollection, and Purification." *Phronesis* 17 (1972): 198-218.

Eberle, Rolf. "Universals as Designata of Predicates."

Edel, Abraham. "Metaphors, Analogies, Models, and All That, in Ethical Theory." In *Philosophy, Science, and Method: Essays in Honor of*

Ernest Nagel, edited by S. Morgenbesser, P. Suppes, and M. White, 364-381. New York: St. Martin's Press, 1969.

Else, G. F. "Imitation in the Fifth Century." *Classical Philology* 53 (1958): 73-90.

Findlay, J. N. *Plato: The Written and Unwritten Doctrines.* New York: Humanities Press, 1974.

Fine, Gail, "The One Over Many." *Philosophical Review* 89 (1980): 197-240.

Forrester, J. W. "Some Perils of Paulinity." *Phronesis* 20 (1975): 11-21.

Fodor, Jerry. *The Language of Thought.* New York: Thomas Y. Crowell, 1975.

Frede, Michael. *Prädikation und Existenzaussage.*

Frege, Gottlob. "The Thought." Translated by A. and M. Quinton. *Mind* n. s. 65 (1956): 289-311.

Gallop, David. "Image and Reality in Plato's *Republic.*" *Archiv für Geschichte der Philosophie* 47 (1965): 113-131.

Goldschmidt, Victor. *Le Paradigme Dans la Dialectique Platonicienne.* Paris: Presses Universitaires de France, 1947.

Goodman, Nelson. "Seven Strictures on Similarity." In *Problems and Projects.* Indianapolis: Hackett, 1973.

Gosling, J. "Similarity in *Phaedo* 73b seq." *Phronesis* 10 (1965): 151-161.

Grote, George. *Plato and the other Companions of Sokrates.* 2d ed. London, 1867.

Grey, D. R. "Art in the *Republic.*" *Philosophy* 27 (1952): 291-310.

Grube, G. M. A. *Plato's Thought.* London: Methuen, 1935. Reprint. Indianapolis: Hackett, 1980.

Hackforth, R., ed. *Plato's "Phaedo."* Cambridge: Cambridge University Press, 1955.

Irwin, Terence. *Plato's Moral Theory: The Early and Middle Dialogues.* Oxford: Oxford University Press, 1977.

Keul, Eva. *Plato and Greek Painting.* Columbia Studies in the Classical Tradition, vol 5. Leiden, 1978.

Lee, E. N. "On the Metaphysics of the Image in Plato's *Timaeus.*" *Monist* 50 (1966): 341-368.

―――. "The Second 'Third Man': An Interpretation." In *Patterns in Plato's Thought,* edited by J. M. E. Moravcsik. 101-122. Dordrecht: D. Reidel, 1973.

―――, A. P. D. Mourelatos, and R. M. Rorty, eds. *Exegesis and Argument: Studies in Greek Philosophy Presented to Gregory Vlastos.* 1973.

Martin, R. "Selbstprädikation bei Platon." *Kantstudien* 58 (1967): 209-228.

Meinhardt, Helmut. *Teilhabe bei Platon. Symposium*, 1967.

Mills, Kenneth. "Plato's *Phaedo*, 74b7-c6." Parts 1, 2. *Phronesis* 2 (1957): 128-147; 3 (1958): 40-58.

Moline, John. *Plato's Theory of Understanding*. Madison: The University of Wisconsin Press, 1981.

Moravcsik, J. M. E., ed. *Patterns in Plato's Thought*. Dordrecht: D. Reidel, 1973.

————. "The 'Third Man' Argument and Plato's Theory of Forms." *Phronesis* 8 (1963): 50-62.

Moreau, Joseph. "Sur la Signification du *Parmenide*." *Revue Philosophique* 1944: 97-131.

Natorp, Paul. *Platos Ideenlehre*. Leipzig: 1903.

Nehamas, Alexander. "Self-Predication and Plato's Theory of Forms." *American Philosophical Quarterly* 16 (1979): 93-103.

————. "Plato on Imitation and Poetry in *Republic* 10." In *Plato on Beauty, Wisdom, and the Arts*, edited by J. Moravcsik and P. Temko, Totowa, N. J.: Rowman and Littlefield, 1982.

————. "Participation and Predication in Plato's Late Dialogues." *Review of Metaphysics* 36 (1982): 343-374.

————. "Plato on the Imperfection of the Sensible World." *American Philosophical Quarterly* 12 (1975): 105-117.

————. "Confusing Universals and Particulars in Plato's Early Dialogues." *Review of Metaphysics* 29 (1975): 287-306.

O'Brien, D. "A Metaphor in Plato: 'Running Away' and 'Staying Behind' in the *Phaedo* and *Timaeus*." *Classical Quarterly* n. s. 27 (1977): 297-299.

Patterson, Cynthia. *Pericles' Citizenship Law of 451-450 B. C.* New York: Arno Press, 1981.

Patterson, Richard. "The Eternality of Platonic Forms." *Archiv für Geschichte der Philosophie*. Forthcoming.

————. "The Unique Worlds of the *Timaeus*." *Phoenix* 35 (1981): 105-119.

Patzig, Gunther. "Platons Ideenlehre, kritisch betrachtet." *Antike und Abendlände* 16 (1978): 113ff.

Pemberton, Elizabeth G. "A Note on *Skiagraphia*." *American Journal of Philology* 80 (1976): 82-92.

Pollitt, J. J. *The Ancient View of Greek Art*. New Haven: Yale University Press, 1974.

Putnam, Hilary. "On Properties." In *Mathematics, Matter, and Method*. 2d ed. Cambridge: Cambridge University Press, 1979: 305-322. (First published in *Essays in Honor of Carl G. Hempel*, edited by Nicholas Rescher. Dordrecht: D. Reidel, 1970.)

Quine, W. V. O. *Word and Object*. Cambridge, Mass.: MIT Press, 1960.

Ringbom, Sixten. "Plato on Images." *Theoria* 31 (1965): 86-109.

Robinson, Richard. *Plato's Earlier Dialectic*. 2d ed. Oxford: Oxford University Press, 1953.

Rohr, Michael. "Empty Forms in Plato." *Archiv für Geschichte der Philosophie* 60 (1980): 268-283.

Ross, Sir David. *Plato's Theory of Ideas*. Oxford: Clarendon Press, 1953.

_____, ed. *Aristotle's Metaphysics I*. Oxford: Oxford University Press, 1924.

Rumsey, William. "A Commentary on Plato's Sophist." Ph.D. diss., Columbia University, 1980.

Ryle, Gilbert. *Plato's Progress*. Cambridge: Cambridge University Press, 1966.

Shimony, Abner, "The Nature and Status of Essences." *Review of Metaphysics* 1 (1948): 38-79.

Shorey, Paul. *The Unity of Plato's Thought*. Chicago: University of Chicago Press, 1903. Reprint. Garden City, N. Y.: Anchor Books, 1968.

_____. *What Plato Said*. Chicago: University of Chicago Press, 1965.

Smith, J. A. "General Relative Clauses in Greek." *Classical Review* 31 (1917): 69-71.

Sonnenschein, E. A. "The Indicative in Relative Clauses." *Classical Review* 32 (1918): 68-69.

Stenzel, Julius. *Plato's Method of Dialectic*. Translated by D. J. Allen. New York: Arno Press, 1973.

Stough, Charlotte. "Forms and Explanation in the *Phaedo*." *Phronesis* 21 (1976): 1-30.

Suhr, Martin. *Platons Kritik an den Eleaten*. Hamburg, 1969.

Taylor, A. E. *Plato: The Man and His Work*. Cleveland: Meridian Books, 1956.

_____. *The Parmenides of Plato*. Oxford: Oxford University Press, 1934.

Taylor, C. C. W., ed. *Plato: Protagoras*. Oxford: Oxford University Press, 1976.

Teloh, Henry. *The Development of Plato's Metaphysics*. College Park, Penn.: The Pennsylvania State University Press, 1981.

Turnbull, Robert. "Aristotle's Debt to the Natural Philosophy of the *Phaedo*." *Philosophical Quarterly* 8 (1958): 131-146.

Vater, Hans. *Die Dialectic von Idee und Teilhabe in Platons "Parmenides."* Hamburg, 1972.

Vlastos, G., ed. *Plato I*. Garden City, N. Y.: Doubleday and Co., 1971.

_____. "A Note on 'Pauline Predications' in Plato." *Phronesis* 19 (1974): 95-101.

_____. *Platonic Studies*. Princeton: Princeton University Press, 1973.

_____. "Self-Predication and Self-Participation in Plato's Later Period."
    The Philosophical Review 78 (1969): 74-78.
Wedin, Michael. "*auta ta isa* and the Argument at *Phaedo* 74b-c5."
    Phronesis 22 (1977): 191-205.
Weizäcker, Carl Friedrich von, "Platonic Natural Science in the Course
    of History," *Main Currents in Modern Thought* 29 (1972): 3-13.
Werkmeister, W. H., ed. *Facets of Plato's Philosophy*. Assen, 1976.
White, Nicholas. *Plato on Knowledge and Reality*. Indianapolis: Hackett
    Publishing Co., 1976.
White, F. C. "The *Phaedo* and *Republic V* on Essences." *Journal of
    Hellenic Studies* 98 (1978): 142-156.
_____. "Plato's Middle Dialogues and the Independence of Particulars."
    Philosophical Quarterly 27 (1977): 193-213.
Whitehead, A. N. *Science and the Modern World*. New York: The Mac-
    millan Company, 1925.
Wilson, John Cook. *On the Interpretation of Plato's "Timaeus."* London,
    1899.
_____. "On the Platonist Doctrine of the ἀσυμβλζτοι ἄριθμοι." *Classi-
    cal Review* 18 919040: 247-260.
Wittgenstein, Ludwig. *Philosophical Investigations*. 3d ed. Translated by
    G. E. M. Anscombe. New York: The Macmillan Company, 1971.

Index